ON
EARTH
AS IN
HEAVEN

ON EARTH AS IN HEAVEN

Daily Wisdom for
Twenty-First-Century Christians

N. T. WRIGHT

Edited by Oliver Wright

HarperOne

An Imprint of HarperCollinsPublishers

HarperCollins books may be purchased for educational, business, or sales promotional use. For information, please email the Special Markets Department at SPsales@harpercollins.com.

FIRST HARPERCOLLINS PAPERBACK PUBLISHED IN 2025

Designed by SBI Book Arts, LLC
Illustrations by Jamie Clarke

Library of Congress Cataloging-in-Publication Data is available upon request.

ISBN 978-0-06-321091-2

24 25 26 27 28 LBC 5 4 3 2 1

CONTENTS

PREFACE

Like time itself, certain ideas creep up on you and, before you know it, they have changed the way you think about everything else.

That's how it was for me with the resurrection of Jesus. Brought up to go to church, to sing the hymns and say the prayers, I knew the story. "On the third day he rose again" and all that. But the sermons I heard and most of the hymns we sang around Eastertime were not actually about resurrection itself. They were about "going to heaven." We assumed that talking about Jesus's resurrection was simply vivid picture language for saying that he was now "alive," and that this meant that we, his followers, would "go to heaven," to be with him in the end.

One of the regular Easter hymns said as much:

> May we go where he is gone,
> Rest and reign with him in heaven.

Adding "Alleluia" to that (as you do) simply reinforced that message: "resurrection" = "life after death" = "going to heaven." End of story.

Except that it isn't. The last scene in the Bible isn't about "saved souls" going up to heaven. It is about the New Jerusalem coming *down* from heaven to earth as the centerpiece of the "new heaven and new earth" promised by the prophets and reaffirmed by Jesus himself and his first followers. That didn't fit the story line we had been taught. So most of us just treated it as a bit of flowery decoration around the edge.

But the more I tried to preach and teach the message of the New Testament in various church and university settings in the first twenty years or so of my public ministry (I was ordained in 1975), the more I came to realize that the old picture wouldn't do. In particular, I found myself trying to think through what the original gospel meant, first personally and pastorally and then with regard to culture and politics. And one day it dawned on me: I was glimpsing in a whole new way what Jesus meant when he taught us to pray that God's kingdom would come *on earth as in heaven*.

Up till then, I had vaguely thought of this as a temporary measure. Until we go to heaven ourselves, it would be nice if "earth" (at least, our little bit of it) could be a bit more, well, heavenly. But that makes nonsense not only of the Lord's Prayer, but also of Jesus's whole announcement of God's kingdom. And, ultimately, of his death, through which—in his own teaching and in the eager and excited teaching of his first followers—that kingdom had been established, though not in the way anyone had imagined before.

At the heart of that new way was a new sense of time itself. The Jewish people, unlike most other ancient cultures, thought of time as a line. It had a beginning (creation), an end (when God would put the whole world right), and a middle—the confused and dangerous period they themselves were living in. But now, principally because of Jesus's resurrection, his followers came to believe that the "end" had already arrived, while the "middle" was still going on. Time itself got muddled up—or, as they came to see it, time itself was redeemed, given back to us in a new mode. The prayer had been answered, in advance of the final putting right of all things. God's new world had indeed begun, "on earth as in heaven." Jesus's bodily resurrection from the dead was an event that so comprehensively shattered the normal patterns of this world that it launched nothing short of new creation.

The first Easter, then, was par excellence the event of God's kingdom coming on earth as it is in heaven. As we pray every day for God's kingdom to come, we are praying that we will be shaped more and more by that Easter reality, rather than by the prevailing and sometimes persuasive "realities" that the present world tries to offer us.

So how does this work?

When you get off the plane in a new time zone, you adjust your watch to the right time in the new location. One of the most striking things Jesus's first followers did was to adjust their watches to this belief that God's ultimate future had arrived in the present.

They didn't, of course, have literal "watches." But they measured time, as we still do, in seven-day weeks, and they made a radical change in how they marked those weeks. For the Jewish people, the sabbath at the end of the week functions as a forward signpost to God's ultimate new world. The early Christians, however, changed that—and if you know anything about traditional societies, you will see what a dramatic thing this was to do. They met for worship on the *first* day of every week. And they did so because they believed that with Jesus's resurrection *God's new world had already begun*. They were living in a new time zone, with new possibilities, challenges, encouragements, and obligations. They had to adjust their sense of time itself.

Within two or three generations, this sense of living in a new time zone developed its own new styles of annual celebration. An annual cycle, focused on Jesus's death and particularly his resurrection, became a way of telling the all-important story of those events, not just in words but in acted-out drama. The whole point was, and is, that these events are not simply things to think about, though, of course, they are that as well. They form a story within which we are called to live, a play in which we discover ourselves already on stage, trying to learn our lines even as the drama unfolds.

The putting right of all creation has begun. Jesus's people, themselves having been put right, are to live as signposts to God's final new creation. Thus, to celebrate Easter itself and to highlight it in the way we organize the whole year, weaving it into our collective consciousness, is to plant the truth of the gospel deeply into our imaginations and assumptions.

The world, of course, will shriek that this is all fantasy. Horrors and disasters fill our newspapers and televisions screens. Murder, disease, violence, and oppression continue as before. But the early Christians show us the way. They knew, better than most of us, that idolatry and injustice are still powerful. But they celebrated the new day, the new time, the new Easter reality, the new Easter and Pentecost reality.

And, despite the chorus of skepticism, the world really has changed. It is still changing. God's kingdom is coming on earth as in heaven—in the ways Jesus said it would, through the pure in heart, the meek, the mourners, the people hungry for justice, and so on. And these changes are signposts to the ultimate transformation, when Jesus comes again to implement fully and finally the victory he won on the cross, the victory whose most stunning immediate result was his own resurrection. In the meantime, millions of Jesus's followers find, year by year and season by season, that telling *and living* the great story, as an annual cycle whose launch and whose climax is Easter itself, is a great way of keeping ourselves oriented to God's time, of keeping our heads and our hearts in the right time zone.

This present book is, on one level, a collection of short passages taken from several of my books. They have been organized so that readers are encouraged to reflect more deeply on what God's kingdom coming on earth as in heaven might look like—when seen through the lens of Easter itself. The truth of Jesus's resurrection is the starting point for every day, week, month, and year of Christian living. It is in the resurrection that we find our hope, our mission, and our love. It is the event above all that calls us to worship God the creator, the life-giver. So, quite deliberately, this book does not run from January 1 to December 31. It begins with the first day of new creation, Easter Day; it ends with a second Easter, coming full circle, always with the Easter invitation to begin again.

The kingdom coming "on earth as in heaven" thus invites those of us who pray these words into a new experience of time. In several churches, including the Anglican Church, which has been my home throughout my life, the church's calendar provides a rich, subtle, and powerful way of making the gospel our own. This book follows that calendar, taking us through seven feasts and fasts in the Christian calendar, Easter, Ascension, Pentecost, Advent, Christmas, Lent, Passiontide, and returning at last to Easter again. (Easter is, of course, a "moveable feast." Those who use this book in any given year are encouraged to make any necessary adjustments, to stretch or shrink the selections to fit.)

These highlights of the year point us to particular readings and themes. Interspersed within these are sections that invite us deeper into the meaning of the various seasons. Here I follow the "signposts" I outlined originally in my book *Simply Christian* and then more fully (with the help of John's gospel) in *Broken Signposts*. The "signposts" in question are beauty, power, spirituality, justice, truth, freedom, and love. Many Christians, in my experience, give little thought to these signposts. When we think of them, however, within the framework I am proposing— namely, an experience of time, and within that of seasons, rooted in and returning to Easter itself—these signposts point in new and deeper ways to the reality of God's new world, the Easter reality, and the consequent renewal of human life that is ours for the asking.

I am very grateful to my son Oliver for taking time out of his own theological studies to select and arrange these passages from my writings. It has been exciting for me to see, through someone else's eyes, the ways in which over the years my thinking, speaking, and writing has increasingly highlighted the all-important theme of what it might look like for God's kingdom to come on earth as in heaven. I hope and pray that this book will help many people to move away from unbiblical or subbiblical ways of thinking about the Christian faith and to embrace more fully the reality of Jesus's victory over evil and the launching of God's new world. It's about time.

Tom Wright
Oxford, Michaelmas 2021

ON
EARTH
AS IN
HEAVEN

EASTER

On the first day of the week, very early, Mary Magdalene came to the tomb while it was still dark. She saw that the stone had been rolled away from the tomb. So she ran off, and went to Simon Peter, and to the other disciple, the one Jesus loved.

"They've taken the master out of the tomb!" she said. "We don't know where they've put him!"

So Peter and the other disciple set off and went to the tomb. Both of them ran together. The other disciple ran faster than Peter, and got to the tomb first. He stooped down and saw the linen cloths lying there, but he didn't go in. Then Simon Peter came up, following him, and went into the tomb. He saw the linen cloths lying there, and the napkin that had been around his head, not lying with the other cloths, but folded up in a place by itself.

Then the other disciple, who had arrived first at the tomb, went into the tomb as well. He saw, and he believed. They did not yet know, you see, that the Bible had said he must rise again from the dead.

Then the disciples returned to their homes.

But Mary stood outside the tomb, crying. As she wept, she stooped down to look into the tomb. There she saw two angels, clothed in white, one at the head and one at the feet of where Jesus's body had been lying.

"Woman," they said to her, "why are you crying?"

"They've taken away my master," she said, "and I don't know where they've put him!"

As she said this she turned around and saw Jesus standing there. She didn't know it was Jesus.

"Woman," Jesus said to her, "why are you crying? Who are you looking for?"

She guessed he must be the gardener.

"Sir," she said, "if you've carried him off somewhere, tell me where you've put him, and I will take him away."

"Mary!" said Jesus.

She turned and spoke in Aramaic.

"Rabbouni!" she said (which means "Teacher").

"Don't cling to me," said Jesus. "I haven't yet gone up to the father. But go to my brothers and say to them, 'I'm going up to my father and your father—to my God and your God.'"

Mary Magdalene went and told the disciples, "I've seen the master!" and that he had said these things to her.

On the evening of that day, the first day of the week, the doors were shut where the disciples were, for fear of the Judaeans. Jesus came and stood in the middle of them.

"Peace be with you," he said.

—John 20:1–19, *The Kingdom New Testament* 219–20

Now Is the Time

This whole book attempts to reflect the Lord's Prayer itself when it says, "Thy kingdom come, on earth as in heaven." That remains one of the most powerful and revolutionary sentences we can ever say. As I see it, the prayer was powerfully answered at the first Easter and will finally be answered fully when heaven and earth are joined in the new Jerusalem. Easter was when Hope in person surprised the whole world by coming forward from the future into the present. The ultimate future hope remains a surprise, partly because we don't know when it will arrive and partly because at present we have only images and metaphors for it, leaving us to guess that the reality will be far greater, and more surprising, still. And the intermediate hope—the things that happen in the present time to implement Easter and anticipate the final day—are always surprising because, left to ourselves, we lapse into a kind of collusion with entropy, acquiescing in the general belief that things may be getting worse but that there's nothing much we can do about them. And we are wrong. Our task in the present—of which this book, God willing, may form part—is to live as resurrection people in between Easter and the final day, with our Christian life, corporate and individual, in both worship and mission, as a sign of the first and a foretaste of the second.

—*Surprised by Hope* 29–30

Easter Transforms Good Advice into Good News

Without Easter—that is, without Jesus being raised from the dead into a new bodily life—nobody would ever have imagined that God's saving plan had been fulfilled. No first-century Jew would ever have said that the shameful execution of a would-be leader could complete the centuries-old, long-prophesied new exodus, rescuing Israel from its long exile and the human race from sin and death. The Jews of the day did, from time to time, tell stories about suffering, describing righteous martyrs whose tribulations would somehow contribute to God's eventual plan. But one more martyr wouldn't mean that the kingdom of God *had* come. It would mean that it hadn't. Israel, and the world, would still be waiting.

Without Easter, in fact, the movement that came into existence around Jesus would not have been about good *news*. At most, it would have been about good *advice* ("here's how Jesus taught us to live our lives"). Some might well doubt whether this advice was actually good in the first place: look what happened to Jesus himself! But even if the advice was good, it would still mean that people were waiting for the great day to dawn, not that they were celebrating its arrival.

—Simply Good News 46–47

Easter Is the Center

Christmas itself has now far outstripped Easter in popular culture as the real celebratory center of the Christian year—a move that completely reverses the New Testament's emphasis. We sometimes try, in hymns, prayers, and sermons, to build a whole theology on Christmas, but it can't, in fact, sustain such a thing. We then keep Lent, Holy Week, and Good Friday so thoroughly that we have hardly any energy left for Easter except for the first night and day. Easter, however, should be the center. Take that away and there is, almost literally, nothing left.

—Surprised by Hope 23

Easter Launches a New World

The challenge is the challenge of *new creation*. To put it at its most basic: the resurrection of Jesus offers itself, to the student of history or science no less than the Christian or the theologian, not as an odd event within the world as it is but as the utterly characteristic, prototypical, and foundational event within the world as it has begun to be. It is not an absurd event within the old world but the symbol and starting point of the new world. The claim advanced in Christianity is of that magnitude: Jesus of Nazareth ushers in not simply a new religious possibility, not simply a new ethic or a new way of salvation, but a new creation.

—Surprised by Hope 67

Life After Life After Death

Resurrection itself appears as what the word always meant, whether (like the ancient pagans) people disbelieved it or whether (like many ancient Jews) they affirmed it. It wasn't a way of talking about life after death. It was a way of talking about a new bodily life *after* whatever state of existence one might enter immediately upon death. It was, in other words, life *after* life after death.

—Surprised by Hope 151

Resurrection Means Bodies

When the ancients spoke of resurrection, whether to deny it (as all pagans did) or to affirm it (as some Jews did), they were referring to a two-step narrative in which resurrection, meaning new bodily life, would be preceded by an interim period of bodily death. *Resurrection* wasn't, then, a dramatic or vivid way of talking about the state people went into immediately after death. It denoted something that might happen (though almost everyone thought it wouldn't) sometime *after* that. This meaning is constant throughout the ancient world until the post-Christian coinages of second-century Gnosticism. Most of the ancients believed in life after death; some of them developed complex and fascinating beliefs about it, which we have only just touched on; but outside Judaism and Christianity (and perhaps Zoroastrianism, though the dating of that is controversial), they did not believe in resurrection.

In content, *resurrection* referred specifically to something that happened to the body; hence the later debates about how God would do this—whether he would start with the existing bones or make new ones or whatever. One would have debates like that only if it was quite clear that what you ended up with was something tangible and physical. Everybody knew about ghosts, spirits, visions, hallucinations, and so on. Most people in the ancient world believed in some such things. They were quite clear that that wasn't what they meant by *resurrection*. While Herod reportedly thought Jesus might be John the Baptist raised from the dead, he didn't think he was a ghost. Resurrection meant bodies. We cannot emphasize this too strongly, not least because much modern writing continues, most misleadingly, to use the word *resurrection* as a virtual synonym for *life after death* in the popular sense.

—*Surprised by Hope* 36

Future Hope Means Present Mission

A proper grasp of the (surprising) *future* hope held out to us in Jesus Christ leads directly and, to many people, equally surprisingly, to a vision of the *present* hope that is the basis of all Christian mission. To hope for a better future in this world—for the poor, the sick, the lonely and depressed, for the slaves, the refugees, the hungry and homeless, for the abused, the paranoid, the downtrodden and despairing, and, in fact, for the whole wide, wonderful, and wounded world—is not something *else*, something extra, something tacked on to the gospel as an afterthought. And to work for that intermediate hope, the surprising hope that comes forward from God's ultimate future into God's urgent present, is not a *distraction from* the task of mission and evangelism in the present. It is a central, essential, vital, and life-giving part of it. Mostly, Jesus himself got a hearing from his contemporaries because of what he was *doing*. They saw him saving people from sickness and death, and they heard him talking about a salvation, the message for which they had longed, that would go beyond the immediate into the ultimate future. But the two were not unrelated, the present one a mere visual aid of the future one or a trick to gain people's attention. The whole point of what Jesus was up to was that he was doing, close up, in the present, what he was promising long-term, in the future. And what he was promising for that future, and doing in that present, was not saving souls for a disembodied eternity but rescuing people from the corruption and decay of the way the world presently is so they could enjoy, already in the present, that renewal of creation which is God's ultimate purpose—and so they could thus become colleagues and partners in that larger project.

When we turn to Paul, the verse that has always struck me in this connection is 1 Corinthians 15:58. Paul, we remind ourselves, has just written the longest and densest chapter in any of his letters, discussing the future resurrection of the body in great and complex detail. How might we expect him to finish such a chapter? By saying, "Therefore, since you have such a great hope, sit back and relax because you know God's got a great future in store for you"? No. Instead, he says, "Therefore, my beloved ones, be steadfast, immovable, always abounding in the work of the Lord, because you know that in the Lord your labor is not in vain."

—*Surprised by Hope* 191–92

The Dangerous Truth of the Resurrection

Let me put it starkly. *The Bible tells the story of the world as having reached its destiny, its climax, when Jesus of Nazareth came out of the tomb on Easter morning.* The Enlightenment philosophy, however, *tells the story of the world as having reached its destiny, its climax, with the rise of scientific and democratic modernism.* These two stories cannot both be true. World history cannot have two climaxes, two destinies. That is why, for the last two hundred years, people have poured such scorn on the story of Jesus's resurrection. Of course, a dead person being raised to a new sort of bodily life always was extraordinary. But the reason the first Christians believed it wasn't that they didn't know the laws of nature. They believed, on the powerful evidence of eyes and ears and hands as well as hearts, that the God of creation had done something new, though deeply coherent, *in and within* the natural world, launching his long-intended project of world renewal. It wasn't an arbitrary intervention, either simply to rescue Jesus or to display God's omnipotence, or whatever. It was all about *new creation*.

But from the eighteenth century on, people have said that if you believe in modern science—by which they mean the Epicurean project of scient*ism,* which claims empirical evidence for its philosophical worldview—then you can't believe in the resurrection. This skepticism has, however, nothing modern about it. Lucretius, the greatest ancient Epicurean, would have scoffed at the idea of resurrection. So would Homer or Aeschylus or Plato or Pliny. The point is that *the resurrection, if it had occurred, would undermine not only the Enlightenment's vision of a split world but also the Enlightenment's self-congratulatory dream of world history reaching its destiny in our own day and our own systems.* That's why the resurrection has been seen in scholarship not as the launching of new creation but simply as the most bizarre of miracles, then as an impossible miracle, then as a dangerous ideological claim. You bet it's dangerous. If it's true, other ideologies are brought to book.

—*Surprised by Scripture* 137–38

Jesus Is Raised . . . So We Have a Job to Do!

A strange feature of the resurrection accounts in the gospels is the fact that they never mention the future Christian hope. Almost everywhere else in the New Testament, the resurrection of Jesus is spoken of in connection with the final hope that those who belong to Jesus will one day be raised as he has been, adding that this must be anticipated in the present in baptism and behavior. Despite a thousand Easter hymns and a million Easter sermons, the resurrection narratives in the gospels never, ever say anything like, "Jesus is raised, therefore there is a life after death," let alone,

"Jesus is raised, therefore we shall go to heaven when we die." Nor even, in a more authentic first-century Christian way, do they say, "Jesus is raised, therefore we shall be raised from the dead after the sleep of death."

No. Insofar as the event is interpreted, Easter has a very this-worldly, present-age meaning: Jesus is raised, so he is the Messiah, and therefore he is the world's true Lord; Jesus is raised, so God's new creation has begun—and we, his followers, have a job to do! Jesus is raised, so we must act as his heralds, announcing his lord-ship to the entire world, making his kingdom come on earth as in heaven! To be sure, as early as Paul, the resurrection of Jesus is firmly linked to the final resurrection of all God's people. Had the stories been invented toward the end of the first century, they would certainly have included a mention of the final resurrection of all God's people. They don't, because they weren't.

—*Surprised by Hope* 56–57

New Physical Bodies and New Patterns of Thought

In 2 Corinthians 5, Paul speaks of the new tent or tabernacle that is waiting for us. There is a new house, a new dwelling, a new body, waiting within God's sphere (again, "heaven"), ready for us to put it on over the present one so that what is mortal may be swallowed up with life. As always, so here, Paul insists that God will accomplish this by the Spirit.

This is the point at which we modern Westerners are called to make a huge leap of the imagination. We have been buying our mental furniture for so long in Plato's factory that we have come to take for granted a basic ontological contrast between "spirit" in the sense of something immaterial and "matter" in the sense of something material, solid, physical. We think we know that solid objects are one sort of thing and ideas or values or spirits or ghosts are a different sort of thing (often not noticing that they are themselves all rather different sorts of things). We know that bodies decay and die; that houses, temples, cities, and civilizations fall to dust; and so we assume that to be bodily, to be physical, is to be impermanent, changeable, transitory, and that the only way to be permanent, unchanging, and immortal is to become nonphysical.

Paul's point here is that this is not so. Actually, it wasn't so even in the dominant cosmology of his day, which was Stoic rather than Platonic. Still less was it so within the Jewish creation theology, which formed the seedbed out of which, because of the resurrection of Jesus himself, Paul grew his theology of new creation. Paul is making his Corinthian readers think in new patterns, and he has the same effect on us.

What Paul is asking us to imagine is that there will be a new mode of physicality, which stands in relation to our present body as our present body does to a ghost. It will be as much more real, more firmed up, more *bodily*, than our present body as our present body is more substantial, more touchable, than a disembodied spirit.

—*Surprised by Hope* 153–54

A Mission-Shaped Church Through Hope-Shaped Mission

The promise of new creation is not and cannot be simply about straightening out ideas about life after death. It is about the mission of the church. There has been a lot of talk where I work about a "mission-shaped church," following a report with that title, urging today's church to regard mission not as an extra, something to fit in if there's any time left over from other concerns, but as the central and shaping dynamic of its life. But if this is to mean what it ought to mean, we must also reshape our ideas of mission itself. It's no good falling back into the tired old split-level world where some people believe in evangelism in terms of saving souls for a timeless eternity and other people believe in mission in terms of working for justice, peace, and hope in the present world. That great divide has nothing to do with Jesus and the New Testament and everything to do with the silent enslavement of many Christians (both conservative and radical) to the Platonic ideology of the Enlightenment. Once we get the resurrection straight, we can and must get mission straight. If we want a mission-shaped church, what we need is a hope-shaped mission. And if that is surprising, we ought to be getting used to it by now.

—*Surprised by Hope* 193–94

Holiness in the New World Created by Easter

The message of Easter is that God's new world has been unveiled in Jesus Christ and that you're now invited to belong to it. And precisely because the resurrection was and is bodily, albeit with a transformed body, the power of Easter to transform and heal the present world must be put into effect both at the macrolevel, in applying the gospel to the major problems of the world—and if Soviet Communism and apartheid don't count on that scale, I don't know what does—and to the intimate details of our daily lives. Christian holiness consists not of trying as hard as we can to be good but of learning to live in the new world created by Easter, the new world we publicly entered in our baptism. There are many parts of the world we can't do anything about except pray. But there is one part of the world, one part of physical reality, that we can do something about, and that is the creature each of us calls "myself." Personal holiness and global holiness belong together. Those who wake up to the one may well find themselves called to wake up to the other as well.

—*Surprised by Hope* 252–53

Building in the Present for God's Future

The point of the resurrection is that *the present bodily life is not valueless just because it will die.* God will raise it to new life. What you do with your body in the present matters because God has a great future in store for it. And if this applies to ethics it certainly also applies to the various vocations to which God's people are called. What you *do* in the present—by painting, preaching, singing, sewing, praying, teaching, building hospitals, digging wells, campaigning for justice, writing poems, caring for the needy, loving your neighbor as yourself—*will last into God's future.* These activities are not simply ways of making the present life a little less beastly, a little more bearable, until the day when we leave it behind altogether (as the hymn so mistakenly puts it, "Until that day when all the blest to endless rest are called away"). They are part of what we may call *building for God's kingdom.*

—*Surprised by Hope* 193

Doubts and New Understanding

The story of Thomas in John 20 serves as a parable. Thomas, like a good historian, wants to see and touch. Jesus presents himself to his sight and invites him to touch, but Thomas doesn't. He transcends the type of knowing he had intended to use and passes into a higher and richer one. In the image I used before, of Israel at the Red Sea, this is how it looks, in words from the *Easter Oratorio*. Thomas begins with doubt:

> The sea is too deep
> The heavens too high
> I cannot swim
> I cannot fly;
> I must stay here
> I must stay here
> Here where I know
> How I can know
> Here where I know
> What I can know.

Jesus then reappears and invites Thomas to see and touch. Suddenly, the new, giddying possibility appears before him:

> The sea has parted. Pharaoh's hosts—
> Despair, and doubt, and fear, and pride—
> No longer frighten us. We must
> Cross over to the other side.
> The heaven bows down. With wounded hands
> Our exiled God, our Lord of shame
> Before us, living, breathing, stands;

The Word is near, and calls our name.
New knowing for the doubting mind,
New seeing out of blindness grows;
New trusting may the sceptic find
New hope through that which faith now knows.

And with that, Thomas takes a deep breath and brings history
and faith together in a rush. "My Lord," he says, "and my God."

That is not an antihistorical statement. The "Lord" in question
is precisely the one who is the climax of Israel's history and the
launch of a new history.

Nor is it an antiscientific statement. The world of new creation
is precisely the world of new *creation*; as such, it is open to, and
indeed eager for, the work of human beings—not to manipulate it
with magic tricks nor to be subservient to it as though the world of
creation were itself divine but to be its stewards.

—*Surprised by Hope* 70–71

Jesus's Unique Resurrection Body

The best explanation by far for the rise of Christianity is that Jesus
really did reappear, not as a battered, bleeding survivor, not as a
ghost (the stories are very clear about that), but as a living, bodily
human being.

But the body was somehow different. The gospel stories are, at
this point, unlike anything before or since. As one leading scholar
has put it, it seems that the gospel writers were trying to explain
something for which they didn't have a precise vocabulary. Jesus's
risen body had many of the same properties as an ordinary body (it

could talk, eat and drink, be touched, and so on), but it had others, too. It could appear and disappear, and pass through locked doors. Nothing in Jewish literature or imagination had prepared people for a portrait like this. If the gospel writers had made something up to fit a preconceived notion, the one thing they would certainly have done is describe the risen Jesus shining like a star. According to Daniel 12:3 (a very influential passage in Jewish thought at the time), this was how the righteous would appear at the resurrection. But Jesus didn't. His body seems to have been transformed in a way for which there was neither precedent nor prophecy, and of which there remains no second example.

That kind of conclusion is always frustrating from a scientific point of view. Science, after all, rightly studies phenomena which can be repeated in laboratory conditions. But history doesn't. Historians study things that happened once and once only; even if there are partial parallels, each historical event is unique. And the historical argument is quite clear. To repeat: far and away the best explanation for why Christianity began after Jesus's violent death is that he really was bodily alive again three days later, in a transformed body.

—*Simply Christian* 113

Take Away the Resurrection, and You Lose the Entire New Testament

In Second-Temple Judaism, resurrection is important, but not that important. There are lots of lengthy works that never mention the question, let alone this answer. It is still difficult to be sure what the authors of the Dead Sea Scrolls thought on the topic. Apart from occasional highlights like 2 Maccabees 7, resurrection is a peripheral topic. But in early Christianity, resurrection moved from the circumference to the center. You can't imagine Paul's thought without it. You shouldn't imagine John's thought without it, though some have tried. It is enormously important in Clement and Ignatius, in Justin and Irenaeus. It is one of the key beliefs that infuriated the pagans in Lyons in AD 177 and drove them to butcher several Christians, including the bishop who preceded the great Irenaeus. Belief in bodily resurrection was one of the two central things that the pagan doctor Galen noted about the Christians (the other being their remarkable sexual restraint). Take away the stories of Jesus's birth, and you lose only two chapters of Matthew and two of Luke. Take away the resurrection, and you lose the entire New Testament and most of the second-century fathers as well.

—*Surprised by Hope* 42–43

God Has Indeed Become King on Earth as in Heaven

The resurrection, in short, is presented by the evangelists not as a "happy ending" after an increasingly sad and gloomy tale, but as the event that demonstrated that Jesus's execution really had dealt the deathblow to the dark forces that had stood in the way of God's new world, God's "kingdom" of powerful creative and restorative love, arriving "on earth as in heaven."

That is why the bodily resurrection matters in a way that it never quite does, even to the devout who insist that they believe it, if all one is interested in is a kingdom "not of this world." The resurrection is, from Mark's point of view, the moment when God's kingdom "comes in power." From John's point of view, it is the launching of the new creation, the new Genesis. From Matthew's point of view, it brings Jesus into the position for which he was always destined, that of the world's rightful Lord, sending out his followers (as a new Roman emperor might send out his emissaries, but with methods that match the message) to call the world to follow him and learn his way of being human. From Luke's point of view, the resurrection is the moment when Israel's Messiah "comes into his glory," so that "repentance for the forgiveness of sins" can now be announced to all the world as the way of life, indeed, as they say in Acts, as the Way.

Once we put kingdom and cross together it is not difficult to see how the resurrection fits closely with that great combined reality. It is the resurrection that declares that the cross was a victory, not a defeat. It therefore announces that God has indeed become king on earth as in heaven.

—*How God Became King* 246

Resurrection Overthrows Those Whose Power Depends on Death

Because of the early Christian belief in Jesus as Messiah, we find the development of the very early belief that Jesus is Lord and that therefore Caesar is not. Already in Paul, the resurrection, both of Jesus and then in the future of his people, is the foundation of the Christian stance of allegiance to a different king, a different Lord. Death is the last weapon of the tyrant, and the point of the resurrection, despite much misunderstanding, is that death has been defeated. Resurrection is not the redescription of death; it is its overthrow and, with that, the overthrow of those whose power depends on it. Despite the sneers and slurs of some contemporary scholars, it was those who believed in the bodily resurrection who were burned at the stake and thrown to the lions. Resurrection was never a way of settling down and becoming respectable; the Pharisees could have told you that. It was the Gnostics, who translated the language of resurrection into a private spirituality and a dualistic cosmology, thereby more or less altering its meaning into its opposite, who escaped persecution. Which emperor would have sleepless nights worrying that his subjects were reading the *Gospel of Thomas*? Resurrection was always bound to get you into trouble, and it regularly did.

—*Surprised by Hope* 50

The Decisive Victory Has Already Been Won

With the resurrection, we uncover the roots of Paul's entire public career. 1 Corinthians 15 is not simply the underlying reasoning behind the whole letter. It is basic to everything Paul believed. It is the reason he became an apostle in the first place. The Messiah's resurrection has constituted him as the world's true Lord, as already the world's rightful ruler, and "He has to go on ruling, you see, until 'he has put all his enemies under his feet.'" Victory *has already* been won over the dark powers of sin and death that have crippled the world and, with it, the humans who were supposed to be God's image-bearers in the world. This victory *will at last* be completed when death itself is destroyed. For Paul, learning to be a Messiah person—learning to live within the great biblical story now culminating in Jesus and the spirit—was all about having the mind and heart, the imagination and understanding transformed, so that it made sense to live in this already/not-yet world.

This was not the easiest place to live, but it was certainly one of the most exhilarating. The Messiah *has already* been raised; all the Messiah's people *will* be raised at his "royal arrival." Christian living, loving, praying, celebrating, suffering, and not least the apostolic ministries that have nothing to do with social prestige or clever rhetoric—all this makes the sense it makes within this eschatological framework. That is the main thing Paul wants to tell the Corinthians. Sitting there in Ephesus, watching the gospel go to work in homes and shops, confronting the powers of the world and seeing magicians burn their books, Paul can sound confident. This is the future, and it works. What they do in the present, within God's new world, is not in vain.

—*Paul: A Biography* 256–57

Time to Wake, Time to Begin Afresh, Time to Flourish

If Lent is a time to give things up, Easter ought to be a time to take things up. Champagne for breakfast again—well, of course. Christian holiness was never meant to be merely negative. Of course, you have to weed the garden from time to time; sometimes the ground ivy may need serious digging before you can get it out. That's Lent for you. But you don't want simply to turn the garden back into a neat bed of blank earth. Easter is the time to sow new seeds and to plant out a few cuttings. If Calvary means putting to death things in your life that need killing off if you are to flourish as a Christian and as a truly human being, then Easter should mean planting, watering, and training up things in your life (personal and corporate) that ought to be blossoming, filling the garden with color and perfume, and, in due course, bearing fruit.

The forty days of the Easter season, until the ascension, ought to be a time to balance out Lent by taking something up, some new task or venture, something wholesome and fruitful and outgoing and self-giving. You may be able to do it only for six weeks, just as you may be able to go without beer or tobacco only for the six weeks of Lent. But if you really make a start on it, it might give you a sniff of new possibilities, new hopes, new ventures you never dreamed of. It might bring something of Easter into your innermost life. It might help you wake up in a whole new way. And that's what Easter is all about.

—Surprised by Hope 257

Singing of God's Reign on the Re-Newed Earth

A good many Easter hymns start by assuming that the point of Easter is that it proves the existence of life after death and encourages us to hope for it. This is then regularly, but ironically, combined with a view of that life after death in which the specific element of resurrection has been quietly removed. "May we go where he is gone," we sing at the end of one well-known hymn, "rest and reign with him in heaven!" But that is precisely *not* the point that the New Testament draws from Jesus's resurrection. Yes, there is a promised rest after the labors of this life, and the word *heaven* may be an appropriate, though vague, way of denoting where this rest takes place. But this time of rest is the prelude to something very

different, which will emphatically involve earth as well. Earth—
the re-newed earth—is where the reign will take place, which is
why the New Testament regularly speaks not of our going to be
where Jesus is but of his coming to where we are, as we saw in the
previous part of the book.

—Surprised by Hope 190

Singing the Right Notes at Easter

There is a many-sided confusion in the hymns we sing, in the way
we celebrate the Christian year, and in the type of funerals or cre-
mations we have. A few words about each of these will show what
I mean.

First, hymns. A glance through the average hymnbook reveals
that a good many references to the future life beyond death are
closer to Tennyson, or even to Shelley, than they are to orthodox
Christianity:

> Till in the ocean of thy love
> We lose ourselves in heaven above.

The words are those of the devout John Keble, but it was he who
was for a moment lost not in Christianity, but in a drop-in-the-
ocean Buddhist eschatology.

And what about his Oxford movement colleague, John Henry
Newman, with his almost Gnostic line?

> So long thy power hath blest me, sure it still
> Will lead me on,

O'er moor and fen, o'er crag and torrent, till
The night is gone.
And with the morn those angel faces smile
Which I have loved long since, and lost awhile.

Did Newman *really* believe that he had a previous life with the angels, whether before his conception or in early childhood, and that he would return there in due course? And—though, of course, the idea of the lonely pilgrim following the "kindly light" across the moors and fens is a powerful, romantic idea—did he really think that the present world and the present life could be described simply as "night"?

Or, what about the blatant Platonism of the hymn "Abide with Me," still a favorite in some circles?

Heaven's morning breaks, and earth's vain shadows flee.

There are entire hymns and anthems that embody this train of thought. In a quick flip through the hymnbook, I noted dozens of other examples, not all explicable by the process of selection at a time when the prevailing theology wanted to say that sort of thing.

Some of the hymns in the revivalist and charismatic traditions slip into the easy mistake, cognate as we shall see with misleading views of the "second coming," of suggesting that Jesus will return to take his people away from earth and "home" to heaven. Thus that wonderful hymn, "How Great Thou Art," in its final stanza, declares:

When Christ shall come, with shout of acclamation,
And take me home, what joy shall fill my heart.

The second line (to anticipate our later argument) might better read, "And heal this world, what joy shall fill my heart." Actually, the original Swedish version of the hymn doesn't talk about Christ coming to take me home; that was the translator's adaptation. Rather, it speaks of the veils of time falling, faith being changed into clear sight, and the bells of eternity summoning us to our sabbath rest, all of which has a lot more to recommend it.

—Surprised by Hope 20–22

Worshipping with Christian Hope

Some hymns, of course, stand out against this trend. "Jerusalem the Golden" draws attention to the decisive final chapters of Revelation. A few hymns speak of being "woken by the last dread call" or of "rising glorious at the last day." One great hymn speaks of God working his purpose out so that "the earth shall be filled with the glory of God as the waters cover the sea." But, towering over all these, is the great All Saints' Day hymn, "For All the Saints," whose sequence of thought catches the New Testament emphasis exactly right. After celebrating the life of the saints in the opening verses, our communion with them in the fourth, and their strengthening of us in the fifth, the sixth verse speaks of our joining them in their present abode, which is *not* the final resting place but rather the intermediate place of rest, joy, and refreshment, for which one name is paradise:

> The golden evening brightens in the west;
> Soon, soon to faithful warriors comes their rest;
> Sweet is the calm of paradise the blest.
> Alleluia, Alleluia!

Only *after* that does the resurrection occur:

> But lo! there breaks a yet more glorious day;
> The saints triumphant rise in bright array;
> The King of glory passes on His way.
> Alleluia, Alleluia!

Which leads in to the triumphant final verse, arriving at last in the new Jerusalem.

—Surprised by Hope 22–23

BEAUTY

So where do you come into it all? Well, you were dead because of your offenses and sins! That was the road you used to travel, keeping in step with this world's "present age"; in step, too, with the ruler of the power of the air, the spirit that is, even now, at work among people whose whole lives consist of disobeying God. Actually, that's how all of us used to behave, conditioned by physical desires. We used to do what our flesh and our minds were urging us to do. What was the result? We too were subject to wrath in our natural state, just like everyone else.

But when it comes to mercy, God is rich! He had such great love for us that he took us at the very point where we were dead through our offenses, and made us alive together with the king. (Yes, you are saved by sheer grace!) He raised us up with him, and made us sit with him—in the heavenly places, in King Jesus! This was so that in the ages to come he could show just how unbelievably rich his grace is, the kindness he has shown us in King Jesus.

How has this all come about? You have been saved by grace, through faith! This doesn't happen on your own initiative; it's God's gift. It isn't on the basis of works, so no one is able to boast. This is the explanation: God has made us what we are. God has created us in King Jesus for the good works that he prepared, ahead of time, as the road we must travel.

—Ephesians 2:1–10, *The Kingdom New Testament* 392–93

The Presence of the Living God in Our Midst

We are all of us hardwired for beauty, searching for a deeper and richer meaning in a world that sometimes seems to overflow with delight but at other times feels dreadful and cold. Beauty—the haunting sense of loveliness, the transient yet utterly powerful stabs of something like love but something more and different as well—is not after all a mere evolutionary twist, an echo of an atavistic urge to hunt prey, to find a mate, or to escape danger. It is a pointer to the strange, gently demanding presence of the living God in the midst of his world.

—Broken Signposts 92–93

Reading Scripture with an Eye for Beauty

If the beauty of creation is a constant pointer to the "glory of God," and if the story of Jesus is the story of his unveiling of that "glory," then we ought to be reading this story with our eyes and ears open for that kind of meaning. And in John's gospel, to be sure, it is. The vivid and haunting exchanges between Jesus and his friends, Jesus and his mother, and Jesus and strangers; Jesus's unexpected actions and flights of explanation—all this suffuses the down-to-earth first-century story with beauty, in the way that twilight invests ordinary objects and scenes with a sudden strange meaning.

—Broken Signposts 96

The Rescuing and Creation-Completing God

The Christian tradition has said, and indeed sung, that glory belongs to God the creator. It is his voice we hear echoing off the crags, murmuring in the sunset. It is his power we feel in the crashing of the waves and the roar of the lion. It is his beauty we see reflected in a thousand faces and forms. And when the cynic reminds us that people fall off crags, get lost after sunset, and are drowned by waves and eaten by lions; when the cynic cautions that faces get old and lined and forms get pudgy and sick—then we Christians do not declare that it was all a mistake. We do not avail ourselves of Plato's safety hatch and say that the *real* world is not a thing of space, time, and matter but another world into which we can escape. We say that the present world is the real one, and that it's in bad shape but expecting to be repaired. We tell, in other words the story of a good Creator longing to put the world back into the good order for which it was designed. We tell the story of a God who does the two things that, some of the time at least, we know we all want and need: a God who completes what he has begun, a God who comes to the rescue of those who seem lost and enslaved in the world the way it now is.

The idea of God coming to the rescue on the one hand, and of God completing creation and putting it to rights on the other, is highlighted in the book of Isaiah. In his eleventh chapter the prophet paints a picture of a world put to rights, of the wolf lying down with the lamb, and of the earth being filled with God's glory as the waters cover the sea. This haunting picture is all the more strange because, five chapters earlier, the prophet had told of seeing angels singing that the whole earth was full of God's glory. As a matter of logic, we want to press the writer: Is the earth *already* full of that glory, or is this something which will only happen in the future? As a matter of understanding beauty, we want to ask: Is the beauty we see at the moment complete, or is it incomplete, pointing to something in the future? And as a matter of far more urgent inquiry, we want to ask the writer, perhaps shaking him by the scruff of the neck: If the earth is full of God's glory, why is it also so full of pain and anguish and screaming and despair?

Isaiah has answers for all these questions, but not the sort of answers you can write on the back of a postcard. The present suffering of the world—about which the biblical writers knew every bit as much as we do—never makes them falter in their claim that the created world really is the good creation of a good God. They live with the tension. And they don't do it by imagining that the present created order is a shabby, second-rate kind of thing, perhaps (as in some kinds of Platonism) made by a shabby, second-rate sort of god. They do it by telling a story of what the one creator God has been doing to rescue his beautiful world and to put it to rights. And the story they tell indicates that the present world really is a signpost to a larger beauty, a deeper truth.

—*Simply Christian* 45–47

The God Who Delights in Beauty

If we read the second half of Exodus straight through, thinking of the slave people who have left the land of the pyramids and are now in the wild and desolate Sinai Peninsula and are about to make something of extraordinary and life-enhancing beauty—we are bound to see this as an amazing and celebratory accomplishment. The Tabernacle was meant to delight the eye, the nose, the ear, and not least the imagination. And part of the point was that it was to be a work of great art and skill. Those involved in the construction and decoration were themselves being ennobled by being involved in God's planned beauty, God's intended dwelling, this "little cosmos," this heaven-and-earth building, they had been instructed to make.

And this is just the start. It is all preparation, again not for a dead king and his potential postmortem existence in some imagined underworld, but for the living God, the powerful and glorious Creator of all, who would come and fill this Tabernacle with his presence. This is a God who delights in beauty and wants his image-bearing human creatures to make more and more of it.

—*Broken Signposts* 101

The Beauty That Points to Its Maker

Our human drive for beauty, for transcendent meaning, turns out to be more than we ever expected. It is God-given: a signpost, designed to lead us back to his presence. Ah, we sigh, but it ends in darkness and horror, with the dust of death covering over the beauty in thick, choking layers of ugliness. Yes, says John, but see what the creator God now does. He makes a way through death and out the other side into new creation, new beauty, new life.

In both the substance of this story and the manner of its telling, John's gospel is speaking of a beauty that had always been pointing back to its maker, even though "the world was made through him, and the world did not know him" (1:10). By focusing our attention, in his telling of Jesus's story, on the Tabernacle and Temple as well as the world of creation, John was picking up their ultimate purpose: to point forward to the coming day when, with the Word having become flesh, beauty itself would become incarnate to make all things new.

We cannot, then, get all the way by argument alone from the human perception and enjoyment of beauty to the existence or character of the Creator. But when, not least through the literary beauty of John's gospel, we are confronted with the beauty of redeeming love in the story of Jesus, we realize, looking back, that the signals we were receiving from all the beauty in the world were telling the truth.

—*Broken Signposts* 110–11

Bearing God's Image as Cocreators

I believe that taking creation and new creation seriously is the way to understand and revitalize aesthetic awareness and perhaps even creativity among Christians today. Beauty matters, dare I say, almost as much as spirituality and justice.

Romans 8, with its rich theology of new creation, offers us a way of appreciating natural beauty. Paul speaks of the creation groaning in travail, waiting to give birth to God's new world. The beauty of the present world, I suggested earlier in the book, has something about it of the beauty of a chalice, beautiful in itself but more hauntingly beautiful in what we know it's meant to be filled with; or that of the violin, beautiful in itself but particularly because we know the music it's capable of. Another example might be the engagement ring, which is meant as it is to delight the eye but which is meant even more to delight the heart because of what it promises.

It is, I believe, part of being made in God's image that we are ourselves creators or at least procreators. The extraordinary ability to bring forth new life, supremely, of course, through begetting children but in millions of other ways as well, is central to the mandate the human race receives in Genesis 1 and 2. To make sense of and celebrate a beautiful world through the production of artifacts that are themselves beautiful is part of the call to be stewards of creation, as was Adam's naming of the animals. Genuine art is thus itself a response to the beauty of creation, which itself is a pointer to the beauty of God.

—Surprised by Hope 222–23

The Vocation of the Artist of Hope

The great promises in Isaiah return to this: YHWH will do a new thing, remaking creation so that the desert blossoms like a rose, and then his glory will be revealed and all flesh will see it together (Isa. 35:2; 40:5; 60:1). And it is out of this matrix of thought that apocalyptic arises, not in itself the dualistic worldview sometimes imagined but rather as a glimpse of the already existing reality of new creation from within the old, so that those living within the old catch sight of the new, inviting them not to escapism but to hope.

The point of art, I believe, is not least to be able to say something like that, to draw attention—not to a shallow or trivial pietistic point, as though to lead the mind away from the world and its problems and into a merely cozy contemplation of God's presence, but rather to the multilayered and many-dimensioned aspects of the present world, to the pains and the terror, yes, but also to the creative tension between the present filling of the world with YHWH's glory and the promised future filling, as the waters cover the sea. When art tries to speak of the new world, the final world, in terms only of the present world, it collapses into sentimentality; when it speaks of the present world only in terms of its shame and horror, it collapses into brutalism. The vocation of the artist is to speak of the present as beautiful in itself but pointing beyond itself, to enable us to see both the glory that fills the earth and the glory that will flood it to overflowing, and to speak, within that, of the shame without ignoring the promise and of the promise without forgetting the shame.

The artist is thus to be like the Israelite spies in the desert, bringing back fruit from the promised land to be tasted in advance.

That story, indeed, is one of the moments when YHWH surprisingly promises that not only the promised land but the whole world will be filled with his glory (Num. 14:21; cf. 14:10). But just as not all the spies brought back an encouraging report, many artists recoil from the challenging vision of the future and prefer to give the apparently more relevant message of despair. Here is the challenge, I believe, for the Christian artist, in whatever sphere: to tell the story of the new world so that people can taste it and want it, even while acknowledging the reality of the desert in which we presently live.

—*Surprised by Scripture* 202–3

Playing Our Part in God's Grand Design

The resurrection, God's re-creation of his wonderful world, which began with the resurrection of Jesus and continues mysteriously as God's people live in the risen Christ and in the power of his spirit, means that what we do in Christ and by the Spirit in the present is not wasted. It will last and be enhanced in God's new world.

I have no idea precisely what this means. I do not know how the painting an artist paints today in prayer and wisdom will find a place in God's new world. I don't know what musical instruments we will have to play Bach, though I'm sure Bach's music will be there. I don't know how my planting a tree today will relate to the wonderful trees that will be in God's recreated world. I don't know how my work for justice for the poor, for remission of global debts, will reappear in that new world. But I know that God's new world of justice and joy, of hope for the whole earth, was launched when Jesus came out of the tomb on Easter morning; I know he calls me and you to live in him and by the power of his spirit, and so to be new-creation people here and now, giving birth to signs and symbols of the kingdom on earth as in heaven. The resurrection of Jesus and the gift of the Spirit mean that we are called to bring forth real and effective signs of God's renewed creation even in the midst of the present age. Not to do so is at best to put ourselves in the position of those Second Temple Jews who believed they had to wait passively for God to act—when God *has* acted in Jesus to inaugurate his kingdom on earth as in heaven. At worst, not to bring forth works and signs of renewal in God's creation is to collude, as gnosticism always does, with the forces of sin and death.

This doesn't mean that we are called to build the kingdom by our own efforts, or even with the help of the Spirit. The final kingdom, when it comes, will be the free gift of God, a massive act of grace and new creation. But we are called to build *for* the kingdom. Like craftsmen working on a great cathedral, we have each been given instructions about the particular stone we are to spend our lives carving, without knowing or being able to guess where it will take its place within the grand design.

—*Surprised by Scripture* 105–6

A Hunger for Beauty

The church should reawaken its hunger for beauty at every level. This is essential and urgent. It is central to Christian living that we should celebrate the goodness of creation, ponder its present brokenness, and, insofar as we can, celebrate in advance the healing of the world, the new creation itself. Art, music, literature, dance, theater, and many other expressions of human delight and wisdom, can all be explored in new ways.

The point is this. The arts are not the pretty but irrelevant bits around the border of reality. They are highways into the center of a reality which cannot be glimpsed, let alone grasped, any other way. The present world is good, but broken and in any case incomplete; art of all kinds enables us to understand that paradox in its many dimensions. But the present world is also designed for something which has not yet happened. It is like a violin waiting to be played: beautiful to look at, graceful to hold—and yet if you'd never heard one in the hands of a musician, you wouldn't believe the new dimensions of beauty yet to be revealed. Perhaps art can show something of that, can glimpse the future possibilities pregnant within the present time. It is like a chalice: again, beautiful to look at, pleasing to hold, but waiting to be filled with the wine that, itself full of sacramental possibilities, gives the chalice its fullest meaning. Perhaps art can help us to look beyond the immediate beauty with all its puzzles, and to glimpse that new creation that makes sense not only of beauty but of the world as a whole, and ourselves within it. Perhaps.

The artist can then join forces with those who work for justice and those who struggle for redemptive relationships, and together encourage and sustain those who are reaching out for a genuine, redemptive spirituality. The way to make sense of it all is to look

ahead. Look to the coming time when the earth shall be filled
with the knowledge and glory of the Lord as the waters cover the
sea; and then live in the present in the light of that promise, sure
that it will come fully true because it was already fulfilled when
God did for Jesus at Easter what he is going to do for the whole
of creation.

—*Simply Christian* 235–36

Describing the World as It Will Be

There is a wonderful opportunity for Christians with an integrated
worldview, and with a theology of both creation and new creation,
to find the way forward, perhaps to *lead* the way forward. When we
read Romans 8, we find Paul affirming that the whole of creation is
groaning in travail as it longs for its redemption. Creation is good,
but it is not God. It is beautiful, but its beauty is at present transient.
It is in pain, but that pain is taken into the very heart of God and
becomes part of the pain of new birth. The beauty of creation, to
which art responds and which it tries to express, imitate, and highlight, is not simply the beauty it possesses in itself but the beauty
it possesses in view of what is promised to it: back to the chalice,
the violin, the engagement ring. We are committed to describing
the world not just as it should be, not just as it is, but as—by God's
grace alone!—one day it will be. And we should never forget that
when Jesus rose from the dead, as the paradigm, first example, and
generating power of the whole new creation, the marks of the nails
were not just visible on his hands and his feet. They were the way
he was to be identified. When art comes to terms with *both* the
wounds of the world *and* the promise of resurrection and learns

how to express and respond to both at once, we will be on the way
to a fresh vision, a fresh mission.

—Surprised by Hope 224

Declaring New Creation Through Artistic Order and Freedom

If the Temple in Jerusalem, the place where God's own glory was
to dwell, was seen as the "little world," the microcosm where the
world's beauty was to be concentrated, then part of the virtue of
the royal priesthood, the new and living Temple, ought to be the
cultivation and celebration of beauty at every level. This calls for the
"royal" virtues of bringing that delicately balanced combination—
order and freedom—to birth, as art has lurched from the over-
ordered world of cubism to the multiply disordered and deliberately
chaotic world of much recent pop art. How can we work in the
present time to anticipate the future of God's remade world, where
the horrors of today's world will at last be overcome? That is the
challenge, as we seek to generate fresh expressions of beauty. Today's aesthetic world lurches to and fro between the brutalism that,
starting with an architectural style, has spilled over into all manner
of sheer tawdry ugliness, and the sentimentalism that, wishing still
to glimpse the loveliness of creation, cannot find a way to express
that without collapsing into kitsch. The virtues of the royal priesthood are called for to declare, in art as well as word, the hard-won
victory of Jesus over the evil that has corrupted and defaced the
world, and to declare the new creation, launched in the resurrection, of a world full of freedom and glory.

—After You Believe 232

The Art of Surprising Hope

A parody of this is found in the passionate belief of many artists and writers of the last generation that the only true art is art that is politically committed. At least the Marxists who thought like that had grasped the point that neither sentimentality nor brutalism will do, but only eschatology in the process of being realized. If Christian artists can glimpse the truth of which that Marxist vision is a parody, they may find a way forward to celebrating beauty without lapsing into either pantheism or cynicism. This will take serious imagination, imagination fueled by reflection and prayer at the foot of the cross and before the empty tomb, imagination that will discern the mysteries of God's judgment on evil and God's reaffirmation, through resurrection, of his beautiful creation. Art at its best draws attention not only to the way things are but also to the way things will be, when the earth is filled with the knowledge of God as the waters cover the sea. That remains a surprising hope, and perhaps it will be the artists who are best at conveying both the hope and the surprise.

—*Surprised by Hope* 224–25

The Beautiful Logic of the Mission of God

What we can and must do in the present, if we are obedient to the gospel, if we are following Jesus, and if we are indwelt, energized, and directed by the Spirit, is to build *for* the kingdom. This brings us back to 1 Corinthians 15:58 once more: what you do in the Lord *is not in vain*. You are not oiling the wheels of a machine that's about to roll over a cliff. You are not restoring a great painting that's shortly going to be thrown on the fire. You are not planting roses in a garden that's about to be dug up for a building site. You are—strange though it may seem, almost as hard to believe as the resurrection itself—accomplishing something that will become in due course part of God's new world.

Every act of love, gratitude, and kindness; every work of art or music inspired by the love of God and delight in the beauty of his creation; every minute spent teaching a severely handicapped child to read or to walk; every act of care and nurture, of comfort and support, for one's fellow human beings and for that matter one's fellow nonhuman creatures; and, of course, every prayer, all Spirit-led teaching, every deed that spreads the gospel, builds up the church, embraces and embodies holiness rather than corruption, and makes the name of Jesus honored in the world—all of this will find its way, through the resurrecting power of God, into the new creation that God will one day make.

That is the logic of the mission of God. God's re-creation of his wonderful world, which began with the resurrection of Jesus and continues mysteriously as God's people live in the risen Christ and in the power of his Spirit, means that what we do in Christ and by the Spirit in the present is not wasted. It will last all the way into God's new world. In fact, it will be enhanced there.

—Surprised by Hope 208–9

The Panoramic View of Ephesians

From where I sit I can see dozens of photographs, mixed in between piles of books and papers, coffee cups and candlesticks.

Most of them are small, particular shots: family members, holiday scenery, a white pony by the seashore, a distant cityscape. There is even a picture of my wife taking a picture of the pope (don't ask).

But in the next room, just out of sight but clear in memory, there is a frame that contains fourteen photographs, cut and joined to make a complete panorama. It was taken on vacation in Switzerland, on the mountain ridge called Schynige Platte in the Bernese Oberland. The camera has swung through a full circle, so that the left end of the panorama actually joins up with the right end. In the center are the great peaks: the Eiger, the Mönch, and the glorious Jungfrau. All around are lesser but still dramatic mountains, snowy and tremendous, bathed in summer sunlight.

It is a different kind of picture altogether from the ones in front of me, though it includes elements familiar from the smaller photos: a family member, holiday scenery, grazing animals (in this case cows), and even, in the far distance, a small town. They are all now in the one frame, and they mean all the more as a result. In a single glance, you can take in an entire world.

Ephesians is like that.

—Paul: A Biography 294–95

Ultimate Beauty

That great vision at the end of the book of Revelation is a vision of ultimate beauty. The word *beauty* doesn't occur much in the Bible, but the celebration of creation all the way from Genesis, through the Psalms and Prophets, on into the gospels and here in Revelation, should alert us to the fact that, though the ancient Jewish people did not theorize about beauty like the Greeks did (that's another story, and a fascinating one, though not for today), they knew a great deal about it and poured their rich aesthetic sensibility not only into poetry but also into one building in particular: the temple in Jerusalem, whose legendary beauty inspired poets, musicians, and dancers alike. This is the temple where YHWH's glory is glimpsed, not as a retreat *from* the world but as a foretaste of what is promised *for* the whole world. In the great vision of John, the temple has disappeared because the whole city has become a temple; the point of the city is not that it is a place of retreat from a wicked world but that its new life is poured out into the whole world, to refresh and heal it.

Sadly, verses 15–21 of Revelation 21 are often omitted in public reading, presumably because those who compose lectionaries suppose these verses to be boring and repetitive. But in passages like this we see, with the eye of the apocalyptic visionary, the astonishingly powerful beauty of God's new creation, beauty that should serve as an inspiration to artists and, through their work, to all of us as we seek to give birth to the life of the new creation within the old. The golden city, perfectly proportioned, equal in length and breadth and even, remarkably, height, has, says John, the glory of God and a radiance like a very rare jewel, like jasper, clear as crystal. The wall is built of jasper, while the city itself is pure gold, clear as glass. The foundations are adorned with jewels: jasper, sapphire, agate, emerald, onyx, cornelian, chrysolite, beryl, topaz, chrysoprase, jacinth, and amethyst. The twelve gates are twelve pearls, while the streets of the city are pure gold, transparent as glass. I confess that my knowledge of jewelry is so poor that I can't at once envisage those shining foundations, but I know that whoever wrote this passage delighted in them and wanted readers to do the same, relishing them one by one and in their glittering combination.

—*Surprised by Scripture* 203–4

ASCENSION

*Because of all this, and because I'd heard that you are loyal and faithful
to Jesus the master, and that you show love to all God's holy people,
I never stop giving thanks for you as I remember you in my prayers. I
pray that the God of King Jesus our Lord, the father of glory, would
give you, in your spirit, the gift of being wise, of seeing things people
can't normally see, because you are coming to know him and to have
the eyes of your inmost self opened to God's light. Then you will know
exactly what the hope is that goes with God's call; you will know the
wealth of the glory of his inheritance in his holy people; and you will
know the outstanding greatness of his power toward us who are loyal
to him in faith, according to the working of his strength and power.*

*This was the power at work in the king when God raised him from
the dead and sat him at his right hand in the heavenly places, above
all rule and authority and power and lordship, and above every name
that is invoked, both in the present age and also in the age to come.
Yes: God has "put all things under his feet," and has given him to the
church as the head over all. The church is his body; it is the fullness of
the one who fills all in all.*

—Ephesians 1:15–23, *The Kingdom New Testament* 392

Rethinking Heaven

If Easter is about Jesus as the *prototype* of the new creation, his as-cension is about his *enthronement* as the one who is now in charge. Easter tells us that Jesus is himself the first part of new creation; his ascension tells us that he is now running it.

Once more, you can only understand the ascension if you push out of your mind the idea of "heaven" you began with and try to imagine a more biblical picture instead. For most people today, as we've said already, "heaven" is a location of a completely different sort from the world in which we live. It is timeless, nonphysical, im-material. (People sometimes say "spiritual" at this point, but that's a misleading description of the way the early Christians thought and spoke. For them, "spiritual" had to do with the work of God's Spirit; and God's Spirit was at work most definitely within, not apart from, the world of space, time, and matter.) So when Luke tells the story of Jesus going up to heaven in a cloud, forty days after his resurrection, and when Paul writes of Jesus being "exalted" to heaven (e.g., Phil. 2:9–11), the one thing we should *not* think of is that, after his death, Jesus is now "going to heaven" in the normal modern sense of that phrase.

—*Simply Jesus* 195

Jesus Is Now in Charge, Not Absent

In both the Nicene and Apostle's Creeds, it also says that Jesus, through his ascension, was "seated at the right hand of the Father."

In ancient Jewish thought, with echoes of Daniel 7, this could only mean that, from that moment, Jesus was the Father's right-hand man, in charge of the whole world. But in our own day the "ascension" is just a way of saying that Jesus "went to heaven when he died." To speak of him "sitting at the Father's right hand" has become simply a fancy, perhaps even a fanciful, way of saying "he entered into a very splendid and glorious position." We have been lured, perhaps by our embarrassment at the literalistic sense of Jesus flying up like a spaceman to a "heaven" located a few miles up within our universe, into ignoring the real meaning both of "heaven" (which is not a place within our universe at all, but God's place, intersecting with our world in all sorts of ways) and of the ascension itself, which is about the sovereignty of Jesus as the Father's accredited and appointed agent. We have, as a result, understood the ascension in vague terms of supernatural glory, rather than in the precise terms (as in Matt. 28:18; Acts 1:6–11) of Jesus's authority over the world. In fact, the ascension, for many people, implies Jesus's absence, not his universal presence and sovereign rule. And this time it isn't only Matthew, Mark, Luke, and John who will raise objections; it's Paul, Hebrews, and Revelation as well. They all think that Jesus is already in charge of the world. (Check out, for instance, 1 Cor. 15:20–28; Heb. 2:5–9; Rev. 5:6–14). That was what they understood by "God's kingdom."

—*How God Became King* 15–16

Four Things About the Ascension

1.

Overlap of Heaven and Earth

There are four things to remember about the ascension. Each of them contributes to its meaning within the story we have been telling. First, to repeat, heaven and earth are not a long way apart. They are meant to overlap and interlock and finally to be joined fully and forever. And the whole point of Jesus's identity, all along, is that he has been a one-man walking Temple; he has been, already, the place where heaven and earth have met, where people on earth have come into contact with the life and power of heaven. So for Jesus, "going to heaven" isn't a matter of disappearing into the far distance. Jesus is like somebody who has two homes. The homes are right next door to each other, and there is a connecting door. One day the partition wall will be knocked down and there will be one, glorious, heaven-and-earth mixture.

What that illustration doesn't quite catch is that heaven and earth are not the same *kind* of space. They are not merely contiguous, like two next-door houses. Heaven permeates earth. If Jesus is now in "heaven," he is present to every place on earth. Had he remained on earth, he wouldn't have been present anywhere except the one place where he was. The ascension enables him to be present everywhere.

—*Simply Jesus* 195–97

2.

A New King on the Throne

Second, and most important for our whole theme, heaven is the place from which the world is run. It is the CEO's office. You can see this in the dramatic scenes in the book of Daniel, where this or that pagan king is warned about "the God of heaven." That doesn't mean, "good, he's safely in heaven, a long way away, so we can do as we like." It means, "God is in the place where he can call the shots, and you'd better watch out!" This is how, in the story of Jesus, the long narrative stretching back to his baptism (and, in Luke particularly, to his birth) comes to its climax. He was born to be king of the world, the king who would upstage Caesar himself; he was baptized as Israel's Messiah, who in Psalm 2 would rule the nations; and now he is enthroned, installed officially as what he already was in theory. This, along with the resurrection, is part of what Jesus meant when he told his followers that the "son of man" would "come in his kingdom" and that they would see it (Matt. 16:28).

—*Simply Jesus* 195–97

3.

The Great Reversal

This, indeed, is part of the point of Luke's description about Jesus being "lifted up" and taken out of sight by a "cloud" (Acts 1:9), which brings us to the third point about ascension. If, as I have stressed, "heaven" and "earth" are not far apart, but are actually meeting and mingling in and through Jesus, why this vertical movement? Here we may want to remain open-minded as to how much Luke intends this description to be a literal account of a concrete reality and how much he is intending primarily to evoke that famous passage in Daniel 7:13 in which "one like a son of man" comes on the clouds of heaven to be presented before and enthroned beside one who is called "the Ancient One."

What I mean is this. Luke certainly intends us to be thinking of Daniel 7 in all its political significance. This is the moment at which Israel's representative is installed as the true world ruler, with all the warring pagan nations made subject to him. How much Luke intends us also to be thinking of an actual physical event it is hard to say. There is no problem, as far as I can see, about it *being* a physical event; as some have suggested, an upward movement is perhaps the best way of indicating a departure from one sphere in order to arrive in another. But neither the ancient Jews nor the early Christians believed that "heaven" was a location within our present continuum of space and matter, a location situated at some distance from our world and to be reached by a primitive form of space travel. We are, after all, at this point at the edge of worldview, of language, of all human thought. We should not expect to be able to put a story like this into easy contemporary categories. Better to stick with this third point about ascension, that it is the fulfillment of Daniel 7. This is the great reversal, the moment when God welcomes the one who has suffered as Israel's representative at the hands of the monsters and is now to exercise judgment over them.

—*Simply Jesus* 195–97

4.

Caesar Radically Upstaged

This brings us to the fourth and last point about the ascension. Anyone reading Luke's account at the beginning of Acts and already being familiar with the world of the early Roman empire would realize what was happening. After the death of Julius Caesar, people swore they had seen his soul ascending to heaven. Augustus, Caesar's adopted son, promptly declared that Julius was therefore a god; which meant that he, Augustus, was now "son of god." This was, to put it mildly, of considerable political advantage. When Augustus himself died, the process was repeated, as it was with many (though not all) of his successors.

Luke's story isn't an exact copy of this tradition. Luke, after all, like all the early Christians, is a monotheist. There is no sense in which he supposes he is describing the adding of another god to the collection of them already "in heaven." And Jesus himself is "son of God" in a sense that would take several generations of prayerful thinkers to explore fully. Nevertheless, the parallel is sufficiently close to make any readers in the Roman world realize what is going on. Jesus is radically upstaging Caesar. Actually, if we think of the story as the opening frame of the book of Acts, we get the point, because the closing frame is Paul in Rome, under Caesar's nose, announcing God as king and Jesus as Lord "with all boldness, and with no one stopping him." The whole book is the story of how Jesus, exercising his power as the CEO of earth as of heaven, sends out his followers as ambassadors to make his kingdom a reality, climaxing with the strange paradox of Paul in chains announcing that the Roman world has a new emperor. It is that paradox, indeed, that sets the tone for all kingdom work in the present time.

—*Simply Jesus* 195–97

Heaven as God's Space,
Not His Location

"God is in heaven," says one of the more hard-nosed biblical writers, "and you are upon earth; so let your words be few" (Eccl. 5:2). That comes as a warning to those of us who write and speak for a living, but it highlights what the biblical tradition always insists upon: that if we are to think of God "living" anywhere, that place is known as "heaven."

Two misunderstandings need clearing up at once. First, despite what some later theologians seem to have imagined, the ancient biblical writers did not suppose that, had they been able to travel in space, they would have come sooner or later to the place where God lived. Granted, the word "heaven" in Hebrew and Greek can mean, effectively, "the sky"; but the biblical writers move more effortlessly than most modern readers between that meaning (a location within the world of space, time, and matter) and the regular meaning of "God's dwelling place"—that is, a different *sort* of "location" altogether. "Heaven" in this latter, very common biblical sense is God's space *as opposed to* our space, not God's location *within* our space-time universe. The question is then whether God's space and our space intersect; and if so how, when, and where.

The second misunderstanding comes about because the word "heaven" is regularly used, misleadingly but very frequently, to mean "the place where God's people will be with him, in blissful happiness, after they die." It has thus come to be thought of as a destination, a final resting place for the souls of the blessed; and, as such, it has regularly been paired with its assumed opposite, "hell." But "heaven" has this meaning, not because, in the earliest Christian traditions, it was the final destination of the redeemed, but because the word offers a way of talking about where God always is, so that the promise held out in the phrase "going to heaven" is more or less exactly "going to be with God in the place where he's been all along." Thus "heaven" is not just a future reality, but a present one. And we then meet the same question as before, from a different angle: How does this "place," this "location" (I use quote marks because I am *not* referring to a place or location within our world of space, time, and matter) interact with our world? Indeed, does it do so at all?

In the Bible, our world is called "earth." Just as "heaven" can refer to the sky, but very commonly refers to God's dimension of reality as opposed to ours, so the word "earth" can refer to the actual soil beneath our feet, but also regularly refers, as in the earlier quotation from Ecclesiastes, to our space, our dimension of reality, as opposed to God's. "The heavens are the Lord's heavens, but the earth he has given to human beings" (Ps. 115:16). Thus, though the Bible can speak of places "under the earth" in addition to heaven and earth themselves, the normal pairing is the one we find in the first line of the Bible: "In the beginning God created the heavens and the earth."

—*Simply Christian* 58–60

All Power and Authority in the Universe Is Now Subject to Jesus

We can sum it all up like this. We live in the period of Jesus's sovereign rule over the world—a reign that has not yet been completed, since, as Paul says in 1 Corinthians 15:20–28, he must reign until "he has put all his enemies under his feet," including death itself. But Paul is clear that we do not have to wait until the second coming to say that Jesus is already reigning. In fact, Paul in that passage says something we might not otherwise have guessed: the reign of Jesus, in its present mode, is strictly temporary. God the father has installed Jesus in power, to act on his behalf; but when his task is complete, "the son himself will be placed in proper order" under God the father, "so that God may be all in all." I do not think that Paul would have quarreled with the Nicene Creed when it says, of Jesus, that his kingdom "will have no end." That, after all, is what the book of Revelation states on page after page. But I stress this point in 1 Corinthians because it makes it very clear that the present age is indeed the age of the reign of Jesus the Messiah.

In trying to understand that present reign of Jesus, though, we have seen two apparently quite different strands. On the one hand, we have seen that all the powers and authorities in the universe are now, in some sense or other, subject to Jesus. This doesn't mean that they all do what he wants all the time, only that Jesus intends that there should be social and political structures of governance. Jesus himself pointed out to Pilate that the authority that the Roman governor had over him had been given to him "from above" (John 19:11). Once that has been said, we should not be shy about recognizing—however paradoxical it seems to our black-and-white minds!—the God-givenness of structures of authority, even when they are tyrannical and violent. Part of what we say when we say that a structure is God-given is also that God will hold it to account. We have trained ourselves to think of political legitimacy simply in terms of the method or mode of appointment (e.g., if you've won an election). The ancient Jews and early Christians were far more interested in holding rulers to account with regard to what they were actually doing. God wants rulers, but God will call them to account.

—*Simply Jesus* 229

The Good Works by Which Jesus's Sovereignty Is Put into Effect

Jesus rules the world today not just through his people "behaving themselves," keeping a code of ethics, and engaging in certain spiritual practices, important though those are. The Beatitudes are much more than a "new rule of life," as though one could practice them in private, away from the world. Jesus rules the world through those who launch new initiatives that radically challenge the accepted ways of doing things: jubilee projects to remit ridiculous and unpayable debt, housing trusts that provide accommodation for low-income families or homeless people, local and sustainable agricultural projects that care for creation instead of destroying it in the hope of quick profit, and so on. We have domesticated the Christian idea of "good works," so that it has simply become "the keeping of ethical commands." In the New Testament, "good works" are what Christians are supposed to be doing in and for the wider community. *That is how the sovereignty of Jesus is put into effect.*

What, then, does it look like when Jesus is enthroned? It looks like new projects that do what Jesus's mother's great song announced: put down the mighty from their seat, exalt the humble and meek, fulfill ancient promises, but send the rich away empty. The church made its way in the world for many centuries by doing all this kind of thing. Now that in many countries the "state" has assumed responsibility for many of them (that's part of what I mean by saying that the state, not least in Western democracies, has become "ecclesial," a kind of secular shadow church), the church has been in danger of forgetting that these are its primary tasks. Jesus went about feeding the hungry, curing the sick, and rescuing lost sheep; his Body is supposed to be doing the same. That is how his kingdom is at work. That is how *he* is at work. Acts begins by saying that in the first book (i.e., the gospel of Luke) the writer described "everything Jesus *began* to do and teach" (Acts 1:1). The implication is clear. The story of Acts, even after Jesus's ascension, is about what Jesus *continued* to do and teach. And the way he did it and taught it was—through his followers.

—*Simply Jesus* 219–20

The Fulfillment of a Dream

The prime example of a movement that held together the themes of God's kingdom, on the one hand, and a messianic kingdom, on the other, was indeed that of Jesus himself. Within a few years of his death, the first followers of Jesus of Nazareth were speaking and writing about him, and indeed singing about him, not just as a great teacher and healer, not just as a great spiritual leader and holy man, but as a strange combination: *both* the Davidic king *and* the returning god. He was, they said, the anointed one, the one who had been empowered and equipped by God's Spirit to do all kinds of things, which somehow meant that he was God's anointed, the Messiah, the coming king. He was the one who had been exalted after his suffering and now occupied the throne beside the throne of God himself.

But they also believed that Jesus had thereby fulfilled the dreams of those who wanted God, and God alone, to be king. Jesus, they believed, had lived and worked within the same overall story as other would-be kings of the time. But he had transformed the story around himself. In Jesus, they believed, God himself had indeed become king. Jesus had come to take charge, and he was now on the throne of the whole world. The dream of a coming king—of

God himself as the coming king, ruling the world in justice and peace—had come true at last. Once we get inside the world of Jesus's day and begin to understand what he might have meant by the word "God," we begin to understand too the breathtaking claim that Jesus was, himself, now in charge. He was the one who had "an everlasting dominion" (Dan. 7:14), a kingship that would never be destroyed.

This claim can never be, in our sense or indeed in the ancient sense, merely "religious." It involves everything, from power and politics to culture and family. It catches up the "religious" meanings, including personal spirituality and transformation, and the philosophical ones, including ethics and worldview. But it places them all within a larger vision that can be stated quite simply: God is now in charge, and he is in charge in and through Jesus. That is the vision that explains what Jesus did and said, what happened to Jesus, and what his followers subsequently did and said. And what happened to them, too.

—*Simply Jesus* 54–55

Joining the Rule of the Enthroned Jesus

Jesus is also at work in all sorts of ways in and through the church itself. We are to be, as Paul says, "renewed in the image of the creator" (Col. 3:10)—renewed, that is, by worship of God and the lamb, so that we are able to serve as "kings and priests," putting Jesus's rule into effect in the world and summing up creation's praise before him. This is what it looks like, today, when Jesus is running the world. This is, after all, what he told us to expect. The poor in spirit will be making the kingdom of heaven happen. The meek will be taking over the earth, so gently that the powerful won't notice until it's too late. The peacemakers will be putting the arms manufacturers out of business. Those who are hungry and thirsty for God's justice will be analyzing government policy and legal rulings and speaking up on behalf of those at the bottom of the pile. The merciful will be surprising everybody by showing that there is a different way to do human relations other than being judgmental, eager to put everyone else down. "You are the light of the world," said Jesus. "You are the salt of the earth." He was announcing a program yet to be completed. He was inviting his hearers, then and now, to join him in making it happen. This is, quite simply, what it looks like when Jesus is enthroned.

—Simply Jesus 231

Christian Faith in Ascension Focus

If the church identifies its structures, its leadership, its liturgy, its buildings, or anything else with its Lord—and that's what happens if you ignore the ascension or turn it into another way of talking about the Spirit—what do you get? You get, on the one hand, what Shakespeare called "the insolence of office" and, on the other hand, the despair of late middle age, as people realize it doesn't work. (I see this all too frequently among those who bought heavily into the soggy rationalism of the 1950s and 1960s.) Only when we grasp firmly that the church is *not* Jesus and Jesus is *not* the church— when we grasp, in other words, the truth of the ascension, that the one who is indeed present with us by the Spirit is *also* the Lord who is strangely absent, strangely other, strangely different from us and over against us, the one who tells Mary Magdalene not to cling to him—only then are we rescued from both hollow triumphalism and shallow despair.

Conversely, only when we grasp and celebrate the fact that Jesus has gone on ahead of us into God's space, God's new world, and is both already ruling the rebellious present world as its rightful Lord and also interceding for us at the Father's right hand—when we grasp and celebrate, in other words, what the ascension tells us about Jesus's continuing *human* work in the present—are we rescued from a wrong view of world history and equipped for the task of justice in the present. We are also, significantly, rescued from the attempts that have been made to create alternative mediators, and, in particular, an alternative mediatrix, in his place. Get the ascension right, and your view of the church, of the sacraments, and of the mother of Jesus can get back into focus.

—*Surprised by Hope* 113

Challenging Contemporary Cosmologies

The ascension speaks of the Jesus who remains truly human and hence in an important sense absent from us while in another equally important sense present to us in a new way. At this point the Holy Spirit and the sacraments become enormously important since they are precisely the means by which Jesus is present. Often in the church we have been so keen to stress the presence of Jesus by these means that we have failed to indicate his simultaneous absence and have left people wondering whether this is, so to speak, "all there is to it." The answer is no, it isn't. The lordship of Jesus; the fact that there is already a human being at the helm of the world; his present intercession for us—all this is over and above his presence with us. It is even over and above our *sense of* that presence, which, of course, comes and goes with our own moods and circumstances.

Now it is of course one thing to say all this, to show how it fits together and sets us free from some of the nonsenses we would otherwise get into. It's quite another to be able to envisage or imagine it, to know what it is we're really talking about when we speak of Jesus being still human, still, in fact, an *embodied* human—actually, a *more solidly embodied* human than we are—but absent from this present world. We need, in fact, a new and better cosmology, a new and better way of thinking about the world than the one our culture, not least post-Enlightenment culture, has bequeathed us.

Surprised by Hope 114–15

POWER

James and John, Zebedee's sons, came up to him.

"Teacher," they said, "we want you to grant us whatever we ask."

"What do you want me to do for you?" asked Jesus.

"Grant us," they said, "that when you're there in all your glory, one of us will sit at your right, and the other at your left."

"You don't know what you're asking for!" Jesus replied. "Can you drink the cup I'm going to drink? Can you receive the baptism I'm going to receive?"

"Yes," they said, "we can."

"Well," said Jesus, "you will drink the cup I drink; you will receive the baptism I receive. But sitting at my right hand or my left—that's not up to me. it's been assigned already."

When the other ten disciples heard, they were angry with James and John.

Jesus called them to him.

"You know how it is in the pagan nations," he said. "Think how their so-called rulers act. They lord it over their subjects. The high and mighty ones boss the rest around. But that's not how it's going to be with you. Anyone who wants to be great among you must become your servant. Anyone who wants to be first must be everyone's slave. Don't you see? The son of man didn't come to be waited on. He came to be the servant, to give his life 'as a ransom for many.'"

—Mark 10:42–45, *The Kingdom New Testament* 88–89

The Power of the Crucified King

The difference between the kingdoms of the world and the kingdom of God lies exactly in this, that the kingdom of God comes through the death and resurrection of his Son, not through naked displays of brute force or wealth.

—Surprised by Hope 245

God's Love Story

The kingdom is radically defined in relation to Jesus's entire agenda of suffering, leading to the cross. This draws the sting of any hint of (what we call) triumphalism. As in the book of Revelation, the victory and sovereignty belong to the slaughtered Lamb—and the slaughtering was not simply a one-time unhappy moment that can now be replaced by the Lamb's followers taking up arms to bring in his kingdom by the methods of Herod and Pilate. Those who would implement Jesus's kingdom are just as prone to forget this as Peter and the others were, trying to dissuade Jesus from his insistence on the suffering and dying vocation with which he interpreted his messiahship, eager to push him toward the vision of a kingdom much more like the kingdoms of the world.

The paradox remains, and those who engage most directly in the work of the kingdom know, again and again, that the principalities and powers they are confronting are cruel, mean, and dirty. Martyrdom of one sort or another, suffering of one sort or another, is what kingdom-bringers must expect. Here, incidentally, is the

Christian answer to the postmodern challenge. Our "big story" is not a power story. It isn't designed to gain money, sex, or power for ourselves, though those temptations will always lie close at hand. It is a love story—God's love story, operating through Jesus and then, by the Spirit, through Jesus's followers. This is the building of the church against which the powers of hell, and for that matter deconstruction, cannot prevail.

—How God Became King 241

The Gift of Power for Creation

Human beings are given power on the very first page of the Bible. In Genesis 1, various features of the newly made world (vegetation, birds, and animals) are given instructions to multiply, to flourish, to get on with being themselves and with propagating their own species. When humans are made, however, there is an extra dimension. Humans too are commanded to be fruitful and multiply (1:28), but they are given an extra awesome and responsible vocation: to "have dominion over the fish of the sea, over the birds of the air, and over the cattle, and over all the wild animals of the earth, and over every creeping thing that creeps upon the earth" (1:26, 28). Power, in other words, comes from God and is given to human beings.

—Broken Signposts 165

The Dominion of Humility and Obedience

When it comes to kings themselves, one psalm holds out a majestic vision of the ways in which "dominion" is supposed to be exercised:

> Give the king your justice, O God,
> and your righteousness to a king's son.
> May he judge your people with righteousness,
> and your poor with justice. . . .
> May he have dominion from sea to sea,
> and from the River to the ends of the earth. . . .
> For he delivers the needy when they call,
> the poor and those who have no helper.
> He has pity on the weak and the needy,
> and saves the lives of the needy.
> From oppression and violence he redeems their life;
> and precious is their blood in his sight. (72:1–2, 8, 12–14)

That's what "dominion" is there for. It can easily be exploited for one's own advantage, as we all know. The stories of monarchies, including the ancient Hebrew monarchies, are full of such abuses, but there is a true use to which rulers can and must be recalled. God wants his world to be ruled wisely, by humble and obedient humans in every sphere, by people who will rely on God's own judgment and wisdom and who will implement it in their communities to bring healing and hope to those most in need of it. The psalm ends with the ultimate promise: under the rule of such a king, God's glory will fill the whole earth (72:19).

—*Broken Signposts* 167

Jesus's Power Is Not "From This World" but Is Certainly For It

A crucial sentence is this one: *My kingdom isn't the sort that grows in this world.* There are two kinds of kingdoms, two kinds of power. Older translations such as the King James Version often gave people the wrong idea in rendering the sentence as, "My kingdom is not of this world." In a culture that positively wants the message of Jesus to have nothing to do with "power" at all, that sounds as though he were saying, "My kingdom is all about going to heaven"—so please don't bother about anything "worldly" at all.

But that's not what the sentence says in the original language. Jesus's kingdom is not "from this world," but it is certainly *for* this world. This is the direct application of the line in the Lord's Prayer that says, "Thy kingdom come on earth as in heaven." The kingdom comes from heaven, but it is designed to take effect on earth. It is designed, in fact, to be the true sort of kingly power, the sort that Psalm 72 was talking about, the sort that is truly a signpost to the reality of God and the truth about the world, however much that signpost has been damaged along the way.

—Broken Signposts 177

The Power of Suffering Love

Jesus's kind of power works the other way. It works through suffering love, through the one who gives his life for his friends, the one who is lifted up like the serpent in the wilderness so that all may see him, believe, and be rescued—rescued from the grip of the other power, the dark power. And the ultimate rescue from the ultimate dark power is, of course, resurrection.

Thus, when Lazarus turned out to be still incorrupt after four days in the tomb and was apparently waiting for Jesus's command to wake him from death, this was the sign to Jesus that his earlier prayers had been answered. When Jesus himself was raised from the dead on the third day, this was the sign that the work of ultimate rescue had indeed been "accomplished," "finished," when he died on the cross (19:30). Easter declares, in power (that is part of the point, as Paul sees it in Rom. 1:3–4), that "the ruler of this world" has indeed been "cast out"—and that now is the time for the Greeks, and anyone else who wants to, to leave their worthless idols and worship the true God.

Ordinary power and the ordinary kingdoms of the world have death as their ultimate weapon. God's kingdom and the power that goes with it can overcome death. The Creator's power renews creation itself. The resurrection is the ultimate answer to Pilate's questions and, with them, to the problem of power itself.

—*Broken Signposts* 183

Real Power

At the heart of the gospel is a redefinition of power. That is one of the central ways in which the early Christians interpreted the death of Jesus. The reason the cross carried such life-changing power, and carries it still, is because it embodied, expressed, and symbolized the true power of which all earthly power is either an imitation or a corrupt parody. It isn't the case that power as we know it in the "real" world is the "norm" and the Christian subversion of it is a kind of bizarre twist that might just work even though we don't see how. The gospel of Jesus summons us to believe that the power of self-giving love unveiled on the cross is the real thing, the power that made the world in the first place and is now in the business of remaking it; and that the other forms of "power," the corrupt and self-serving ways in which the world is so often run, from global empires and multimillion businesses down to classrooms, families, and gangs, are the distortion.

Please note, I am not suggesting (as some have done) that power itself is a bad thing. As I have insisted throughout this book and elsewhere, the creator God wants his world to flourish and be fruitful under human direction, and this applies to communities and human organizations as much as to farms, fields, and gardens. The Bible knows nothing of anarchy, except as the state that results when tyranny collapses under its own weight, leaving a dangerous vacuum behind.

—*The Day the Revolution Began* 398–99

The Power of Vulnerability

How easy it has been, when people have glimpsed the human vocation to exercise this God-given power in the world, for them to "play God"—while forgetting that the God they ought to be imitating is not the God of naked, bullying power, but the God of generous, outgoing love, the power-sharing God, the God who works through vulnerable humans, the God who came and exercised his saving power as an utterly vulnerable human, "a man of sorrows, and acquainted with grief," as the King James Version translates Isaiah 53:3.

One might even say that the abuse of power, which has caused so many in our day to regard power itself not as a signpost to the truth about God and the world but as an unpleasant and regrettable feature of the way the world really is (and perhaps even as an argument against the existence of God!), goes hand in hand with a failure in the Western church and world to understand the doctrine of the Trinity itself. It is through the mysterious truth that God the Creator always intended to come into his creation in and as a human being that we can ultimately understand what power is all about.

—*Broken Signposts* 173–74

The Authentic Voice of Opposition

Power, after all, is frequently held and wielded not by elected officials and politicians, but by well-positioned lobbying groups, on the one hand, and the media, on the other. They will say in their defense that their mandate—sometimes given theoretical justification, more often just quietly assumed—is to hold the elected officials to account (the media) and to remind them of the real needs and interests of their constituents (the lobbyists). There is no doubt a grain of truth in that, but it is almost completely hidden under a ton of unscrutinized agendas. Official oppositions sometimes provide genuine critique, but often they don't. Journalists sometimes do, but often simply reflect their own equally distorted agendas. We should not assume that our systems are automatically the best we could possibly have. This is where those who believe in the victory of the cross have something to say—quite literally. As Christians, our role in society is not to wring our hands at the corruption of power or simply to pick a candidate that supports one or another supposedly Christian policy. The Christian role, as part of naming the name of the crucified and risen Jesus on territory presently occupied by idols, is to *speak the truth to power* and especially to speak up for those with no power at all.

—*The Day the Revolution Began* 400

The Power of Love

When Jesus died, the "powers" lost their power. They can still rage and shout, but the power of Jesus is stronger. And it is the power—to say it again—of *forgiveness*. The past is blotted out. A new world has begun. A *revolution* has begun, in which power itself is redefined as the power of love. Paul had discovered in towns and cities, in private houses and public streets, in formal and informal settings, that the news of Jesus, crucified, risen, and reigning, was "God's power, bringing salvation to everyone who believes" (Rom. 1:16). The reign of the crucified Jesus only had to be announced for it to become effective. The powers that had held people captive were powerless to stop them believing, to prevent them from becoming part of God's new creation. The gospel was—and is—the powerful announcement that the world has a new lord and the summons to give him believing allegiance.

The reason the gospel carries this power is that it's true: on the cross Jesus really did defeat the powers that had held people captive. For the early Christians, the revolution *had happened* on the first Good Friday. The "rulers and authorities" really had been dealt their death blow. This didn't mean, "So we can escape this world and go to heaven," but "Jesus is now Lord of this world, and we must live under his lordship and announce his kingdom." The revolution had begun. It had to continue. Jesus's followers were not simply its beneficiaries. They were to be its agents.

What might it mean for the church today to live by the same belief? It would mean recognizing, for a start, that the "powers," though defeated on the cross, are still capable of enslaving millions. When we in the Western world think of forces that enslave millions we tend to think of the ideologies of the twentieth century, not least Communism, which until 1989 had half the world in its grip and still controls the lives of millions. Many in southern Africa think back to the terrible days of *apartheid* and remember with a shudder how racial segregation and the denial of basic freedoms to much of the nonwhite population were given an apparent Christian justification. Similar reflections continue to be appropriate in parts of the United States, where the victories won by the civil rights movement in the 1960s still sometimes appear more precarious than people had thought.

—*The Day the Revolution Began* 391–92

Victory and Suffering

The victory was indeed won, the revolution was indeed launched, through the suffering of Jesus; it is now implemented, put into effective operation, by the suffering of his people. This is why Paul could write:

> We recommend ourselves as God's servants: with much
> patience, with suffering, difficulties, hardships, beatings,

imprisonments, riots, hard work, sleepless nights, going
without food, with purity, knowledge, great-heartedness,
kindness, the holy spirit, genuine love, by speaking the truth,
by God's power, with weapons for God's faithful work in
left and right hand alike, through glory and shame, through
slander and praise; as deceivers, and yet true; as unknown,
yet very well known; as dying, and look—we are alive; as
punished, yet not killed; as sad, yet always celebrating; as
poor, yet bringing riches to many; as having nothing, yet
possessing everything. (2 Cor. 6:4–10)

It was hard for Paul's audience to understand this. They lived,
as we do, in a competitive society where everyone was eager to
look good, to be successful, to impress the neighbors. The beaten,
bedraggled figure of Paul was hardly that of a leader one might be
proud of. Yet Paul rubs their noses in the point that this is the Messiah pattern, the cross pattern. This is how the victory was won.
Jesus himself went to the place of shame and degradation. This is
how the revolution was launched; this is how it makes its way in
the world. And this is why, for every one person today who reads
Seneca, Plutarch, or Epictetus (among the greatest philosophers of
Paul's day), there are thousands who read Paul and find his message
life-giving. This is why too for every theologian who puzzles over
abstract definitions of "atonement," there are thousands who will
say, with Paul, "The son of God loved me and gave himself for me"
(Gal. 2:20)—and who will then get on with the job of radiating
that same love out into the world.

I suspect that this message about the necessity of suffering has
not been fully understood in today's church, especially in the comfortable Western churches to which I and many of my readers
belong.

—*The Day the Revolution Began* 366–67

"When I'm Weak, Then I Am Strong"

One of the underlying themes in 2 Corinthians is Paul's confrontation with those in Corinth who wanted, as it were, to "make apostleship great again." He disagrees and sets them straight. Although being an apostle of Jesus the crucified Messiah does indeed carry power—and power is necessary if the church is not to collapse back into anarchic paganism—the power in question is that shown by the Messiah himself through his death and resurrection. "When I'm weak," he insists, "then I am strong" (12:10).

The whole letter forms an extended meditation on that theme, applied with great subtlety and pathos. I suspect that many in our churches, including many who think of themselves as "Pauline" Christians, are comparatively unfamiliar with Second Corinthians, perhaps again because the Western church does not expect to learn about power from studying the Bible. But it's time we did.

The initial biblical answer to the question about power, then, is that power undoubtedly has an important place within the Creator's purpose for the world, but that (like justice, freedom, and all the rest) it can be, and regularly is, corrupted in ways that seem to undermine any chance of its being a signpost to ultimate truth about God and the world. But, in fact, power really is a signpost of that kind, since it points to the fact that the Creator intended, and still intends, that his world should be ordered, not chaotic; fruitful, not wasteful; glorifying to him, rather than shameful. And the central design the creator God has put in place to accomplish this is his delegation of his power to his image-bearing human creatures.

—*Broken Signposts* 171–72

God's Weakness Is Stronger Than Human Strength

Apostles are precisely not supposed to be people of great standing in the wider community. They are like bedraggled prisoners at the end of a triumphal procession, on their way to a shameful death. That is part of the point, but it is also the source of the power. This whole opening section of 1 Corinthians is about power, a theme that obviously concerned Paul both as he was thinking about Corinth and as he was dealing with various sorts of power in Ephesus. The foolish gospel of the crucified Messiah is God's power; God's weakness is stronger than human strength; their faith, as evoked by Paul's preaching, did not rest on human wisdom but on God's power; and now, dramatically and with a somewhat shocking threat," the kingdom of God isn't about talk—it's about power," the "power" in question being the power Paul thinks he may have to use in confronting those who are "puffed up" with their own sense of worth and importance.

—*Paul: A Biography* 250

Learning the Hidden Secret

Celebrating the victory of the Messiah, Paul has arrived at a very different place from the one he describes in 2 Corinthians 1. In one of many allusions in Philippians to the great philosophies of his time, Paul declares that being the Messiah's man has

produced the "contentment" for which both Stoics and Epicureans aim:

> I'm not talking about lacking anything. I've learned to
> be content with what I have. I know how to do without,
> and I know how to cope with plenty. In every possible
> situation I've learned the hidden secret of being full and
> hungry, of having plenty and going without, and it's this:
> I have strength for everything in the one who gives me
> power. (4:11–13)

There it is again: *power*. But "the extraordinary quality of the
power belongs to God, not to us." Paul has learned this now. His
meditation on the victory of Jesus, growing out of the scripturally
rooted prayers of many years, with those roots going down into the
dark of suffering and despair, have brought him to a new place. All
power is vested by God in Jesus. Any power Jesus's followers may
have comes only through his work.

—*Paul: A Biography* 279–80

How God Becomes King Today

Some things (like the crucifixion itself) had to be done by Jesus
himself, alone. Other things (like the itinerant ministry around
Galilee) could and should be shared. God and Jesus don't do what
they do by blasting a way through all opposition. They do what they
do by working with the grain of the cosmos, by planting seeds that
grow secretly, by calling humans to be cocreators. God's kingdom
comes like a farmer sowing a fresh crop or like a vineyard owner

looking for workers to pick the grapes, bringing people on board to help. When God goes to work—when Jesus becomes king—human beings are not downgraded, reduced to being pawns or ciphers. In God's kingdom, humans get to reflect God at last into the world, in the way they were meant to. They become more fully what humans were meant to be. That is how God becomes king. That is how Jesus goes to work in the present time. Exactly as he always did.

That is why Jesus answers his followers the way he does at the start of the book of Acts. The disciples ask Jesus if this is now the moment for God's kingdom to be "restored to Israel." Jesus, answering obliquely, as he does so often when correcting the assumptions of questioners, tells them that they are to be his "witnesses":

> So when the apostles came together, they put this question to Jesus.
>
> "Master," they said, "is this the time when you are going to restore the kingdom to Israel?"
>
> "It's not your business to know about times and dates," he replied. "The father has placed all that under his own direct authority. What will happen, though, is that you will receive power when the holy spirit comes upon you. Then you will be my witnesses in Jerusalem, in all Judaea and Samaria, and to the very ends of the earth." (Acts 1:6–8)

—*Simply Jesus* 213–14

The Power of a People of Praise

Our attempts at political theology lurch to and fro between the political equivalents of pantheism (assuming that things must be left to go on under their own steam by the automatic operation of due process) and dualism (assuming that things are so bad that the only solution is either to opt out and retreat into a private sphere or to revolt and change the system entirely).

The Psalms offer a different vision: a people of praise who, out of their celebration of God's goodness in creation and out of their eager anticipation of his coming in judgment at last, speak his word and his truth to those in power, reminding them that they are answerable to the God who will one day hold them accountable.

—Case for the Psalms 151

Both a Kingdom of Faith and a Kingdom of the State

The critical scholarship of the past two hundred years was born in a world (that of the European Enlightenment) where it was felt vitally important to separate religion and politics. Critical biblical scholarship was then nurtured in a world (that of German Lutheranism) where the "two kingdoms" theory, which separated the kingdom of religion/faith and the kingdom of the state, was all but set in stone. Thus, for philosophical, cultural, and theological reasons the inner core of the gospels—the message of god becoming king—remained impenetrable. The story the gospels tell, of a Jesus who embodied the living God of Israel and whose cross and resurrection really did inaugurate the kingdom of that God, remained not only incomprehensible, but unheard.

The New Testament writers did their best to make it heard and to make it understood. Matthew believed that Jesus had already accomplished it: "all authority," declares Matthew's Jesus, "in heaven *and on earth* has been given to me" (28:18). Paul believed Jesus was already reigning; you can't understand Romans or 1 Corinthians or Philippians unless you take that as basic. Revelation celebrates the sovereignty of Jesus from first page to last. But of course neither Matthew nor Paul nor Revelation supposed for a minute that this meant that utopia had already arrived, that the vision of Isaiah 11 was already fully in place. Christians were being persecuted, facing violent opposition, celebrating the lordship of Jesus in a world where Caesar and his type of power still seemed to be solid and unshaken.

—*How God Became King* 161–62

God's Kingdom Will Clash with the Powers of the World

For Matthew, ever conscious of the immediate Jewish surroundings, it is the Herod family who loom darkly on the horizon. Matthew's equivalent of the opening of Luke 2 is the start of his second chapter, where Herod the Great, nearing the end of his increasingly paranoid reign, receives an unexpected and unwelcome visit from eastern sages who claim that the stars are proclaiming the birth of the Jews' rightful king. Herod's instant suspicions and subsequent overreaction indicate well enough the way that pagan power always behaves when confronted with news of the true God and the true king. His son, Herod Antipas, then looms over Jesus's public career, killing his cousin John and providing the threatening backdrop for Jesus's own (implicitly messianic) work (11:1–14; 14:1–12).

This points forward to the larger power, Rome itself, which will close in at the end, only to be symbolically overthrown as the Roman guards at the tomb fail to prevent Jesus's resurrection. Luke has Herod in Jerusalem at this time as well, in league at last with Pontius Pilate (23:1–12). The sense is the same: the powers of the world are waiting there, in the wings, mostly offstage, but ready to pounce at a moment's notice. If this really is the story of God's kingdom arriving on earth as in heaven, sooner or later there will be a confrontation. Again, it doesn't take a Ph.D. in political psychology to know what the world's powers will do to those who act and speak to bring about God's kingdom. As well as all the other elements in the gospel story, we must recognize this for what it is, a telling of the story of Jesus as the clash between the kingdom of God and the kingdoms of the world.

—*How God Became King* 137–38

Following the Way of the Servant

The kings of the earth exercise power one way, by lording it over their subjects, but Jesus's followers are going to do it the other way, the way of the servant. You might almost think Mark (at 10:35–45) thought Jesus had been reading Isaiah 40–55, where the "servant of the Lord" and his shameful death are the means by which, somehow, the gods and rulers of Babylon are overthrown, Israel is rescued, and God himself returns to Zion to renew not only the covenant, but the whole creation. And Mark (followed by Matthew) also highlights Jesus's words about the vindication of the "Son of Man," which by its evocation of the whole narrative of the book of Daniel declares, as powerfully as any statement to a scripture-soaked audience could do, that, despite present suffering and disappointment, Israel's God is indeed going to take his seat and, in vindicating the one who represents his suffering people, pass judgment on the monsters, the pagan powers, that have arrogantly taken charge of the world.

There is, in other words, a clear line all the way from Genesis 11, via Isaiah 40–55 and Daniel 7, to Mark 10, and thereby in turn to Mark 14–15, where Jesus meets his captors, his judges, and his death. He not only theorizes about the difference between pagan power and the kind of power he is claiming; he enacts it. Mark 10:35–45 is not a "political" statement (about different types of power) followed by an "atonement" statement (about how sins would be forgiven), as though the two were entirely separate things. When we put together "kingdom" and "cross" in a way few readers of the gospels have even tried to do, Jesus establishes the new kind of power—God's kingdom as opposed to Caesar's, on earth as in heaven—precisely through his (scripturally interpreted) death. And, to put it the other way around, God rescues his people from their sins, through the work of the Isaianic "servant," precisely in order to establish his rule, his own very different kind of power, in all the world.

—*How God Became King* 139

The Kingdom of God Runs on Love

The clash between Jesus and the powers of the world—between the kingdom of God and the kingdom of humans—was never about God simply having a bit more power than humans, so that he could manage to beat them at their own game. It isn't that God has stronger tanks and bombs than everybody else. That's what people expected in Jesus's day (well, they didn't have tanks and bombs, but you know what I mean). It is also what people expect, and often want, today. ("Why doesn't God do something to stop wicked dictators killing people?") This is why the good news is so often misunderstood. This is why it continues to puzzle and challenge people, as it always did. It's also why people step back from the big claims in the Bible and turn the radical good news into something they find more believable. Something about "me and my relationship to God" or about "going to heaven." Something more like advice than news.

Let's be clear. The relationship each of us has with God is hugely important. It is also vital to insist that God will indeed look after his people following their deaths, all the way to his final new creation. But these are not the center of the good news. We have placed the stress at the wrong point, like people putting the em*pha*sis on the wrong syl*lab*le. The words may be true, but the way we say them gets in the way of that truth coming out clearly. The good news is about the living God overcoming all the powers of the world to establish his rule of justice and peace, *on earth as in heaven*. Not in heaven, later on. And that victory is won not by superior power of the same kind but by a different sort of power altogether.

We know what the power of the world looks like. When push comes to shove, as it often does, it is the power of violence, using the threat of pain and death. It is, yes, the power of tanks and bombs, and also of guns and knives and whips and prisons and barbed wire and bulldozers. Weapons to destroy people's lives; machines to destroy their homes. Cruelty in the home or at work. Malice and manipulation where there should be gentleness, kindness, and wisdom. Jesus's power is of a totally different sort, as he explained to the Roman governor a few minutes before the governor sent him to his death—thereby proving the point. The kingdoms of the world run on violence. The kingdom of God, Jesus declared, runs on love.

That is the good news.

This wasn't a theory. It was and is a general truth, but the only reason for believing it is that it actually happened. In history. "The son of God," wrote Paul in one of his earliest letters, "loved me and gave himself for me" (Gal. 2:20).

—*Simply Good News* 43–44

The God-Given Role of Today's Rulers

The New Testament reaffirms the God-given place even of secular rulers, even of deeply flawed, sinful, self-serving, time-serving, corrupt, and idolatrous rulers like Pontius Pilate, Felix, Festus, and Herod Agrippa. They get it wrong and they will be judged, but God wants them in place because order, even corrupt order, is better than chaos. Here we find, in the gospels, in Acts, and especially in Paul, a tension that cannot be dissolved without great peril. We in the contemporary Western world have all but lost the ability, conceptually as well as practically, to affirm simultaneously that rulers are corrupt and must be confronted and that they are God-given and must be obeyed. That sounds to us as though we are to affirm simultaneously anarchy and tyranny. But that merely shows to what extent our concepts have led us again to muzzle the texts in which both stand together. How can that be?

The answer comes in such passages as John 19 and 1 Corinthians 2 and Colossians 2. The rulers of this age inevitably twist their God-given vocation (to bring order to the world) into the satanic possibility of tyranny. But the cross of Jesus, enthroned as the true Son of God as in Psalm 2, constitutes the paradoxical victory by which rulers' idolatry and corruption are confronted and overthrown. And the result, illustrated in Colossians 1:18–20, is that the rulers are *reconciled*—in some strange sense reinstated as the bringers of God's wise order to the world, whether or not they would see it like that. This is the point where Romans 13 comes in, not as the validation of every program that every ruler dreams up, certainly not as the validation of what democratically elected governments in one country decide to do against other countries, but as the strictly limited proposal, in line with Isaiah's recognition of Cyrus, that the creator God uses even those rulers who do not know him personally to bring fresh order and even rescue to the world.

—*Surprised by Scripture* 176–77

Salvation and Politics

It is in this context that we find the kingdom and the cross in close juxtaposition. Jesus contrasts the normal practice of pagan rulers with his own vision of power and prestige: "Anyone who wants to be great among you must become your servant" (Mark 10:43). This is at the center of his vision of the kingdom. And this is not only illustrated, but instantiated, by Jesus's own vocation: "The son of man didn't come to be waited on. He came to be the servant, to give his life 'as a ransom for many'" (10:45). This saying, so far from being (as has often been suggested) a detached, floating nugget of "atonement theology" within early church tradition that Mark or his source has tacked on to a story about something else (the reversal of normal modes of power), is, in fact, the theologically *and politically* apposite climax to the whole train of thought. What we call "atonement" and what we call "kingdom redefinition" seem, in fact, to be part and parcel of the same thing. Ultimately, the cross *is* the sharp edge of kingdom redefinition, just as the kingdom, in its redefined form, *is* the ultimate meaning of the cross.

—*How God Became King* 227–28

When God Wants to Change the World, He Doesn't Send in the Tanks

This is the point at which a great deal of Jesus's own kingdom agenda comes into its own. His great Sermon on the Mount opens with the Beatitudes, which are normally read either as a special form of "Christian ethic" ("This is how you are to behave, if you want to be really special people") or as the rules you must keep in order to "go to heaven when you die." This latter view has been reinforced by the standard misreading of the first Beatitude. "Blessings on the poor in spirit! The kingdom of heaven is yours" (Matt. 5:3) doesn't mean, "You will go to heaven when you die." It means *you will be one of those through whom God's kingdom, heaven's rule, begins to appear on earth as in heaven.* The Beatitudes are the agenda for kingdom people. They are not simply about how to behave, so that God will do something nice *to* you. They are about the way in which Jesus wants to rule the world. He wants to do it *through* this sort of people—people, actually, just like himself (read the Beatitudes again and see). The Sermon on the Mount is a call to Jesus's followers to take up their vocation as light to the world, as salt to the earth—in other words, as people through whom Jesus's kingdom vision is to become a reality. This is how to be the people through whom the victory of Jesus over the powers of sin and death is to be implemented in the wider world.

The work of the kingdom, in fact, is summed up pretty well in those Beatitudes. When God wants to change the world, he doesn't send in the tanks. He sends in the meek, the mourners, those who are hungry and thirsty for God's justice, the peacemakers, and so on. Just as God's whole *style*, his chosen way of operating, reflects his generous love, sharing his rule with his human creatures, so the way in which those humans then have to behave if they are to be agents of Jesus's lordship reflects in its turn the same sense of vulnerable, gentle, but powerful self-giving love. It is because of this that the world has been changed by people like William Wilberforce, campaigning tirelessly to abolish slavery; by Desmond Tutu, working and praying not just to end apartheid, but to end it in such a way as to produce a reconciled, forgiving South Africa; by Cicely Saunders, starting a hospice for terminally ill patients ignored by the medical profession and launching a movement that has, within a generation, spread right around the globe.

—*Simply Jesus* 218–19

Spectacular Humility

Writing to Corinth in AD 56, Paul seems to be mocking the Corinthians' desire for spectacular "spiritual" events. "All right," he says, "if I must, I must. Someone I know in the Messiah . . ."—he won't even say it's himself, though this becomes clear. "This 'Someone' was snatched up to the third heaven." (Since heaven was often subdivided into seven, this itself might have seemed a bit of a letdown.) "I don't know," he says, "whether this was a bodily experience or one of those out-of-body things; only God knows that. And this 'Someone' heard . . . but actually I'm not allowed to tell you what was heard. Oh, and the most important thing about it all was that I was given 'a thorn in my flesh,' a satanic messenger, to stop me from getting too exalted with it all." The underlying point in the letter is clear: *You shouldn't be asking this kind of question and trying to rank me with other people and their 'experiences.'* If you do, I will only say that yes, these things have happened, but that the real point was that I had to learn humility, to understand that 'when I'm weak, then I am strong'" (2 Cor. 12:1–10).

—Paul: A Biography 69–70

The Defeat of the Power of Darkness

Behind the actual human beings, whether Caiaphas, Pilate, or even Caesar himself, there stand the dark spiritual forces that they have implicitly invoked. As many scholars have argued, this should not be seen as an either/or (*either* "human authorities" *or* "spiritual powers"). No doubt the "powers" can work independently too; but, like Rome itself in its outlying provinces, the shadowy powers of evil seem to prefer to do their dark deeds through the agency of willing collaborators. Each of the four evangelists highlights this in his own way.

Luke's Jesus declares that he saw the Satan fall like lightning from heaven, though this is clearly not the end of the matter; he also says, with a wry solemnity, that the moment of his arrest is the moment when darkness does its worst (10:18; 22:53). Mark's Jesus explains that the rulers of the nations use ordinary power, but that he will use servant power instead (10:35–45). John's Jesus explains to Pilate that his kingdom is of a different sort and so does not use violence (18:36). Matthew's Jesus explains that he is casting out demons by the power of God's Spirit, so that God's kingdom has arrived on their doorstep (12:28); and he then warns that, like an unclean spirit returning with seven worse ones after a temporary exorcism, Israel itself ("this wicked generation") will find that it will end up worse off than it was to start with (12:43–45). All the evangelists see Jesus going to his death in order to win the deeply paradoxical victory over the forces of evil that, throughout Israel's long story, have gathered themselves together to do their worst to the people of God.

—How God Became King 206–7

Sharing One Another's Jesus-Shaped Suffering

This is the clue that enables us to understand the whole New Testament vision of the church. It grows directly out of the vision of God's holy ones "receiving the kingdom" in Daniel 7. But it does so insofar as, and only insofar as, the category of the "holy ones" is first shrunk right down to the one man, Jesus himself, and opened up thereafter to his followers. Once this is clear, the way is open for a fresh understanding of the kingdom-and-cross combination, as we find it, for instance, in Revelation:

> Glory to the one who loved us, and freed us from our sins
> by his blood, and made us a kingdom, priests to his God
> and father. (1:5–6)

> You are worthy to take the scroll;
> You are worthy to open its seals;
> For you were slaughtered and with your own blood
> You purchased a people for God,
> From every tribe and tongue,
> From every people and nation,
> And made them a kingdom and priests to our God
> And they will reign on the earth. (5:9–10)

This vision, of a community rescued by the cross and transformed into kingdom-bringers, follows directly from the story the four evangelists are telling. It is, once more, a measure of how far the Western church has drifted from those moorings that it has been possible for Christians in our own day to think of bringing "justice and peace" into the world by the normal, disastrous means of bombs and bullets. Not so. The implicit ecclesiology of all four gospels is a picture of a community sharing the complex vocation of Jesus himself: to be kingdom-bringers, yes, but to do this first because of Jesus's own suffering and second by means of their own. The slaughtered and enthroned lamb of Revelation 5 is not only the shepherd of his people; he is also their template. Sharing his suffering is the way in which they are to extend his kingdom in the world. As I write this I am conscious that today's Western church, and I myself as part of it, has suffered remarkably little by comparison with Christians of other times and, today, other places. I honor those who are leading the way as today's kingdom-bringers and pray for them in their courage and steadfast witness.

—*How God Became King* 202–3

PENTECOST

Let me explain. We know that the entire creation is groaning together, and going through labor pains together, up until the present time. Not only so: we too, we who have the first fruits of the spirit's life within us, are groaning within ourselves, as we eagerly await our adoption, the redemption of our body. We were saved, you see, in hope. But hope isn't hope if you can see it! Who hopes for what they can see? But if we hope for what we don't see, we wait for it eagerly—but also patiently.

In the same way, too, the spirit comes alongside and helps us in our weakness. We don't know what to pray for as we ought to; but that same spirit pleads on our behalf, with groanings too deep for words. And the Searcher of Hearts knows what the spirit is thinking, because the spirit pleads for God's people according to God's will.

—Romans 8:22–27, *The Kingdom New Testament* 324

An Outburst of New Life

I have just thrown open the window on a glorious spring morning. A fresh breeze is stirring around the garden. In the distance there is a crackle of bonfire as a farmer clears away some winter rubbish. Near the path down to the sea, a skylark is hovering over its nest. All around, there is a sense of creation throwing off its wintry coverings and getting ready for an outburst of new life.

All these (I didn't make them up, by the way) are images the early Christians used to describe something just as strange as the story of Jesus, but just as real in their own lives. They spoke of a powerful wind rushing through the house and entering them. They spoke of tongues of fire resting on them and transforming them. They picked up, from the ancient creation story, the image of a bird brooding over the waters of chaos, bringing to birth a new world of order and life.

How else can we explain the inexplicable, except in a rush of images from the world we already know?

—*Simply Christian* 121

New Energy

The odd sense of a new kind of life, as in all the very early Jesus communities, was heavily dependent (they would have said) on the powerful presence and guidance of the Holy Spirit. Whatever account we want to give of this phenomenon today, we cannot begin to understand Saul, Barnabas, and their colleagues without recognizing that as they prayed, sang, studied scripture, organized their community life, and (not least) went about talking to both Jews and non-Jews about Jesus, they were conscious of an energy and a sense of direction unlike anything they had known before. They had no hesitation in ascribing that energy and leading to the divine spirit, which had been promised in the scriptures and then again, only a few years before, by Jesus's own forerunner, John the

Baptist. These early Jesus-followers were not naive "enthusiasts." Already within the first decades it became necessary to challenge some claims about the work of the spirit and to warn against the likelihood of deceit, and indeed of self-deceit. But we cannot understand the things that now happened unless we allow that Saul and the others really did believe they were being led and energized by the personal presence of the One God.

—*Paul: A Biography* 93–94

In the Spirit, the Future's Reality Comes to the Present

The Spirit is given to begin the work of making God's future real in the present. That is the first, and perhaps the most important, point to grasp about the work of this strange personal power for which so many images are used. Just as the resurrection of Jesus opened up the unexpected world of God's new creation, so the Spirit comes to us from that new world, the world waiting to be born, the world in which, according to the old prophets, peace and justice will flourish and the wolf and the lamb will lie down side by side. One key element of living as a Christian is learning to live with the life, and by the rules, of God's future world, even as we are continuing to live within the present one (which Paul calls "the present evil age" and Jesus calls "this corrupt and sinful generation").

That is why St. Paul, our earliest Christian writer, speaks of the Spirit as the *guarantee* or the *down-payment* of what is to come. The Greek word he uses is *arrabon*, which in modern Greek means an engagement ring, a sign in the present of what is to come in the future.

Paul speaks of the Spirit as the guarantee of our "inheritance" (Eph. 1:14). He isn't simply using an image taken from the ordinary human transaction whereby, when a person dies, someone else inherits his or her wealth—an "inheritance" from which one might perhaps receive something in advance, an early first installment. Nor is he simply speaking, as many Christians have supposed, of our "going to heaven," as though celestial bliss were the full "inheritance" God had in mind for us. No. He is drawing on a major biblical theme—the Exodus—and taking it in a striking new direction. To grasp this is to see why the Spirit is given in the first place, and indeed who the Spirit actually is.

But if that "inheritance" isn't a disembodied heaven, neither is it simply one small country among others. *The whole world is now God's holy land.* At the moment the world appears as a place of suffering and sorrow as well as of power and beauty. But God is reclaiming it. That's what Jesus's death and resurrection were all about. And we are called to be part of that reclaiming. One day all creation will be rescued from slavery, from the corruption, decay, and death which deface its beauty, destroy its relationships, remove the sense of God's presence from it, and make it a place of injustice, violence, and brutality. That is the message of rescue, of "salvation," at the heart of one of the greatest chapters Paul ever wrote, the eighth chapter of his Letter to the Romans.

—*Simply Christian* 124–26

The Theology of the Spirit on Every Page

All this demands, of course, a strong theology of the Holy Spirit as the one who dwells in Jesus's followers and enables them in turn to be kingdom-bringers. Without that, the vocation would encourage either arrogance or despair. And that theology of the Spirit is, of course, what the New Testament supplies, on page after page.

—*How God Became King* 202

We Have the Living Presence of God with and in Us

If the Temple was always the sign and the means of the true theocracy, then the Temple-in-person, that is, Jesus himself, is now that sign. The one who sits in heaven is the one who rules on earth. He therefore sends out his followers, equipped by his own Spirit (if the ascension locates a part of "earth" in "heaven," Pentecost sends the breath of heaven to earth), to celebrate his sovereignty over the world and make it a reality through the founding of communities rescued by his love, renewed by his power, and loyal to his name. Jesus's followers, equipped with his Spirit, are to become in themselves, individually and together, little walking temples, rescued themselves from sin through Jesus death, and with the living presence of God going with them and in them.

—*How God Became King* 247

Holiness and Prayer

The present anticipation of the future glory consists not in lording it over creation, imagining ourselves already its masters, able to tyrannize it and bend it to our will. It consists, rather, in the humble, Christlike, Spirit-led activity of prayer, the prayer in which the love of God is poured into our hearts by the Spirit (Rom. 5:5) so that the extraordinary and almost unbelievable hope that is set before us is nevertheless firm and secure (5:1–5; 8:28–30). Thus, at the heart of arguably the greatest chapter of certainly his greatest letter, Paul sets out the pattern of *present anticipation of future hope.* This is what virtue is all about. The hope is that all those who are "in Christ" and are indwelt by the Spirit will eventually reign in glory over the whole creation, thereby taking up at long last the role commanded for humans in Genesis 1 and Psalm 8 and sharing the inheritance, and the final rescuing work, of the Messiah himself, as in Psalm 2. And if that is the *telos,* the goal, it is to be anticipated in the present by the settled habits of holiness and prayer.

If this is what Paul means by the final "reign," and its present strange anticipation, we observe that alongside this vision at every point in his writings is his equal emphasis that the Spirit comes to "dwell" in the hearts and lives of believers, inspiring precisely this holiness, this prayer, this love, and this hope. But this theme of the "indwelling" of the Spirit (see Rom. 8:5–11; Eph. 3:17) is nothing other than Paul's vision of the church, Christ's people, as the "new Temple," as in 1 Corinthians 3:10–17, 6:19–20, and Ephesians 2:11–22. Just as Israel's God "dwelt" in the old Temple (and its predecessor, the wilderness tabernacle), leading the people from Egypt to the promised land, so now God's own Spirit dwells within his people, leading them from previous slavery to future ultimate freedom. The Spirit thus enables God's people to be a community of priests, gathering up the worship of creation, just as the Spirit also constitutes God's people as rulers, bringing God's wise, healing order to the world.

—After You Believe 94–95

Easter Commissions, Pentecost Equips

The resurrection has little to do with showing that we "go to heaven when we die" and a great deal to do with the new commission of the disciples to be for the world what Jesus was for Israel: "As the father sent me," he says, "so I send you" (John 20:21). And, as in Luke, the commission is accompanied by the necessary equipment: to be Jesus's agents in the world, his followers need, and are given, his own Spirit. Easter and Pentecost belong together. Easter commissions Jesus's followers for a task; Pentecost gives them the necessary equipment to accomplish it.

—Surprised by Hope 239

Living at the Intersection of Heaven and Earth

The point is not that the Law is a convenient moral guide, ancient and venerable. It is that the Torah, like the Temple, *is one of the places where heaven and earth meet,* so that, as some Jewish teachers had suggested, those who study and keep the Torah are like those who worship in the Temple. And the early Christians are encouraging one another to live as points of intersection, points of overlap, between heaven and earth. Again, this sounds fearsomely difficult, not to say downright impossible. But there is no getting around it. Fortunately, as we shall see, what ought to be normal Christianity is actually all about finding out how to sustain this kind of life and even grow in it.

The fulfillment of the Torah by the Spirit is one of the main themes underlying the spectacular description, in Acts 2, of the day of Pentecost itself. To this day, Pentecost is observed in Judaism as the feast of the giving of the Law. First comes Passover, the day when the Israelites leave their Egyptian slavery behind for good. Off they go through the desert, and fifty days later they reach Mount Sinai. Moses goes up the mountain and comes down with the Law, the tablets of the covenant, God's gift to his people of the way of life by which they will be able to demonstrate that they really are his people.

This is the picture we ought to have in mind as we read Acts 2. The previous Passover, Jesus had died and been raised, opening the way out of slavery, the way to forgiveness and a new start for the whole world—especially for all those who follow him. Now, fifty days later, Jesus has been taken into "heaven," into God's dimension of reality; but, like Moses, he comes down again, to ratify the renewed covenant and to provide the way of life, written not on stone but in human hearts, by which Jesus's followers may gratefully demonstrate that they really are his people. That is the underlying theology by which the remarkable phenomenon of Pentecost as Luke tells it—the wind, the fire, the tongues, and the sudden, powerful proclamation of Jesus to the astonished crowds—is given its deepest meaning. Those in whom the Spirit comes to dwell are to be people who live at the intersection between heaven and earth.

—*Simply Christian* 132–33

The Spirit and the Creed

> I believe in the Holy Ghost, the holy catholic church,
> the communion of saints, the forgiveness of sins . . .

For anyone who has grasped the picture of the kingdom so far, each of these elements has a *missionary* orientation. The Holy Spirit is given not simply so that God's redeemed people may be blessed with his presence and love, though that does indeed follow, but so that we may be witnesses to Jesus and his resurrection, so that we may be for the world what Jesus was for Israel (John 20:19–24). The Spirit is the one who enables the church to extend the work of the kingdom, and the transformation that takes place personally and corporately within and among those who are thus energized for the work is the necessary by-product of that vocation. To read the creed from a "kingdom" point of view is thus to look outward and to invoke the Spirit, not to provide private "blessings" (they may or may not come; they are not the point), but to glorify Jesus in the wider world.

That too is the reason why there is a "holy catholic church." It isn't there because God simply wanted to found an institution in which his people could sit down and feel safe. It is a worldwide community that (as has been rightly said) exists by mission as fire exists by burning. And that, in turn, is why the "communion of saints" matters; read the book of Revelation and see. Those who have gone before us include, especially, those who have lived, suffered, and died to bear witness to Jesus as the world's true Lord over against the other "lords" that try to claim our allegiance. To be "in communion" with them is far more than simply hoping that our departed loved ones will actually still, in some sense, be in touch with us, that there will be some kind of mystical contact beyond the grave. It is to share in fellowship and solidarity with all those who have been the "kingdom people" of their day and to gain strength and courage from them for our own witness.

Within this context, the "forgiveness of sins" gains an entirely new dimension. It includes, of course, just what it says to most of us: we are all overdrawn at the moral bank, and need to know again and again that God wipes out the debt and fills the account with his own freely given treasure. But when we step back from our own personal anxieties and awareness of guilt, we recognize that the world as a whole needs, longs for, aches and yearns and cries out for *forgiveness*—for that collective, global sigh of relief that means that nobody need seek vengeance ever again; that nobody will bear a grudge ever again; that the million wrongs with which the world has been so horribly defaced will be put right at last; that in God's ultimate new world there will be no moral shadow, no lingering resentment, no character warped by another's wrong.

—*How God Became King* 270–72

The Spirit-Fired Church

The Holy Spirit and the task of the church. The two walk together, hand in hand. We can't talk about them apart. Despite what you might think from some excitement in the previous generation about new spiritual experiences, God doesn't give people the Holy Spirit in order to let them enjoy the spiritual equivalent of a day at Disneyland. Of course, if you're downcast and gloomy, the fresh wind of God's Spirit can and often does give you a new perspective on everything, and above all grants a sense of God's presence, love, comfort, and even joy. But the point of the Spirit is to enable those who follow Jesus to take into all the world the news that he is Lord, that he has won the victory over the forces of evil, that a new world has opened up, and that we are to help make it happen.

Equally, the task of the church can't be attempted without the Spirit. I have sometimes heard Christian people talk as though God, having done what he's done in Jesus, now wants us to do our part by getting on with things under our own steam. But that is a tragic misunderstanding. It leads to arrogance, burnout, or both. Without God's Spirit, there is nothing we can do that will count for God's kingdom. Without God's Spirit, the church simply can't be the church.

I use the word "church" here with a somewhat heavy heart. I know that for many of my readers that very word will carry the overtones of large, dark buildings, pompous religious pronouncements, false solemnity, and rank hypocrisy. But there is no easy alternative. I, too, feel the weight of that negative image. I battle with it professionally all the time.

But there is another side to it, a side which shows all the signs of the wind and fire, of the bird brooding over the waters and bringing new life. For many, "church" means just the opposite of that negative image. It's a place of welcome and laughter, of healing and hope, of friends and family and justice and new life. It's where the homeless drop in for a bowl of soup and the elderly stop by for a chat. It's where one group is working to help drug addicts and another is campaigning for global justice. It's where you'll find people learning to pray, coming to faith, struggling with temptation, finding new purpose, and getting in touch with a new power to carry that purpose out. It's where people bring their own small faith and discover, in getting together with others to worship the one true God, that the whole becomes greater than the sum of its parts. No church is like this all the time. But a remarkable number of churches are partly like that for quite a lot of the time.

—*Simply Christian* 122–23

The Spirit, the Cloud, and the Fire

So what does it mean to say that this future has begun to arrive in the present? What Paul means is that those who follow Jesus, those who find themselves believing that he is the world's true Lord, that he rose from the dead—these people are given the Spirit as a fore-taste of what that new world will be like. If anyone is "in the Messiah" (one of Paul's favorite ways of describing those who belong to Jesus), what they have and are is . . . new creation (2 Cor. 5:17)! Your own human self, your personality, your body, is being reclaimed, so that instead of being simply part of the old creation, a place of sorrow and injustice and ultimately the shame of death itself, you can be both part of the new creation in advance and someone through whom it begins to happen here and now.

What does this say about the Holy Spirit? It says that the Spirit plays the same role in our pilgrimage from Passover to the Promised Land—from Jesus's resurrection, in other words, to the final moment when all creation will be renewed—that was played in the old story by the pillar of cloud and fire. The Spirit is the strange, personal presence of the living God himself, leading, guiding, warning, rebuking, grieving over our failings, and celebrating our small steps toward the true inheritance.

But if the Spirit is the personal presence of God himself, what does this say about us as Christians? Let Paul again give the answer. You, he says, are the Temple of the living God.

—*Simply Christian* 126

The Voice of a New Community

It should be obvious that the Spirit enables Jesus's followers to do and say things that the authorities, both Jewish and pagan, see as dangerous nonsense—just as they did with Jesus himself. When many people today think of the Holy Spirit, they think simply of personal spiritual experience (perhaps including "charismatic" gifts such as "speaking in tongues") or powerfully effective spiritual gifts such as healing. These are there in Acts, to be sure. But the story line is not about the church discovering these gifts and simply enjoying them for their own sake. It is about the church living as a new community, giving allegiance to Jesus as Lord rather than to the kings and chief priests who rule the Jewish world or the emperor or magistrates who rule the non-Jewish world. "We must obey God," declares Peter, "not human beings!" (Acts 5:29).

—*Simply Jesus* 204

Spirit–Filled Image Bearing

God builds God's kingdom. But God ordered his world in such a way that his own work within that world takes place not least through one of his creatures in particular, namely, the human beings who reflect his image. That, I believe, is central to the notion of being made in God's image. God intends his wise, creative, loving presence and power to be *reflected*—imaged, if you like—into his world *through* his human creatures. He has enlisted us to act as his stewards in the project of creation. And, following the disaster of rebellion and corruption, he has built into the gospel message the fact that through the work of Jesus and the power of the Spirit, he equips humans to help in the work of getting the project back on track. So the objection about us trying to build God's kingdom by our own efforts, though it seems humble and pious, can actually be a way of hiding from responsibility, of keeping one's head well down when the boss is looking for volunteers. Not that one can go on eluding God's call forever . . . but still.

—*Surprised by Hope* 207

Take the Kingdom Out into the World

The *method* of the kingdom will match the *message* of the kingdom. The kingdom will come as the church, energized by the Spirit, goes out into the world vulnerable, suffering, praising, praying, misunderstood, misjudged, vindicated, celebrating: always—as Paul puts it in one of his letters—bearing in the body the dying of Jesus so that the life of Jesus may also be displayed.

—*Surprised by Hope* 112

The Charter of All Jesus Followers

The four gospels were never meant as "historical reminiscence" for its own sake. Just because we are (in my view) right to insist that, in supporting and sustaining the life of the early church, the gospels are precisely telling the story of Jesus, we are not for that reason to swing the other way and imagine that their writers are not aware, constantly, of their task of writing foundational documents for God's renewed people. The gospels are, and were written to be, fresh tellings of the story of Jesus designed to be the charter of the community of Jesus's first followers and those who, through their witness, then and subsequently, have joined in and have learned to hear, see, and know Jesus in word and sacrament.

—How God Became King 125

Announcing a World-Changing Event

Despite Paul's talk about God, he was not telling people about a new religious system. Nor was he urging them to adopt a new type of morality. He wasn't offering them a new philosophy—a theory about the world, how it worked, how we could know things, how we should behave. Other teachers at the time were offering things like that, but Paul's approach was different. True, his message would eventually affect those areas, too. But many people today assume that Christianity is one or more of these things—a religion, a moral system, a philosophy. In other words, they assume that Christianity is about advice.

But it wasn't and isn't.

Christianity is, *simply, good news*. It is the news that *something has happened as a result of which the world is a different place*. That is what the apostle Paul—Paul the royal commissioner—was announcing.

To many people then, and to many today, this was and is either nonsense or offensive or both. One can debate the merits of a religion, moral system, or philosophy, but a news event is discussed in a different way. Either the event happened or it didn't; if it did happen, either it means what people say it means or it doesn't. So we begin to see the enormity of Paul's challenge. He is announcing that a world-changing event has happened, and he is announcing it to an audience composed of people who assume they would have heard of a world-changing event if one had really occurred. And they hadn't.

—*Simply Good News* 16–17

God Is God, Jesus Is Lord, God's New World Has Begun

The power of the gospel lies not in the offer of a new spirituality or religious experience, not in the threat of hellfire (certainly not in the threat of being "left behind"), which can be removed if only the hearer checks this box, says this prayer, raises a hand, or whatever, but in the powerful announcement that God is God, that Jesus is Lord, that the powers of evil have been defeated, that God's new world has begun. This announcement, stated as a fact about the way the world is rather than as an appeal about the way you might like your life, your emotions, or your bank balance to be, is the foundation of everything else. Of course, once the gospel announcement is made, in whatever way, it means instantly that all people everywhere are gladly invited to come in, to join the party, to discover forgiveness for the past, an astonishing destiny in God's future, and a vocation in the present. And in that welcome and invitation, all the emotions can be, and one hopes will eventually be, fully engaged.

But how can the church announce that God is God, that Jesus

is Lord, that the powers of evil, corruption, and death itself have
been defeated, and that God's new world has begun? Doesn't this
seem laughable? Well, it would be if it wasn't happening. But if
a church is working on the issues we've already looked at—if it's
actively involved in seeking justice in the world, both globally and
locally, and if it's cheerfully celebrating God's good creation and
its rescue from corruption in art and music, and if, in addition, its
own internal life gives every sign that new creation is indeed happening, generating a new type of community—then suddenly the
announcement makes a lot of sense.

—Surprised by Hope 227–28

Following Jesus Is for Life, Not Just for Decision Day

To become a Christian is not to say no to the good world, which
God has made. It is, of course, to turn one's back on all the cor-
ruptions into which the world has fallen and into which each individual has fallen. Sometimes converts will need to say a firm no to
things that are not evil in themselves (alcohol, for instance) in order
to put a clear space between themselves and habits and patterns of
life that previously held them in their grip. But to think in terms of
a new creation avoids the problem of supposing for a moment that
one could forget earth and concentrate on heaven.

Second, to see evangelism in terms of the announcement of
God's kingdom, of Jesus's lordship and of the consequent new creation, avoids from the start any suggestion that the main or central thing that has happened is that the new Christian has entered
into a private relationship with God or with Jesus and that this

relationship is the main or only thing that matters. Seeing evangelism and any resulting conversions in terms of new creation means that the new convert knows from the start that he or she is part of God's kingdom project, which stretches out beyond "me and my salvation" to embrace, or rather to be embraced by, God's worldwide purposes. Along with conversion there will then go, at least in principle, the call to find out where in the total project one can make one's own contribution.

Third, putting evangelism and conversion within the context of new creation means that the convert, who has heard the message in terms of the sovereign and saving lordship of Jesus himself, will never be inclined to think that Christian behavior—saying no to the things that diminish human flourishing and God's glory and saying yes to the things that enhance them—is an optional extra or simply a matter of wrapping your head around some rather strange rules and regulations. To speak, rather, of Jesus's lordship and of the new creation, which results from his victory on Calvary and at Easter, implies at once that to confess him as Lord and to believe that God raised him from the dead is to allow one's entire life to be reshaped by him, knowing that though this will be painful from time to time, it will be the way not to a diminished or cramped human existence but to genuine human life in the present and to complete, glorious, resurrected human life in the future. As with every other aspect of new creation, there will be surprises on the way. But Christian ethics will only gain from being understood as one expression of Christian hope.

—*Surprised by Hope* 228–30

Moving Straight from Worship to Mission

When the church is seen to move straight from worship of the God we see in Jesus to making a difference and effecting much-needed change in the real world; when it becomes clear that the people who feast at Jesus's table are the ones in the forefront of work to eliminate hunger and famine; when people realize that those who pray for the Spirit to work in and through them are the people who seem to have extra resources of love and patience in caring for those whose lives are damaged, bruised, and shamed, then it is not only natural to speak of Jesus himself and to encourage others to worship him for themselves and find out what belonging to his family is all about but it is also natural for people, however irreligious they may think of themselves as being, to recognize that something is going on that they want to be part of. In terms that the author of Acts might have used, when the church is living out the kingdom of God, the word of God will spread powerfully and do its own work.

—*Surprised by Hope* 267

Declaring Your Allegiance

If someone went about the communities of diaspora Jews declaring that God had at last sent Israel's Messiah, this would not have seemed at the time to be a message either about "religion" (the Messiah was never supposed to start a new "religion"!) or about "life after death" (devout Jews had long believed that God would take care of them hereafter). Nor would it involve a new philosophy. It would be what we would call "political," though as always for the Jews of the day this would also be profoundly theological. It would be perceived as the announcement of a new state of affairs, a new community owing allegiance to a new Master, the unveiling, at last, of the covenant faithfulness of the One God. That is exactly what Paul intended.

If you use the word "political" to refer to a new state of affairs in which people give their ultimate and wholehearted allegiance to someone other than the ordinary local ruler or someone other than Caesar on the throne in Rome—and if you call "political" the establishment of cells of people loyal to this new ruler, celebrating his rescuing rule and living in new kinds of communities as a result—then what Paul was doing was inescapably "political." It had to do with the foundation of a new *polis,* a new city or community, right at the heart of the existing system. Paul's "missionary" journeys were not simply aimed at telling people about Jesus in order to generate inner personal transformation and a new sense of ultimate hope, though both of these mattered vitally as well. They were aimed at the establishment of a new kind of kingdom on earth as in heaven. A kingdom with Jesus as king. The kingdom—Paul was quite emphatic about this—that Israel's God had always intended to set up.

—*Paul: A Biography* 105–7

Think Eschatologically: Turn the World's Standards Upside Down

Here and throughout 1 Corinthians Paul is teaching the Corinthians, as he had surely been teaching them in person earlier, to *think eschatologically,* that is, to imagine a world quite unlike the world of ordinary Greco-Roman paganism, a world in which the One God was living and active and had started up something quite new, something that would be complete on the coming day. That something involved the creation of the new Temple; the church, which the Corinthians were pulling apart in their search for the ideal clever teacher, was the new Temple, the place where the living God had come to dwell by the spirit. No first-century Jew could use imagery like that as a mere "illustration" of a different kind of truth. Paul's vision of the church picked up the ancient Jewish hope of an ultimate Temple and put forth a new creation for which the Jerusalem Temple and the wilderness Tabernacle were advance signposts. This is it, says Paul. And if they belonged to it—if they belonged to the Messiah—then they should be above these petty squabbles:

> Everything belongs to you, whether it's Paul or Apollos or Cephas, whether it's the world or life or death, whether it's the present or the future—everything belongs to you! And you belong to the Messiah; and the Messiah belongs to God. (1 Cor. 3:21–23)

And if they all belong to the Messiah—the *crucified* Messiah, as Paul never lets them forget—then they should expect the world's standards to be stood on their heads.

—*Paul: A Biography* 249–50

The Church Is a River,
the Church Is a Tree

The river and the tree appear to be opposites.

The river begins, quite literally, all over the place. A tiny spring way up in the hills; a distant lake, itself fed by streams; a melting glacier—all of them and a thousand more contribute to the babble and rush of water, the smooth flow here and the swirling rapids there. Gradually other streams, other whole rivers, make their contribution. Out of many there emerges the one. I lived for a time by the banks of the Ottawa River in Canada, just upstream from where it joins the St. Lawrence. It is, at that point, over a mile wide. Many streams have made it what it is.

The tree begins with a single seed. An acorn or its equivalent falls into the earth: tiny, vulnerable, alone. It germinates and puts out roots down into the dark earth. Simultaneously it sends up a shoot into the light and air. The roots quickly diverge and probe all over the place, looking for nourishment and water. The shoot becomes a trunk, again a single upright stalk, but this, too, quickly diverges. An oak or a cedar will spread far and wide in all directions. Even the tall, narrow poplar is far more than just a single trunk. The river flows from many into one; the tree grows from one into many.

We need both images if we are to understand the church.

—*Simply Christian* 199

The Church: From Abraham to the Whole of Creation

The church is the single, multiethnic family promised by the creator God to Abraham. It was brought into being through Israel's Messiah, Jesus; it was energized by God's Spirit; and it was called to bring the transformative news of God's rescuing justice to the whole creation. That's a tightly packed definition, and every bit of it matters.

—*Simply Christian* 200

The Church Is a Missional Body

Many people today find it difficult to grasp the sense of corporate Christian identity. We have been so soaked in the individualism of modern Western culture that we feel threatened by the idea of our primary identity being that of the family we belong to—especially when the family in question is so large, stretching across space and time. The church isn't simply a collection of isolated individuals, all following their own pathways of spiritual growth without much reference to one another. It may sometimes look like that, and even feel like that. And it's gloriously true that each of us is called to respond to God's call at a personal level. You can hide in the shadows at the back of the church for a while, but sooner or later you have to decide whether this is for you or not. But we need to learn again the lesson (to take St. Paul's image of the Body of Christ) that a hand is no less a hand for being part of a larger whole, an entire body. The foot is not diminished in its freedom to be a foot by being part of a body which also contains eyes and ears. In fact, hands and feet are most free to be themselves when they coordinate properly with eyes, ears, and everything else. Cutting them off in an effort to make them truly free, truly themselves, would be truly disastrous.

In particular, it would deny the very purpose for which the church was called into being. According to the early Christians, the church doesn't exist in order to provide a place where people can pursue their private spiritual agendas and develop their own spiritual potential. Nor does it exist in order to provide a safe haven in which people can hide from the wicked world and ensure that they themselves arrive safely at an otherworldly destination. Private spiritual growth and ultimate salvation come rather as the by-products of the main, central, overarching purpose for which God has called and is calling us. This purpose is clearly stated in various places in the New Testament: that through the church God will announce to the wider world that he is indeed its wise, loving, and just creator; that through Jesus he has defeated the powers that corrupt and enslave it; and that by his Spirit he is at work to heal and renew it.

The church exists, in other words, for what we sometimes call "mission": to announce to the world that Jesus is its Lord. This is the "good news," and when it's announced it transforms people and societies.

—*Simply Christian* 203–4

Kingdom Worship, Kingdom Work, and Kingdom Fellowship

The church exists primarily for two closely correlated purposes: to worship God and to work for his kingdom in the world. You can and must worship, and work for God's kingdom, in private and in ways unique to yourself, but if God's kingdom is to go forward, rather than around and around in circles, we must work together as well as apart.

The church also exists for a third purpose, which serves the other two: to encourage one another, to build one another up in faith, to pray with and for one another, to learn from one another and teach one another, and to set one another examples to follow, challenges to take up, and urgent tasks to perform. This is all part of what is known loosely as *fellowship*. This doesn't just mean serving one another cups of tea and coffee. It's all about living within that sense of a joint enterprise, a family business, in which everyone has a proper share and a proper place.

It is within this context that the different "ministries" within the church have grown up. From the very earliest evidence we have, in the Acts of the Apostles and the letters of Paul, the church has recognized different callings within its common life. God has given different gifts to different people so that the whole community may flourish and take forward the work with which it has been entrusted.

Worship, fellowship, and the work of reflecting God's kingdom into the world flow into and out of one another. You can't reflect God's image without returning to worship to keep the reflection fresh and authentic. In the same way, worship sustains and nourishes fellowship; without it, fellowship quickly deteriorates into groups of the like-minded, which in turn quickly become exclusive cliques—the very opposite of what Jesus's people should be aiming at.

—*Simply Christian* 211

"And Earth and Heaven Be One"

A little over a hundred years ago, an American pastor in upstate New York celebrated in a great hymn both the beauty of creation and the presence of the creator God within it. His name was Maltbie Babcock, and his hymn "This Is My Father's World" points beyond the present beauty of creation, through the mess and tragedy with which it has been infected, to the ultimate resolution. There are different versions of the relevant stanza, but this one is the clearest:

> This is my Father's world; O let me ne'er forget
> That though the wrong seems oft so strong,
> God is the ruler yet.
> This is my Father's world; the battle is not done;
> Jesus, who died, shall be satisfied,
> And earth and heaven be one.

And earth and heaven be one: that is the note that should sound like a clear, sweet bell through all Christian living, summoning us to live in the present as people called to that future, people called to live in the present in the light of that future.

—*Simply Christian* 217–18

Living in the Fifth Act of God's Story

Within the scheme of God's whole story seen as a five act play, we are currently living in the fifth act, the time of the church. This act began with Easter and Pentecost; its opening scenes were the apostolic period itself; its charter text is the New Testament; its goal, its intended final scene, is sketched clearly in such passages as Romans 8, 1 Corinthians 15, and Revelation 21–22. The key point of the whole model, which forms the heart of the multilayered view of how "the authority of scripture" actually works, runs as follows: Those who live in this fifth act have an ambiguous relationship with the four previous acts, not because they are being disloyal to them but precisely because they are being loyal to them as part of the story. If someone in the fifth act of *All's Well That Ends Well* were to start repeating speeches from earlier acts, instead of those which belonged to the fifth act itself, the whole play would begin to unravel. We must act in the appropriate manner for *this* moment in the story; this will be in direct continuity with the previous acts (we are not free to jump suddenly to another narrative, a different play altogether), but such continuity also implies discontinuity, a moment where genuinely new things can and do happen. We must be ferociously loyal to what has gone before and cheerfully open about what must come next.

—*Scripture and the Authority of God* 122–23

An Announcement, Not a Sermon

Something else happened at the same time: Saul received Jesus's own spirit. The point of immense significance in Ananias's visit to Straight Street is that Saul was promised the gift of the spirit, and everything in his subsequent life and writings indicates that he believed this had happened then and there. The story in Acts doesn't say that Saul spoke in tongues or prophesied. The idea that things like that had to happen for the spirit's gift to be genuine is a much later fiction. What Acts offers instead is the remarkable statement that Saul went at once to the synagogue in Damascus and announced that Jesus was the son of God (a theme to which we shall return in due course). There was a new power coupled with a new sense of direction.

Paul's powerful, spirit-driven proclamation of Jesus as "son of God" can hardly be called "preaching," if by "preaching" we mean the sort of thing that goes on in churches week by week in our world. This was a public announcement, like a medieval herald or town crier walking through the streets with a bell, calling people to attention and declaring that a new king had been placed on the throne. This was, indeed, how the word "gospel" would be heard right across the Roman world of the day: as the announcement of a new emperor. Paul's proclamation was not, then, a fresh twist on the regular teaching work of the local Jewish community. He wasn't offering advice on how to lead a more holy life. He certainly wasn't telling people how to go to heaven when they died. He was making the all-time one-off announcement: Israel's hope has been fulfilled! The King has been enthroned! He was declaring that the crucified Jesus was Israel's long-awaited Messiah.

—*Paul: A Biography* 58

SPIRITUALITY

"I am the true vine," said Jesus, "and my father is the gardener. He cuts off every branch of mine that doesn't bear fruit; and he prunes every branch that does bear fruit, so that it can bear more fruit. You are already clean. That's because of the word that I've spoken to you.

"Remain in me, and I will remain in you! The branch can't bear fruit by itself, but only if it remains in the vine. In the same way, you can't bear fruit unless you remain in me. I am the vine; you are the branches. People who remain in me, and I in them, are the ones who bear plenty of fruit. Without me, you see, you can't do anything.

"If people don't remain in me, they are thrown out, like a branch, and they wither. People collect the branches and put them on the fire, and they are burned. If you remain in me, and my words remain in you, ask for whatever you want and it will happen for you. My father is glorified in this: that you bear plenty of fruit, and so become my disciples."

—John 15:1–8, *The Kingdom New Testament* 208–9

God's Gift of New Life

There are a great many people in today's world who do *not* think of themselves as either "religious" or indeed "Christian," but who *do* think of themselves as somehow "spiritual"—any kind of spirituality, as long as isn't "religious." Particularly *as long as it's not Christian*, the thinking goes.

Yet Christianity speaks uniquely to the broken signpost that is spirituality. God answers our longing for spiritual connection by interjecting glimpses of heaven on earth. That is what the Jerusalem Temple was all about, and for John that was what Jesus was all about. Nor does the fresh vision of spirituality stop there. God calls us to active participation, to a new life that is both God's gift and a deeply humanizing power, a new breath within us. John's vision is of the often puzzling quest for spirituality, the need to know and be known at the deepest levels, being fulfilled at last.

—*Broken Signposts* 65

The Challenge of Faith and an Active Spirituality

The rescue and transformation that God effected in the death and resurrection of Jesus is to become the rescue and transformation of every person. That is the challenge of faith, because the gospel message, working powerfully through God's Spirit in the hearts and minds of human beings, produces that faith: the confession that Jesus is Lord and the heartfelt belief that God really did raise him from the dead. That faith is the first sign of new life, and Paul declares that God will complete in the end the work he has begun in us.

Christian spirituality—an awareness of the loving and guiding presence of God, sorrow for sin and gratitude for forgiveness, the possibility and challenge of prayer, a love for God and for our neighbors, the desire for holiness and the hard moral work it requires, the gradual or sudden emergence of particular vocations, a lively hope for God's eventual new creation—is generated by the good news of what *has* happened in the past and what *will* happen in the future. All this and much, much more is what is meant by the good news in the present.

—*Simply Good News* 121

Rejecting Platonic Shrinkage

How fatally easy it would be for us Westerners to sigh with relief at this point. Ah, we think, God's kingdom is simply the sum total of all the souls who respond in faith to God's love. It isn't a real kingdom in space, time, and matter. It's a spiritual reality, "not of this world." John, though, will not collude with this Platonic shrinkage. We remind ourselves of the earlier passages about the ruler of this world being cast out, condemned, and overthrown. These appear to refer to a being that stands behind the present earthly rulers, but also incarnates itself in them; we are not simply talking about a "spiritual" victory that leaves the present human rulers unaffected.

—*How God Became King* 231–32

The Absolute Demands of Worship

All kingdom work is rooted in *worship*. Or, to put it the other way around, worshipping the God we see at work in Jesus is the most politically charged act we can ever perform. Christian worship declares that *Jesus* is Lord and that therefore, by strong implication, nobody else is. What's more, it doesn't just declare it as something to be believed, like the fact that the sun is hot or the sea wet. It commits the worshipper to allegiance, to following this Jesus, to being shaped and directed by him. Worshipping the God we see in Jesus orients our whole being, our imagination, our will, our hopes, and our fears away from the world where Mars, Mammon, and Aphrodite (violence, money, and sex) make absolute demands and punish anyone who resists. It orients us instead to a world in which love is stronger than death, the poor are promised the kingdom, and chastity (whether married or single) reflects the holiness and faithfulness of God himself. Acclaiming Jesus as Lord plants a flag that supersedes the flags of the nations, however "free" or "democratic" they may be. It challenges *both* the tyrants who think they are, in effect, divine *and* the "secular democracies" that have effectively become, if not divine, at least ecclesial, that is, communities that are trying to do and be what the church was supposed to do and be, but without recourse to the one who sustains the church's life. Worship creates—or should create, if it is allowed to be truly itself—a community that marches to a different beat, that keeps in step with a different lord.

Ideally, then—I shall come to the problems with this in a moment—the church, the community that hails Jesus as Lord and king, and feasts at his table celebrating his victorious death and resurrection, is constituted as the "body of the Messiah." This famous Pauline image is not a random "illustration." It expresses Paul's conviction that *this is the way in which Jesus now exercises his rule in the world—through the church, which is his Body.*

—*Simply Jesus* 217–18

Love Taking Thought

That is the difference between liturgy and spontaneous worship. There is nothing wrong with spontaneous worship, just as there's nothing wrong with two friends meeting by chance, grabbing a sandwich from a shop, and going off together for an impromptu picnic. But if the friends get to know one another better and decide to meet more regularly, they might decide that, though they could indeed repeat the picnic from time to time, a better setting for their friendship, and a way of showing that friendship in action, might be to take thought over proper meals for one another and prepare thoroughly. In the same way, good Christian liturgy is friendship in action, love taking thought, the covenant relationship between God and his people not simply discovered and celebrated like the sudden meeting of friends, exciting and worthwhile though that is, but thought through and relished, planned and prepared—an ultimately better way for the relationship to grow and at the same time a way of demonstrating what the relationship is all about.

In particular, Christian worship is all about the church celebrating God's mighty acts, the acts of creation and covenant followed by the acts of new creation and new covenant. The church needs constantly to learn, and constantly to be working on, the practice of telling and retelling the great stories of the world and Israel, especially the creation and the Exodus; the great promises that emerged from those stories; and the ways in which those promises came to their fruition in Jesus Christ.

The reading of scripture—the written account of those stories—has therefore always been central to the church's worship. It isn't only that people need to be reminded what the stories say. It's that these stories should be rehearsed in acts of celebration and worship, "telling out the greatness of the Lord," as Mary sang in the Magnificat. Good liturgy uses tried and tested ways of making sure that scripture is read thoroughly and clearly, and is constantly on the lookout for ways of doing it even more effectively—just as good liturgy is also eager to discover better and better ways of singing and praying the Psalms together, so that they come to be "second nature" within the memory, imagination, and spirituality of all the worshipping faithful, not just of a few musically minded leaders.

It's interesting to study the scriptural account of the early church at worship in the Acts of the Apostles, which describes the first Christians drawing on the Psalms and other scriptures to celebrate God's love and power and to be strengthened and sustained in mission. Because the early Christians were attempting to live as the true Temple, filled with the Spirit, we ought not to be surprised that the major confrontations they incurred were with existing temples and their guardians—the Jewish Temple in Jerusalem, and the whole culture of pagan temples in Athens and elsewhere.

—*After You Believe* 222–23

The Heavenly Dimension of Our Present Life

The pictures of heaven in the book of Revelation have been much misunderstood. The wonderful description in Revelation 4 and 5 of the twenty-four elders casting their crowns before the throne of God and the lamb, beside the sea of glass, is not, despite one of Charles Wesley's great hymns, a picture of the last day, with all the redeemed in heaven at last. It is a picture of *present* reality, the heavenly dimension of our present life. Heaven, in the Bible, is not a future destiny but the other, hidden, dimension of our ordinary life—God's dimension, if you like. God made heaven and earth; at the last he will remake both and join them together forever. And when we come to the picture of the actual end in Revelation 21–22, we find not ransomed souls making their way to a disembodied heaven but rather the new Jerusalem coming down from heaven to earth, uniting the two in a lasting embrace.

Most Christians today, I fear, never think about this from one year to the next. They remain satisfied with what is at best a truncated and distorted version of the great biblical hope. Indeed, the popular picture is reinforced again and again in hymns, prayers, monuments, and even quite serious works of theology and history. It is simply assumed that the word *heaven* is the appropriate term for the ultimate destination, the final home, and that the language of resurrection, and of the new earth as well as the new heavens, must somehow be fitted into that.

—Surprised by Hope 18–19

The Whole-Person Vocation of Worship

When human beings worship God the creator, articulating their praise and adoration because of who he is and what he's done, they are, whether or not they realize it, summing up the praises and adoration of the whole creation. That is another reason why the *physical* expression of worship, in liturgy and especially in the sacraments, remains important. We shouldn't expect to worship as disembodied souls who happen to be temporarily resident in these strange things called physical bodies, and then to be able to do our job as God's royal priesthood, picking up creation's praises and presenting them before God's throne. Remember: that is what we are called to do and to be. Don't be surprised if the body language of worshippers expresses something of what is being said and done.

No doubt this, too, can become a hollowed-out habit, to be challenged from time to time in the name of authenticity. But to frown on the physical expression of worship (gestures of hand and arm, of head and knee, whatever)—as though all such things were signs of hypocrisy or the attempt to put God in our debt—would be as ridiculous as to suppose that such expressions were all that was required, without the devotion of the heart and mind. As we have seen frequently in this book, the church is called to be the new Temple, the place where the living God dwells by the Spirit. This is a whole-person vocation.

The life of worship, then, is itself a corporate form of virtue. It expresses and in turn reinforces the faith, hope, and love which are themselves the key Christian virtues. From this activity there flow all kinds of other things in terms of Christian life and witness. But worship is central, basic, and in the best sense habit-forming. Every serious Christian should work at having worship become second nature.

—*After You Believe* 224–25

The Intimate Presence of God

Christian spirituality combines a sense of the awe and majesty of God with a sense of his intimate presence. This is hard to describe but easy to experience. As Jesus addressed God by the Aramaic family word *Abba*, "Father," so Christians are encouraged to do the same: to come to know God in the way in which, in the best sort of family, the child knows the parent. From time to time, I have met Christians who look puzzled at this, and say that they have no idea what all that stuff is about. I have to say that being a Christian without having at least something of that intimate knowledge of the God who is at the same time majestic, awesome, and holy sounds like a contradiction in terms.

I freely grant that there may be conditions under which, because of wounds in the personality, or some special calling of God, or some other reason, people may genuinely believe in the gospel of Jesus, strive to live by the Spirit, and yet have no sense of God's intimate presence. There is, after all, such a thing as the "dark night of the soul," reported by some who have probed the mysteries of prayer further than most of us. But Jesus declares that the Holy Spirit will not be denied to those who ask (Luke 11:13). One of the characteristic signs of the Spirit's work is precisely that sense of the intimate presence of God.

Second, Christian spirituality normally involves a measure of suffering. One of the times when Jesus is recorded as having used the *Abba* prayer was when, in Gethsemane, he asked his Father if there was another way, if he really had to go through the horrible fate that lay in store for him. The answer was yes, he did. But if Jesus prayed like that, we can be sure that we will often have to as well. Both Paul and John lay great stress on this. Those who follow Jesus are called to live by the rules of the new world rather than the old one, and the old one won't like it. Although the life of heaven is designed to bring healing to the life of earth, the powers that presently run this earth have carved it up to their own advantage, and they resent any suggestion of a different way.

But the point is this: it is precisely when we are suffering that we can most confidently expect the Spirit to be with us. We don't seek, or court, suffering or martyrdom. But if and when it comes, in whatever guise, we know that, as Paul says toward the end of his great Spirit-chapter, "in all these things we are more than conquerors through him who loved us" (Rom. 8:37).

—*Simply Christian* 137–38

The Two Golden Rules of Spirituality

I have been to many concerts of music ranging from major symphonic works to big-band jazz. I have heard world-class orchestras under world-famous conductors. I have been in the audience for some great performances that have moved me and fed me and satisfied me richly. But only two or three times in my life have I been in an audience which, the moment the conductor's baton came down for the last time, leaped to its feet in electrified excitement, unable to contain its enthusiastic delight and wonder at what it had just experienced. (American readers might like to know that English audiences are very sparing with standing ovations.)

That sort of response is pretty close to genuine worship. Something like that, but more so, is the mood of Revelation 4–5. That is what, when we come to worship the living God, we are being invited to join in.

What happens when you're at a concert like that is that everyone present feels that they have grown in stature. Something has happened to them: they are aware of things in a new way; the whole world looks different. It's a bit like falling in love. In fact, it *is* a kind of falling in love. And when you fall in love, when you're ready to throw yourself at the feet of your beloved, what you desire, above all, is union.

This brings us to the first of two golden rules at the heart of spirituality. *You become like what you worship.* When you gaze in awe, admiration, and wonder at something or someone, you begin to take on something of the character of the object of your worship. Those who worship money become, eventually, human calculating machines. Those who worship sex become obsessed with their own attractiveness or prowess. Those who worship power become more and more ruthless.

So what happens when you worship the creator God whose plan to rescue the world and put it to rights has been accomplished by the Lamb who was slain? The answer comes in the second golden rule: because you were made in God's image, *worship makes you more truly human.* When you gaze in love and gratitude at the God in whose image you were made, you do indeed grow. You discover more of what it means to be fully alive.

—*Simply Christian* 147–48

The Truth About the One We Worship

When you give total worship to anything or anyone else other than God, you shrink as a human being. It doesn't, of course, feel like that at the time. When you worship part of the creation as though it were the Creator himself—in other words, when you worship an idol—you may well feel a brief "high." But, like a hallucinatory drug, that worship achieves its effect at a cost: when the effect is over, you are less of a human being than you were to begin with. That is the price of idolatry.

The opportunity, the invitation, the summons is there before us: to come and worship the true God, the creator, the redeemer, and to become more truly human by doing so. Worship is at the very center of all Christian living. One of the main reasons that theology (trying to think straight about who God is) matters is that we are called to love God with all our heart, mind, soul, and strength. It matters that we learn more about who God is so that we can praise him more appropriately. Perhaps one of the reasons why so much worship, in some churches at least, appears unattractive to so many people is that we have forgotten, or covered up, the truth about the one we are worshipping. But whenever we even glimpse the truth, we are drawn back. Like groupies sneaking off work to see a rock star who's in town for just an hour or so, like fans waiting all night for a glimpse of a football team returning in triumph—only much more so!—those who come to recognize the God we see in Jesus, the Lion who is also the Lamb, will long to come and worship him.

—*Simply Christian* 148–49

True Worship Entails Unity Across Traditional Boundaries

Paul was determined *to establish and maintain Jew-plus-Gentile communities, worshipping the One God in and through Jesus his son and in the power of the spirit, ahead of the catastrophe.* Only so could this potential split—the destruction of the "new Temple" of 1 Corinthians

3 and Ephesians 2, no less—be averted. This is why Paul insisted, in letter after letter, on *the unity of the church across all traditional boundaries.* This was not about the establishment of a new "religion." It had nothing to do—one still meets this ill-informed slur from time to time—with Paul being a "self-hating Jew." Paul affirmed what he took to be the central features of Jewish hope: one God, Israel's Messiah, and resurrection itself. For him, what mattered was *messianic eschatology* and the community that embodied it. The One God had fulfilled, in a way so unexpected that most of the guardians of the promises had failed to recognize it, not only a set of individual promises, but the entire narrative of the ancient people of God. That, after all, was what Paul had been saying in one synagogue after another. And it was because of that fulfillment that the Gentiles were now being brought into the single family.

—*Paul: A Biography* 404–5

A New Family, a Genuine Identity, and a Gift

God is calling out a new family, and though the members of the old family (Abraham's physical descendants) are of course eagerly invited to belong, there is no guarantee they will avail themselves of this. Every Jewish renewal movement of the period thought like this: when God did the new thing he had promised, you had to get on board or you would miss out. John had already said as much in the prologue: "his own people" didn't receive Jesus, but anyone and everyone who did so gained the right to Israel's title, "children of God." And "they were not born from blood, or from fleshly desire, or from the intention of a man, but from God" (John 1:13). This offers the ultimate response to the puzzled spirituality questions of our day: a personal heaven-and-earth link, a new genuinely human "identity" of the highest order, a gift from the Creator himself.

—*Broken Signposts* 79–80

Worshipping with One Mind and One Mouth

It is noticeable that, right up to the end of Romans 14:1–15:13, Paul does not mention the underlying problem: that some of the house-churches are Jewish and some are Gentile. (Of course, things may well have been more complicated than that. Some of the Gentile Christians may, like some in Galatia, have been eager to take on the Jewish Torah; some of the Jewish Christians may, like Paul himself, have embraced what he calls the "strong" position.) But Paul will not address the questions in those terms. "Some of us prefer to do this . . . some of us prefer to do that," he says.

Paul wants the members of the Roman churches to respect one another across these differences. (We note, to ward off a very different problem in today's contemporary Western churches, that this supposed "tolerance" does not extend to all areas of behavior, as the closing lines of chapter 13 and the equivalent sections of other letters make abundantly clear.) And, once again, he reminds them they are living out the pattern of the Messiah. The death and resurrection of Jesus is, for Paul, not simply a historical reality that has created a new situation, but a pattern that must be woven into every aspect of church life. For Paul, what matters is the life of praise and worship that now, in the spirit, couples Jesus with God the father himself. This is the worship that, when united across traditional barriers, will shake Caesar's ideology to its foundations:

> Whatever was written ahead of time, you see, was written for us to learn from, so that through patience, and through the encouragement of the Bible, we might have hope. May the God of patience and encouragement grant you to come to a common mind among yourselves, in accordance with the Messiah, Jesus, so that, with one mind and one mouth, you may glorify the God and father of our Lord Jesus the Messiah. (15:4–6)
>
> —*Paul: A Biography* 336–37

Read Scripture Aloud and Celebrate

Telling the story, rehearsing the mighty acts of God: this is near the heart of Christian worship, a point not always fully appreciated in the enthusiastic, free-flowing worship common in many circles today. We know God through what he has done in creation, in Israel, and supremely in Jesus, and what he has done in his people and in the world through the Holy Spirit. Christian worship is praise of *this* God, the one who has done *these* things. And the place we find the God-given account of these events is, of course, scripture: the Bible.

I shall say more in due course about what the Bible itself is, but my point at the moment is simply this: reading the Bible aloud is always central to Christian worship. Cutting back on this for whatever reason—trimming readings so that the service doesn't go on too long, chanting scripture passages so that they become merely part of a musical performance, or reading only the few verses the preacher intends to preach about—misses the point. The reason we read scripture in worship isn't primarily to inform or remind the congregation about some biblical passage or theme they might have forgotten. Likewise, it's much more than a peg to hang a sermon on, though preaching from one or more of the readings is often a wise plan. Reading scripture in worship is, first and foremost, the central way of celebrating who God is and what he's done.

—*Simply Christian* 150

The Public Reading of Scripture

The question of how we might then read the gospels, publicly and privately, is a challenging one. I have enjoyed exploring, over many years now, different ways of undertaking this central task. Most congregations, I think, have never heard a gospel read, or "performed," all the way through. There are plenty of people in our churches who have the dramatic talent to undertake that. Many clergy have never thought of allowing large sections of scripture to frame their liturgy, rather than the other way around; that was done as an experiment in one of the Durham churches in Lent 2010, and it worked wonderfully well. Equally—and this is really astonishing when you stop to think about it—most practicing Christians, including most clergy, have never sat down privately and read right through one or more of the gospels in a single sitting. These books are not long. They are hardly *War and Peace*—but they are every bit as much page-turners as some of the great novels. We need to shed some inhibitions and experiment with ways of allowing the gospels to speak their message afresh. Preachers and teachers too need to face the challenge of communicating the excitement and drama of an entire book, so that hearers are led both into fresh worship then and there and into an eagerness to read it, and live it, for themselves.

Equally, we need to try new ways of *praying* the gospels. Many have used, with great profit, the Ignatian method of entering into a story, becoming a character within it. Think of yourself as a by-stander or onlooker as you watch Jesus asleep in the boat with the disciples panicking all around him, or as an extra guest at the sup-per table, suddenly wondering, "Lord, it's not me, is it?" Stay there long enough to hear what he has to say to you in particular. That method is well known, and rightly so. But there are ways of doing this corporately, too. Again, be innovative. Read the gospels for all they're worth; and they're worth a lot more than we have usually supposed. Consider, for instance, reading through Matthew and allowing the Lord's Prayer, which Matthew puts at the center of the Sermon on the Mount, to become the prayer you pray after each chapter or section to sum up and draw together all that you've been reading. Or try doing the same with John's gospel, using Jesus's great High-Priestly Prayer in chapter 17. The point is that if it's true that in Jesus God was genuinely "becoming king," that is something that cannot remain a matter of mere "information," something we learn about with our heads. It's something we must pray, something that, through prayer, must become a new reality in our lives and our communities.

—*How God Became King* 274–75

Reading Scripture in Communion with All Christians

The primary place where the church hears scripture is during corporate worship. This is itself a practice in direct descent from the public reading of the law by Ezra, Jesus's own reading of Isaiah in the synagogue at Nazareth, the reading of Paul's letters in the assembled church, and so on. However different we may be personally, contextually, culturally, and so on, when we read scripture we do so in communion with other Christians across space and time. This means, for instance, that we must work at making sure we read scripture properly in public, with appropriate systems for choosing what to read and appropriate training to make sure those who read do so to best effect. If scripture is to be a dynamic force within the church, it is vital that the public reading of scripture does not degenerate into what might be called "aural wallpaper," a pleasing and somewhat religious noise which murmurs along in the background while the mind is occupied elsewhere.

—*Scripture and the Authority of God* 130

Reading Scripture: Loving God with Our Mind and Heart

For all this to make the deep, life-changing, kingdom-advancing sense it is supposed to, it is vital that ordinary Christians read, encounter and study scripture for themselves, in groups and individually. The famous passage about the inspiration of scripture in 2 Timothy 3:16–17 was written, not so much to give people the right belief *about* scripture, as to encourage them to study it for themselves. Western individualism tends to highlight individual reading as the primary mode, and liturgical hearing as secondary, encouraging an Enlightenment-driven fragmentation of the witness of the whole church; by reversing this order, I do not for a moment mean to downgrade the importance of private reading. Study at all levels, with others and by oneself, is part of the church's continual calling to listen more closely to scripture as a whole and in its parts.

Indeed, scripture is a key means by which we can grow, as we are bidden, in loving God with our mind (through study) and with our heart (through devotional reading). It forms part of that complex pathway whereby each Christian is simultaneously called to worship and prayer, supplied with fresh understanding, puzzled by new questions (and so stimulated to yet more study and questioning), and equipped to take their own place in the ongoing story of God's people as they engage in his mission to the world. This is precisely what the authority of scripture looks like in practice, day by day and week by week, in the life of the ordinary Christian—and *all* Christians are ordinary Christians.

—*Scripture and the Authority of God* 133–34

Swallow the Bible Whole

Many children in many countries are functionally multilingual. In the longer perspective of history, in fact, it is those who know only one language who are the odd ones out. But the mature Paul has something else of which fewer people, even in his world, could boast. He gives every impression of having swallowed the Bible whole. He moves with polished ease between Genesis and the Psalms, between Deuteronomy and Isaiah. He knows how the story works, its heights and depths, its twists and turns. He can make complex allusions with a flick of the pen and produce puns and other wordplays across the languages. The radical new angle of vision provided by the gospel of Jesus is a new angle on texts he already knows inside out. He has pretty certainly read other Jewish books of the time, books like the Wisdom of Solomon, quite possibly some of the philosophy of his near contemporary Philo. They too knew their Bibles extremely well. Saul matches them stride for stride and, arguably, outruns them.

What is more, whether Saul has read the non-Jewish philosophers of his day or the great traditions that go back to Plato and Aristotle, he knows the ideas. He has heard them on the street, discussed them with his friends. He knows the technical terms, the philosophical schemes that probe the mysteries of the universe and the inner workings of human beings, and the theories that hold the gods and the world at arm's length like the Epicureans or that draw them into a single whole, *to pan*, "the all," like the Stoics.

—Paul: A Biography 16

What Is the Bible For?

It helps to remind ourselves constantly what the Bible is given to us *for*. One of the most famous statements of "inspiration" in the Bible itself puts it like this: "All scripture is inspired by God and is useful for teaching, for reproof, for correction, and for training in righteousness, so that everyone who belongs to God may be proficient, equipped for every good work" (2 Tim. 3:16–17). *Equipped for every good work;* there's the point. The Bible is breathed out by God (the word for "inspired" in this case is *theopneustos*—literally, "God-breathed") so that it can fashion and form God's people to do his work in the world.

In other words, the Bible isn't there simply to be an accurate reference point for people who want to look things up and be sure they've got them right. It is there to equip God's people to carry forward his purposes of new covenant and new creation. It is there to enable people to work for justice, to sustain their spirituality as they do so, to create and enhance relationships at every level, and to produce that new creation which will have about it something of the beauty of God himself. The Bible isn't like an accurate description of how a car is made. It's more like the mechanic who helps you fix it, the garage attendant who refuels it, and the guide who tells you how to get where you're going. And where you're going is *to make God's new creation happen in his world,* not simply to find your own way unscathed through the old creation.

That is why, though I'm not unhappy with what people are trying to affirm when they use words like "infallible" (the idea that the Bible won't deceive us) and "inerrant" (the stronger idea, that the Bible can't get things wrong), I normally resist using those words myself. Ironically, in my experience, debates about words like these have often led people away from the Bible itself and into

all kinds of theories which do no justice to scripture as a whole—
its great story, its larger purposes, its sustained climax, its haunting
sense of an unfinished novel beckoning us to become, in our own
right, characters in its closing episodes.

Such debates, in my view, distract attention from the real point
of what the Bible is there for. Squabbling over particular definitions
of the qualities of the Bible is like a married couple squabbling
over which of them loves the children more, when they should be
getting on with bringing them up and setting them a good example. The Bible is there to enable God's people to be equipped to do
God's work in God's world, not to give them an excuse to sit back
smugly, knowing they possess all God's truth.

—*Simply Christian* 182–84

Grow in the Love of God

Scripture has never, in any major part of the Christian church,
been simply a book to be referred to when certain questions are
to be discussed. From the very beginning, it has been given a key
place in the church's worshipping life, indicating that it has been
understood not only as part of the church's *thinking* but also as part
of the church's *praise and prayer*. As well as the obvious use of the
Psalms at the heart of Christian worship in many traditions, the
reading of the gospel within the eucharistic liturgy in many if not
most branches of the church indicates the implicit but powerful belief that the Bible continues to be both a central way in which God
addresses his people and a central way in which his people respond.
The widespread habit of private reading and study of scripture,
once a more particularly Protestant phenomenon but now widely

encouraged among Roman Catholics as well, has a long track re-
cord as a central part of Christian devotion.

Not only devotion: discipleship. Reading and studying scripture
has been seen as central to how we are to grow in the love of God;
how we come to understand God and his truth more fully; and how
we can develop the moral muscle to live in accordance with the gospel of Jesus even when everything seems to be pulling the other way.
Since these remain vital aspects of Christian living, the Bible has
been woven into the fabric of normal Christian life at every point.

—Scripture and the Authority of God 5

Scripture Plays an Active Part Within God's New Creation

What *role* does scripture play *within* God's accomplishment of this
goal? It is enormously important that we see the role of scripture
not simply as being to provide *true information about,* or even an
accurate running commentary upon, the work of God in salvation and new creation, but as taking an active part *within* that ongoing purpose. If we are to discover a fully rounded—and itself
biblical!—meaning of "the authority of scripture," it will be within
this setting. Short-circuiting the question of biblical authority by
ignoring these opening moves is one of the root causes of our continuing puzzles and polarizations. Scripture is there to be a means
of God's action in and through us—which will include, but go far
beyond, the mere conveying of information.

—Scripture and the Authority of God 30

The God Who Speaks, Renews Minds, and Empowers Mission

In particular, the role of the Bible within the church and the individual Christian life indicates three things which are of central importance as we proceed. To begin with, it reminds us that the God Christians worship is characterized not least as a God who *speaks*, who communicates with his human creatures in words. This differentiates the God of the Old and New Testaments from some other gods known in the worlds of the time, and indeed today. It means that the idea of reading a book to hear and know God is not far-fetched, but cognate with the nature of God himself.

Second, it is central to early Christian instruction that we be transformed by the renewal of our minds (Rom. 12:1–2). In other words, it is important that God's transforming grace is given to us not least through enabling us to *think* in new ways. Again, this means that the idea of reading a book in order to have one's life reordered by the wisdom of God is not counter-intuitive, but is cognate with the nature of Christian holiness itself.

Third, it reminds us that the God we worship is the God whose world-conquering power, seen in action in the resurrection of Jesus, is on offer to all those who ask for it in order thereby to work for the gospel in the world (Eph. 1:15–23). The idea of reading a book in order to be energized for the task of mission is not a distraction, but flows directly from the fact that we humans are made in God's image, and that, as we hear his word and obey his call, we are able to live out our calling to reflect the creator into his world.

—*Scripture and the Authority of God* 33–34

A Christian Theology of Scriptural Authority

Here we have the roots of a fully Christian theology of scriptural authority: planted firmly in the soil of the missionary community, confronting the powers of the world with the news of the Kingdom of God, refreshed and invigorated by the Spirit, growing particularly through the preaching and teaching of the apostles, and bearing fruit in the transformation of human lives as the start of God's project to put the whole cosmos to rights. God accomplishes these things, so the early church believed, through the "word": the story of Israel now told as reaching its climax in Jesus, God's call to Israel now transmuted into God's call to his renewed people. And it was this "word" which came, through the work of the early writers, to be expressed in writing in the New Testament as we know it.

The church was thus from the very beginning characterized precisely as the transformed people of God, as the community created by God's call and promise, and summoned to hear the "word" of the gospel in all its fullness. The earliest church was centrally constituted as the people called into existence, and sustained in that existence, by the powerful, effective and (in that sense and many others) "authoritative" word of God, written in the Old Testament, embodied in Jesus, announced to the world, taught in the church. This was the heart of the church's mission (Israel's story has been fulfilled; the world must therefore hear of it); of its common life (the first "mark of the church" in Acts 2:42 is "the teaching of the apostles"); and of the call to a holiness which would express both the true Israel and the newly human dimensions ("renewed according to God's image") characteristic of the new identity. Some of the major disputes in the early church were precisely about what this holiness meant in practice.

—Scripture and the Authority of God 50

Matter Matters

Jesus's announcement that God is now in charge, that God is becoming king on earth as in heaven, means that we can glimpse, fitfully and in flashes, something of what the prophetic vision might mean—where Jesus is and what he is doing. We can see *the material world itself* being transformed by the presence and power of Israel's god, the creator.

We see it already, to be sure, in the healing stories. In them the physical matter of someone's body is being transformed by a strange power, which, in one telling scene, Jesus feels going out of him (Mark 5:30). But then, to the astonishment of the first onlookers and the scornful skepticism of Epicureans ancient or modern, we see creation, as it were, under new management. The professional fishermen who caught nothing during the night are overwhelmed with the catch they get when Jesus tells them where to cast the net. Jesus not only heals the sick; he raises the dead. He feeds a hungry crowd with a few loaves and a couple of fish. Something new is happening, and it's happening to the material world itself. He commands the raging storm to be quiet, and it obeys. Then, worse still, he walks on the lake and invites Peter to do it, too.

As with the resurrection itself, which forms the climax to this whole sequence, it is no use trying to rationalize these events. Disbelieve them if you will; retain the Epicurean detachment, the belief that if there is a God he (or she, or it) is a long way away and doesn't get involved with this world. But at least see what is being claimed. These "miracles" make little or no sense within the present world of creation, where matter is finite, humans do not walk on water, and storms do what storms will do, no matter who, Canute-like, tries to tell them not to.

But suppose, just suppose, that the ancient prophetic dream had glimpsed a deeper truth. Suppose there *were* a god like Israel's God. Suppose this God did after all make the world. And suppose he were to claim, at long last, his sovereign rights over that world, not to destroy it (another philosophical mistake) or merely to "intervene" in it from time to time (a kind of soggy compromise position), but to fill it with his glory, to allow it to enter a new mode in which it would reflect his love, his generosity, his desire to make it over anew. Perhaps these stories are not, after all, the sort of bizarre things that people invent in retrospect to boost the image of the dead hero. Perhaps they are not even evidence of the kind of "interventionist," miracle-working, "supernatural" divinity of some "conservative" speculation. Perhaps they are, instead, the sort of things that might just be characteristic of *the new creation*, of the fulfilled time, of what happens when heaven and earth come together.

—*Simply Jesus* 140–41

Spirituality as Holistic Mission, Not Capitulation or Withdrawal

The kingdom that Jesus inaugurated, that is implemented through his cross, is emphatically *for* this world. The four gospels together demand a complete reappraisal of the various avoidance tactics Western Christianity has employed rather than face this challenge head-on. It simply won't do to line up the options, as has normally been done, into either a form of "Christendom," by which people normally mean the capitulation of the gospel to the world's way of power, or a form of sectarian withdrawal. Life is more complex, more interesting, and more challenging than that. The gospels are there, waiting to inform a new generation for holistic mission, to embody, explain, and advocate new ways of ordering communities, nations, and the world. The church belongs at the very heart of the world, to be the place of prayer and holiness at the point where the world is in pain—not to be a somewhat "religious" version of the world, on the one hand, or a detached, heavenly minded enclave, on the other. It is a measure of our contemporary muddles that we find it very difficult to articulate, let alone to live out, a vision of church, kingdom, and world that is neither of these.

—*How God Became King 241–42*

Not "Just Passing Through"

Most Western Christians—and most Western non-Christians, for that matter—suppose that Christianity was committed to at least a soft version of Plato's position. A good many Christian hymns and poems wander off unthinkingly in the direction of Gnosticism. The "just passing through" spirituality (as in the spiritual "This world is not my home, / I'm just a'passin' through"), though it has some affinities with classical Christianity, encourages precisely a Gnostic attitude: the created world is at best irrelevant, at worst a dark, evil, gloomy place, and we immortal souls, who existed originally in a different sphere, are looking forward to returning to it as soon as we're allowed to. A massive assumption has been made in Western Christianity that the purpose of being a Christian is simply, or at least mainly, to "go to heaven when you die," and texts that don't say that but that mention heaven are read as if they did say it,

and texts that say the opposite, like Romans 8:18–25 and Revelation
21–22, are simply screened out as if they didn't exist.

—*Surprised by Hope* 90

The Eucharist as the Arrival of God's Future in the Present

When Jews celebrate Passover they don't suppose they are essen-
tially doing something *different from* the original event. "This is the
night," they say, "when God brought us out of Egypt." The people
sitting around the table become not the distant heirs of the wilderness generation but the same people. Time and space telescope
together. Within the sacramental world, past and present are one.
Together they point forward to the still-future liberation.

What happens in the Eucharist is that through the death and
resurrection of Jesus Christ, this future dimension is brought
sharply into play. We break this bread to share in the body of
Christ; we do it in remembrance of him; we become for a moment
the disciples sitting around the table at the Last Supper. Yet if we
stop there we've only said the half of it. To make any headway in
understanding the Eucharist, we must see it as the arrival of God's
future in the present, not just the extension of God's past (or of
Jesus's past) into our present. We do not simply remember a long-
since dead Jesus; we celebrate the presence of the living Lord. And
he lives, through the resurrection, precisely as the one who has
gone on ahead *into the new creation*, the transformed new world, as
the one who is himself its prototype. The Jesus who gives himself to
us as food and drink is himself the beginning of God's new world.
At communion we are like the children of Israel in the wilderness,

tasting fruit plucked from the promised land. It is the future coming to meet us in the present.

This perspective is a far more helpful way to talk about the presence of Christ in the Eucharist than trying to redefine the old language of transubstantiation. The problem with the old language was not that it was the wrong answer but that it was the right answer to the wrong question.

—Surprised by Hope 274

Jesus Wants to Feed Us

First, we break bread and drink wine together, telling the story of Jesus and his death, because Jesus knew that this set of actions would explain the meaning of his death in a way that nothing else—no theories, no clever ideas—could ever do. After all, when Jesus died for our sins it wasn't so he could fill our minds with true ideas, however important they may be, but so he could *do* something, namely, rescue us from evil and death.

Second, it isn't a piece of sympathetic magic, as suspicious Protestants have often worried it might be. This action, like the symbolic actions performed by the ancient prophets, becomes one of the points at which heaven and earth coincide. Paul says that "as often as you eat the bread and drink the cup, you *proclaim* the Lord's death until he comes" (1 Cor. 11:26). He doesn't mean that it's a good opportunity for a sermon. Like a handshake or a kiss, *doing* it *says* it.

Third, therefore, nor is the bread-breaking a mere occasion for remembering something that happened a long time ago, as suspicious Catholics sometimes suppose Protestants believe. When we break the bread and drink the wine, we find ourselves joining the disciples in the Upper Room. We are united with Jesus himself as he prays in Gethsemane and stands before Caiaphas and Pilate. We become one with him as he hangs on the cross and rises from the tomb. Past and present come together. Events from long ago are fused with the meal we are sharing here and now.

But it isn't only the past that comes forward into the present. If the bread-breaking is one of the key moments when the thin partition between heaven and earth becomes transparent, it is also one of the key moments when God's future comes rushing into the present. Like the children of Israel still in the wilderness, tasting food which the spies had brought back from their secret trip to the Promised Land, in the bread-breaking we are tasting God's new creation—the new creation whose prototype and origin is Jesus himself.

That is one of the reasons why he said "This is my body" and "This is my blood." We don't need elaborate metaphysical theories with long Latin names to get the point. Jesus—the real Jesus, the living Jesus, the Jesus who dwells in heaven and rules over earth as well, the Jesus who has brought God's future into the present—wants not just to influence us, but to rescue us; not just to inform us, but to heal us; not just to give us something to think about, but to feed us, and to feed us with himself. That's what this meal is all about.

—*Simply Christian* 153–54

We Are All Brothers and Sisters in Christ

Along with Eucharist there goes, of course, baptism. Again, many Christians couldn't easily explain what happens in baptism or why they do it. That doesn't necessarily mean that the practice has become a mere bit of formal ritual (though that, too, does happen). It may well mean that, as with virtue itself, it has become second nature. This is how we join the family: by plunging into water and coming up again! By dying and rising with Jesus the Messiah! I sense that, at least in the churches I know best, baptism may, in fact, need more explanation, and more working through in terms of how its meaning becomes a living reality for the core congregation and also for those on the fringe who want their baby baptized but are far from clear why. But the regular practice of baptism says something to the congregation, something that should go deeper and deeper until it becomes second nature.

So what does it say to them? First, nobody drifts into the kingdom of God. Sooner or later there must be a dying and a rising. Christian living, "virtue" included, is never a matter simply of discovering what I feel like doing and seeing how to do it. No: "You have died, and your life is hidden with Christ in God" (Col. 3:3). Baptism makes it crystal clear that all Christian life is a matter of being signed with the cross, of sharing in the cross, of taking up the cross and following Jesus. This needs emphasizing today in view of the extraordinary idea which has crept in to some churches that baptism simply means God's acceptance of everybody as is, with no need for repentance or for dying to self and rising to God in Christ.

Second, baptism is the same for everybody, marking out the church decisively as a single body. We don't have a different rite for adults and children, or for men and women, or for rich and poor, or for people from different nations, races, and cultures. Yes, there are different modes of baptism—some people don't think it's real baptism unless the person gets wet from head to toe, for example, while most of us think it's enough if a handful of water is splashed on the head (just as the Eucharist is a real meal even if you have only a tiny bit of bread and a small sip of wine). But the point is that baptism, by being the same for everyone alike, reminds us at a deep level, informing the heart and mind of every Christian, that we are all brothers and sisters in Christ. There are, in that sense, no "special" Christians. Every Christian has a different calling. But all callings are marked with the same water, the same cross.

—After You Believe 280–82

Relax and Enjoy the Sacraments

But to reject, marginalize, trivialize, or be suspicious of the sacraments (and quasi-sacramental acts such as lighting a candle, bowing, washing feet, raising hands in the air, crossing oneself, and so forth) on the grounds that such things *can* be superstitious or idolatrous or that some people might suppose that by doing them they are putting God in their debt, is like rejecting sexual relations in marriage on the grounds that it's the same act that in other circumstances constitutes immorality. (I am always amused, on this point, when I visit churches that carefully abandoned all signs of professional worship from a former age—robed choirs, processions, organists, and the like—and then invented new forms of worship that demand just as much professionalism in terms of competent people managing sound systems, lighting, overhead projection and PowerPoint, and so on. There is nothing wrong with either. All can and should be done to the glory of God. But the implication that older styles of worship are somehow less spiritual and the modern electronic worship is somehow more worthy is sheer cultural prejudice and should be happily laughed at whenever it emerges.)

Try looking at it like this (shortening, for the moment, a much longer case that could be argued). In the Eucharist, the bread and the wine come to us as part of God's new creation, the creation in whose reality Jesus already participates through the resurrection. They speak powerfully, as only encoded actions can speak (whether a handshake, a kiss, the tearing up of a contract, or whatever), both of the death he suffered, through which idolatry and sin have been defeated, and of his future arrival in which creation is to be renewed (1 Cor. 11:26). We feed on that reality even though we may find it difficult to conceptualize what *sort* of reality it is. Knowing that we are thereby renewed as the people of Jesus who live and work in the tension between Easter and the final renewal enables us at least to relax and enjoy all that the sacrament has to offer.

—*Surprised by Hope* 263–64

Paul Had His Sleeves Rolled Up

When people in churches today discuss Paul and his letters, they often think only of the man of ideas who dealt with lofty and difficult concepts, implying a world of libraries, seminar rooms, or at least the minister's study for quiet sermon preparation. We easily forget that the author of these letters spent most of his waking hours with his sleeves rolled up, doing hard physical work in a hot climate, and that perhaps two-thirds of the conversations he had with people about Jesus and the gospel were conducted not in a place of worship or study, not even in a private home, but in a small, cramped workshop. Saul had his feet on the ground, and his hands were hardened with labor. But his head still buzzed with scripture and the news about Jesus. His heart was still zealous, loyal to the One God.

A second thing we can be sure of is that he prayed, he studied, and he figured out all sorts of things.

—*Paul: a Biography* 68–69

Following Paul's Example of Prayer

While he was traveling—on the sea, on the roads—Paul prayed. We know this. When he tells people that they should "never stop praying," this can hardly be something that applies to everybody else but not to himself. But how do you go on praying all the time? Is it simply ceaseless chatter, a stream-of-consciousness monologue (or indeed dialogue) with the God who through the spirit was as present as breath itself? This may have been part of it, but reading back from the letters Paul wrote I think we can be much more precise and focused. At several points in his letters he seems to be adapting Jewish prayers and liturgies to include Jesus in recognition of the new life that had erupted into the ancient tradition. We know from many passages in the letters that he prayed the Psalms, focusing them on Jesus; Jesus was the promised king, the ultimate sufferer, the truly human one who would now be crowned with glory and honor. We can guess, from the easy way he weaves it into his argument, that the astonishing adaptation of the *Shema* prayer had already been Paul's daily, perhaps thrice-daily, way of invoking Jesus, of expressing his loyalty to him and his kingdom: *For us there is one God . . . and one Lord . . .*

So too the "benedictions" in Jewish liturgy ("Blessed be the God who . . . ") had become part of his celebration of the way in which the One God had fulfilled his purposes in Jesus. They were Exodus prayers, kingdom prayers, messianic prayers, Jesus prayers. Paul's experience of articulating the crazy, nonsensical message about Jesus and watching as it grasped and gripped and changed people's lives had given him concrete reasons to pray like this, to invoke the name and power of Jesus, to seek his protection, his guidance, his encouragement, his hope, to know his presence as the focus of what in Paul's earlier life he had experienced as the covenant love of the One God.

It is easy as we follow the outward course of Paul's life to forget that the inward course was just as important. But unless we step to one side from his relentless journeyings and imagine him praying like this, praying as he and his friends break bread in Jesus's name; praying as he waits for the next ship, for the turn of the tide, for the right weather to sail; praying for sick friends and for newly founded little churches; praying as he makes his way toward what may be a wonderful reunion with old friends or an awkward confrontation with old enemies—unless we build this into the very heart of our picture of this extraordinary, energetic, bold, and yet vulnerable man, we will not understand him at all.

—*Paul: A Biography* 231–32

An *"Earth as It Is in Heaven"* Prayer

The Lord's Prayer says: I want to be part of his kingdom movement. I find myself drawn into his heaven-on-earth way of living. I want to be part of his bread-for-the-world agenda, for myself and for others. I need forgiveness for myself—from sin, from debt, from every weight around my neck—and I intend to live with forgiveness in my heart in my own dealings with others. (Notice how remarkable it is that, at the heart of the prayer, we commit ourselves to live in a particular way, a way we find difficult.) And because I live in the real world, where evil is still powerful, I need protecting and rescuing. And, in and through it all, I acknowledge and celebrate the Father's kingdom, power, and glory.

Most of the things we might want to pray about are taken care of within that prayer. Like Jesus's parables, it is small in scale but huge in coverage. Some people find that it helps to pray the Lord's Prayer slowly, pausing every few words to hold before God the particular things on their hearts which come into that category. Some people prefer to use it at the beginning or the end of a more extended time of prayer, either to set the context for everything else or to sum things up. Some people find that saying it slowly, over and over again, helps them to go down deeply into the love and presence of God, into the place where the spheres overlap, into the power of the gospel to bring bread and forgiveness and rescue. However you want to use it, use it. Start here and see where it takes you.

—*Simply Christian* 160–61

The Freedom of Formal Prayer

There's nothing wrong with having a form of words composed by somebody else. Indeed, there's probably something wrong with *not* using such a form. Some Christians, some of the time, can sustain a life of prayer entirely out of their own internal resources, just as there are hardy mountaineers (I've met one) who can walk the Scottish highlands in their bare feet. But most of us need boots; not because we don't want to do the walking ourselves, but because we do.

This plea, it will be obvious, is aimed in one particular direction: at the growing number of Christians in many countries who, without realizing it, are absorbing an element of late modern culture (the Romantic-plus-Existentialist mixture) as though it were Christianity itself. To them I want to say: there is nothing wrong, nothing sub-Christian, nothing to do with "works-righteousness," about using words, set forms, prayers, and sequences of prayers written by other people in other centuries. Indeed, the idea that I must always find my own words, that I must generate my own devotion from scratch every morning, that unless I think of new words I must be spiritually lazy or deficient—that has the all-too-familiar sign of human pride, of "doing it my way": of, yes, works-righteousness. Good liturgy—other people's prayers, whether for corporate or individual use—can be, *should* be, a sign and means of grace, an occasion of humility (accepting that someone else has said, better than I can, what I deeply want to express) and gratitude. How many times have I been grateful, faced with night-falls both metaphorical and literal, for the old Anglican prayer that runs,

> Lighten our darkness, we beseech thee, O Lord;
> and by thy great mercy
> defend us from all perils and dangers of this night;
> for the love of thy only Son,
> our Savior Jesus Christ. Amen.

I didn't write it, but whoever did has my undying gratitude. It's just what I wanted.

Of course, there's a plea to be directed the other way as well. The Romantics and the Existentialists were not fools. Some suits of clothes don't fit; they constrict both movement and personality.

Some walking boots are too cumbersome. When David went off to fight Goliath, he couldn't wear the heavy armor that tradition suggested. He had to use the simpler weapons he already knew. They worked for him. If it weren't so tragic, it would be hugely comic to watch many people in traditional churches clumping around in suits of armor made for serious warfare—in other words, using ancient liturgies and traditional practices—without much apparent idea where they're going or what to do when they get there.

—*Simply Christian* 165–67

The Creeds Are Common Faith Markers, Not Theological Syllabi

The creeds were remarkable, a unique postbiblical innovation to meet a fresh need. They have functioned as the badge and symbol of the Christian family (not for nothing is the creed referred to in Latin as a *symbolum*) for a millennium and a half. They are more than merely a list of things we happen to believe. Saying we believe these things marks us out as standing in continuity with those who went before us as well as with those around the world who today, in other places very different from our own, share this common faith and life.

And yet. As we observed in the first part of this book, it simply won't do to say that the Bible and the creeds can come together in that ultimate, intimate way. The creeds simply do *not* "let scripture come to its natural, two-testament expression." Indeed, for many who have said the creeds down the years, the Old Testament has remained a largely closed book. There are many who would be horrified to have their status as catholic, creedal Christians questioned, but in whose life, worship, teaching, prayer, and Christian thinking the scriptures of Israel play no visible part. The creeds do virtually nothing to challenge this form of truncated, quasi-Marcionite Christianity. (When I say "virtually nothing," I allow the two exceptions: that calling God the "maker of heaven and earth" at once invokes Genesis 1, for those who have ears to hear; and saying, in the Nicene Creed, that the Holy Spirit "spoke by the prophets" acknowledges—assuming with most that the reference is to the "prophets" of the Old Testament, not the new—that the gift of Pentecost was simply the universalizing of the special inspiration of the ancient biblical writers.)

But that is only the start of it. As we saw, directly following from the creeds' nonmention of the whole story of Israel is the complete absence of anything to do with God's kingdom. This is fine so long as the creeds are regarded as the key markers in areas where there had been serious controversy. But as soon as they are made *the* syllabus, the master list of vital topics, there is a major gap.

—How God Became King 256

Praying for the Return of the King

Some of the regular prayers, in my tradition, let us down with a bump—which is actually the wrong metaphor because what they do is to say, in effect, "Jesus has been raised to heaven, and we pray that we may be raised there, too." There is indeed a sense in which this is true, as in Ephesians 2:6 and Colossians 3:1–4. But when people hear those prayers today (speaking of Jesus being exalted to heaven and of us going in heart and mind to be with him forever; or speaking of the Holy Spirit as the one who will exalt us to the place where he has gone before), they are almost bound, within today's muddled worldview, to be reinforced in their view that the whole point of the Christian faith is to follow Jesus away from earth to heaven and stay there forever. And the New Testament insists, on the contrary, that the one who has gone into heaven will come back. At no point in the gospels or Acts does anyone say anything remotely like, "Jesus has gone into heaven, so let's be sure we can follow him." They say, rather, "Jesus is in heaven, ruling the whole world, and he will one day return to make that rule complete."

—Surprised by Hope 116–17

Do Not Neglect the Church's Original Hymnbook

In some parts of contemporary Christianity, the Psalms are no longer used in daily and weekly worship. This is so especially at points where there has been remarkable growth in numbers and energy, not least through the charismatic movements in various denominations. The enormously popular "worship songs," some of which use phrases from the Psalms here and there but most of which do not, have largely displaced, for thousands of regular and enthusiastic worshippers, the steady rhythm and deep soul-searching of the Psalms themselves. This, I believe, is a great impoverishment.

By all means write new songs. Each generation must do that. But to neglect the church's original hymnbook is, to put it bluntly, crazy. There are many ways of singing and praying the Psalms; there are styles to suit all tastes. That, indeed, is part of their enduring charm. I hope that one of the effects of this little book will be to stimulate and encourage those who lead worship in many different settings to think and pray about how to reintegrate the church's ancient prayer book into the regular and ordinary life of their fellowships. The Psalms represent the Bible's own spiritual root system for the great tree we call Christianity. You don't have to be a horticultural genius to know what will happen to the fruit on the tree if the roots are not in good condition.

—Case for the Psalms 4–5

The Taproot of Christian Mission

The Psalms stand at the intersection of both time and space, of the present Jerusalem Temple and the future cosmic Temple. That is close to what Paul is saying in Romans 8:18–27; it is at the heart of what John the Visionary is saying when he sketches his vision of the New Jerusalem in the form of a gigantic Holy of Holies (Rev. 21), where, as at the end of Ezekiel, the city will be known by the fact that "YHWH is There" (Ezek. 48:35).

The New Testament picks up all of these themes, so central to the Psalter, and sings them in a new key. There is, of course, still a definite future focus to it all. The early Christians did not imagine for a moment that they had "arrived" at the ultimate new creation. But with the resurrection of Jesus and the gift of the Spirit, that new creation had already broken into the world, and they were able to sing the ancient songs with, as it were, a whole new set of harmonies. Learning to sing them that way formed the heart of early Christian spirituality and the taproot of early Christian mission.

—The Case for the Psalms 111

Multidimensional Worship

Most of all, once more, they are designed as *worship:* the multidimensional worship in which every aspect of human life, love, fear, delight, anger, despair, and gratitude is laid as an offering before the God who himself comes to stand at the crossroads of time, space, and matter. The Psalms might not always seem to us particularly pure or worthy, as sacrifices should be. But I think part of the point is that they are *truthful,* the sincere outpourings of who and what the worshipper actually is. And when we worship the creator God with our whole, truthful self, we trust—and the Psalms strongly encourage this trust—that we will be remade. As Paul puts it, we are to be "renewed in the image of the creator, bringing us into possession of new knowledge" (Col. 3:10).

—Case for the Psalms 29

Worshipping with the Praise of All Creation Through the Psalms

> The pastures of the wilderness overflow,
> the hills gird themselves with joy,
> the meadows clothe themselves with flocks,
> the valleys deck themselves with grain,
> they shout and sing together for joy.
> (Ps. 65:9–13)

The whole countryside, in fact, is putting on its fine clothes as if getting ready for a party: God's party, the harvest season that humans facilitate but do not create.

I have learned, in my advancing years, to take all this more seriously than a normal Western worldview would suggest. The old Anglican prayer book prescribes, to be prayed daily, Psalm 95 with its celebration of God's creative power:

> For YHWH is a great God,
> and a great King above all gods.
> In his hand are the depths of the earth;
> the heights of the mountains are his also.
> The sea is his, for he made it,
> and the dry land, which his hands have formed.
> (95:3–5)

The service of morning prayer then moves on, after the reading from the Old Testament, to the ancient hymn called "Te Deum," which begins in similar fashion:

We praise thee, O God,
we acknowledge thee to be the Lord;
all the earth doth worship thee,
the Father everlasting.

All the earth! Well, the seraphim in Isaiah's vision declared that the whole earth was full of YHWH's glory (Isa. 6:3). With that to one side of us and the answering hymn in Revelation 4 to the other, why should we not look out on the fruitful earth around us, whether it be mountains and lakes or simply a plant on a windowsill, and celebrate the fact that it is all singing praise to its maker? That, indeed, is part of what it means when we say in the creed that we believe in "God the Father almighty, *Maker of heaven and earth*." Unless our worship is joined—more or less consciously—with the praises of all creation, there should be a question mark as to whether it really is genuine Christian worship.

—*Case for the Psalms* 122–24

Joining the Worship of Every Creature in Heaven and on Earth

In Revelation, "every creature in heaven and on earth and under the earth and in the sea, and all that is in them," join in the song:

To the one seated on the throne and to the Lamb
be blessing and honor and glory and might, forever and
ever! (5:13)

That is what worship is all about. It is the glad shout of praise that arises to God the creator and God the rescuer from the creation that recognizes its maker, the creation that acknowledges the triumph of Jesus the Lamb. That is the worship that is going on in heaven, in God's dimension, all the time. The question we ought to be asking is how best we might join in.

—*Simply Christian* 146–47

The Psalms Are Agents of Change

The Psalms speak of change, but more importantly they are *agents* of change: change within the humans who sing them, and change *through* those humans, as their transformed lives bring God's kindness and justice into the world. The Psalms do much more than inform the singer and the listener of the truth of Israel's worldview, in which past, present, and future, heaven and earth, creation and new creation all overlap. They are part of the means by which this happens. It is as though the same Schubert song that spoke of the lover's yearning for his beloved was also used as the means of successfully wooing her.

—*Case for the Psalms* 164–65

The Challenge of All 150 Psalms

I find it impossible, therefore, to imagine a growing and maturing church or individual Christian doing without the Psalms. And that is why (to be frank) a fair amount of contemporary Christian music has worried me for some time.

The last generation in the Western churches has seen an enormous explosion in "Christian music," with hundreds of new songs written and sung, often with great devotion and energy. That is wonderful; like all new movements, it will no doubt need to shake down and sift out the wheat from the chaff, but one would much rather have all these new signs of life than the sterile repetition of stale traditions.

Until very recently, though, the kind of traditions from which this new music has emerged, traditions that think of themselves as "biblical," after all, would always have included solid doses of psalmody. If that has changed, the sooner it changes back the better, with, of course, all the resources of fresh musical treatments upon which to draw. To worship without using the Psalms is to risk planting seeds that will never take root.

There is then a further point. Much of what the Psalms are designed to do, they are designed to do *as a complete set*. We should resist, as a general or normal practice, the picking and choosing, the dotting here and there, the selection of a few scattered psalm verses, which has become commonplace in some circles where the Psalms are still used. We should do our best to find ways to use the whole Psalter.

We should say or sing the puzzling and disturbing bits along with the easy and "nice" ones. We should allow the flow and balance of the entire set to make their points, with the sharp highs and lows of the Psalter all there to express and embody the highs and lows of all human life, of our own human lives.

This is a challenge, and different Christian communities will work out different ways of doing this that will be appropriate for them.

—*Case for the Psalms* 165–56

Go Deeper!

Of course, we will never understand everything in the Psalms. Of course, there will be puzzles and problems. Some churches, some congregations, and some Christians will find that this ancient poetry contains passages they can't use in good conscience—particularly those lines that call down bitter curses on their enemies. That's a decision that must be made in each local church. But no Christian congregation ought to deny itself regular and thorough use of the Psalms. One of the great tragedies in much contemporary free-church worship is the great void at this point. Here is a challenge for a new generation of musicians to take up. And here, too, is a challenge for those traditions, like my own, in which the Psalms have always been front and center: Are we making the best use of them? Are we going deeper and deeper into them, or simply round and round in circles?

—*Simply Christian* 152–53

It's Time to Wake Up

We may be prepared to grant that the resurrection of Jesus has opened a new era in world history. Even this, however, takes some doing. The anti-Christian rhetoric of the last two hundred years in the Western world has done its best to deny such a thing. Most of us have a Pavlovian reaction to the claim about the present kingdom that the New Testament makes. We instantly want to talk about the ambiguities of the Constantinian settlement, the connivance of many churches in twentieth-century atrocities, and much in between. But we shouldn't let a proper penitence for past wickedness turn into a false humility about the extraordinary achievements of the church in both the past and the present.

The William Wilberforces and the Desmond Tutus are real, and they matter, and so do a million others who are less well known but equally signs of the strange lordship of Jesus over the world. We are all called to live within the world where these things are possible and to be agents of such things insofar as they lie in our calling and sphere. But for Paul, the resurrection is not just about large-scale or public work. It is about the personal and intimate life of resurrection to which each of us is called. It is, in other words, about baptism and holiness. This is where his bracing command comes home to us: it's time to wake up.

—Surprised by Hope 248

ADVENT

This is all the more important because you know what time it is. The hour has come for you to wake up from sleep. Our salvation, you see, is nearer now than it was when first we came to faith. The night is nearly over; the day is almost here. So let's put off the works of darkness and put on the armor of light. Let's behave appropriately, as in the daytime: not in wild parties and drunkenness, not in orgies and shameless immorality, not in bad temper and jealousy. Instead, put on the Lord Jesus, the Messiah, and don't make any allowance for the flesh and its lusts.

—Romans 13:11–14, *The Kingdom New Testament* 333

Confused by Advent?

"Christ has died," we say in the Anglican Eucharist, "Christ is risen; *Christ will come again.*" And, of course, in the creed too: "He will come again in glory to judge the living and the dead." If we sing it once during the season of Advent, we sing it a dozen times. "Alleluia! Come, Lord, come!"

And if we are ordinary mainstream Christians in Britain today—and in many other places too, including parts of North America—we may well add under our breath, "even though I haven't a clue what it means." The so-called second coming of Jesus is not a hot topic in the preaching of the mainstream churches, even in Advent. (Some churches, of course, speak of little else; I shall come to them presently.) The more recent lectionaries we use in my church rather steer us away from it. What's more, the revival of a lively eucharistic life in the Church of England in the postwar years carried with it, in some circles at least, a theology that seemed to leave no room for a final coming.

—Surprised by Hope 117

Escorting the Rightful King Back into the World

The word *parousia,* "royal appearing," was regularly used to describe Caesar's "coming" or "royal appearing" when visiting a city or when returning home to Rome. And what happened at such a *parousia* was that the leading citizens would go out to meet him, the technical term for such a meeting being *apantçsis,* the word Paul uses here for "meeting," as in "meeting the Lord in the air." But when the citizens went out to meet Caesar, they didn't stay there in the countryside. They didn't have a picnic in the fields and then bid him farewell; they went out *to escort their Lord royally into their city.* In other words, Paul's picture must not be pressed into the nonbiblical image of the second coming according to which Jesus is "coming back to take us home"—swooping down, scooping up his people, and zooming back to heaven with them, away from the wicked earth forever.

As Revelation makes clear in several passages, with echoes in other New Testament books, the point is that Jesus will reign on the earth, and at his royal appearing the faithful will go to meet him, like the disciples on the road to Jerusalem only now in full-blooded triumph, and escort him back into the world that is rightfully his and that he comes to claim, to judge, to rule with healing and wise sovereignty.

"When Christ shall come," we sing in a favorite hymn, "with shout of acclamation, and take me home, what joy shall fill my heart." What we ought to sing is, "When Christ shall come, with shout of acclamation, *and heal his world*, what joy shall fill my heart." In the New Testament, the second coming is not the point at which Jesus snatches people up, away from the earth, to live forever with him somewhere else, but the point at which he returns to reign not only in heaven but upon the earth.

—*Surprised by Scripture* 101–2

The Great Day of Jesus's Reappearing

Thinking of the second coming or of Jesus "returning" often raises the same kind of problems that we saw with the ascension. People who still think that "heaven" is a long way away, up in the sky, and that that's where Jesus has gone, imagine that the second coming will be an event somewhat like the return of a space shuttle from its far-off orbit. Not so. *Heaven is God's space, God's dimension of present reality*, so that to think of Jesus "returning" is actually, as both Paul and John say in the passages just quoted, to think of him presently invisible, but one day *reappearing*.

It won't be the case that Jesus will simply reappear within the world the way it presently is. His return—his reappearing—will be the central feature of the much greater event that the New Testament writers promise, based on Jesus's resurrection itself: heaven and earth will one day come together and be present and transparent to each other. That's what they were made for, and that's what God will accomplish one day. It has, in fact, already been accomplished in the person of Jesus himself; and what God has done in Jesus, bringing heaven and earth together at immense cost and with immense joy, will be achieved in and for the whole cosmos at last. That is what Paul says at the heart of one of his great visionary prayers:

> His plan was to sum up the whole cosmos in the king—yes, everything in heaven and on earth, in him. (Eph. 1:10)
>
> —*Simply Jesus* 202

A Reappearance, Not the Descent of a Spaceman from the Sky

Notice a significant pair of passages. First, at the end of 1 Corinthians, Paul suddenly writes a phrase in Aramaic: *Marana tha*. It means, "Our Lord, come!" and goes back (like the word *Abba*, "father") to the very early Aramaic-speaking church. There is no reason why the Greek-speaking church would have invented a prayer in Aramaic; we must be in touch at this point with extremely early and pre-Pauline tradition. The early church was from the beginning praying to Jesus that he would return.

Second, a very different passage in Colossians 3. Here we have in a nutshell Paul's theology of resurrection and ascension as applied to present Christian living and future Christian hope:

If you've been raised with the Messiah, seek the things that are above, because that's where the Messiah is, sitting at God's right hand. Think about the things above, not about the things below; for you died, and your life is hidden with the Messiah in God. When the Messiah appears, the one who is your life, then you too will appear with him in glory. (3:1–4)

Notice the key thing: that instead of "coming," or the blessed word *parousia*, Paul can here use the word *appear*. It's the same thing from a different angle, and this helps us to demystify the idea that the "coming" of Jesus means that he will descend like a spaceman from the sky. Jesus is at present in heaven. But, as we saw earlier, heaven, being God's space, is not somewhere within the space of our world but is rather a different though closely related space. The promise is not that Jesus will simply reappear within the present world order, but that when heaven and earth are joined together in the new way God has promised, then he will appear to us—and we will appear to him, and to one another, in our own true identity.

—*Surprised by Hope* 134–35

Be Ready for the Earthquakes!

We are called to live at the overlap both of heaven and earth—the earth that has yet to be fully redeemed as one day it will be—and of God's future and this world's present. We are caught on a small island near the point where these tectonic plates—heaven and earth, future and present—are scrunching themselves together. Be ready for earthquakes!

When Paul writes his greatest chapter about life in the Spirit and the coming renewal of the whole cosmos, he points out at the heart of it all that, while we don't know how to pray as we ought, the Spirit—God's very own Spirit—intercedes for us according to God's will. It's a small passage (Rom. 8:26–27), but it's extremely important both for what it says and for where it says it. Here's the context: God's whole creation is groaning in labor pains, says Paul, waiting for the new world to be born from its womb. The church, God's people in the Messiah, find themselves caught up in this, as we, too, groan in longing for redemption. (Paul was talking, a few verses earlier, about sharing the sufferings of the Messiah. Did he, perhaps, have Gethsemane in mind?)

Christian prayer is at its most characteristic when we find ourselves caught in the overlap of the ages, part of the creation that aches for new birth.

—*Simply Christian* 161–62

Advent Lies Between Inauguration and Consummation

The early Christian writers were setting forth an eschatology that had been inaugurated, but not fully consummated; they were celebrating (Paul is quite explicit on this point in 1 Cor. 15:20–28) something that *has already happened,* but at the same time something that *still has to happen in the future.* They believed themselves to be living between Jesus's *accomplishment* of the reign of God and its full *implementation.* But the eschatology in question was not just the personal or "spiritual" eschatology of so much Western thought ("going to heaven" in the future, but with a taste of "heaven," of "eternal life," already in the present), but the social, cultural, political, and even cosmic eschatology of Matthew, Paul, Revelation, and of course—perhaps above all—the fourth gospel.

New creation itself has begun, they are saying, and will be completed. Jesus is ruling over that new creation and making it happen through the witness of his church. "The ruler of this world" has been overthrown; the powers of the world have been led behind Jesus's triumphal procession as a beaten, bedraggled rabble. *And that is how God is becoming king on earth as in heaven.* That is the truth the gospels are eager to tell us, the truth the past two hundred years of European and American culture has been desperately trying to stifle.

And, of course, as we've seen already, the world of the Enlightenment has been ready with its counter-Christian polemic. "What good," it asks, "has the church ever done for us? It's produced nothing but squabbles, crusades, inquisitions, and witch burnings. The church is part of the problem, not part of the solution." Well, of course you have to tell the story that way if you are Voltaire, eager to wipe out the "scandal" of the church, or indeed if you are a postmodern journalist ready to sneer at God's apparent representatives (the often muddled clergy) to stop yourself from having to take God himself seriously. But the failure of Christianity is a modern myth, and we shouldn't be ashamed of telling the proper story of church history, which, of course, has plenty of muddle and wickedness, but also far more than we normally imagine of love and creativity and beauty and justice and healing and education and hope. To imagine a world without the gospel of Jesus is to imagine a pretty bleak place, the cultural and ideological equivalent of those horrible 1960s buildings that were structures without spirit, boxes without beauty, all function and no flourish.

—*How God Became King* 162–63

Our Times Are in His Hand

We are called to stretch out the arms of our minds and hearts, and to find ourselves, Christ shaped, cross shaped, at the intersection of the past, present, and future of God's time and our own time. This is a place of intense pain and intense joy, the sort that perhaps only music and poetry can express or embody. The Psalms are gifts that help us not only to think wisely about the overlaps and paradoxes of time, but to live within them, to reach out in the day of trouble and remind ourselves—and not only ourselves, but also the mysterious one whom the Psalms call "you"—of the story in which we live. Past, present, and future belong to him. We are called to live, joyfully and painfully, in the story that is both his and ours. Our times are in his hand.

—Case for the Psalms 75

The Life of the Age to Come
Has Already Broken In

The *time* of the church, the long story of church history and the tradition that has accrued during it, must be taken seriously in any eschatologically based and mission-shaped view of the church. Once again, we must, of course, beware of idolatry, the hallowing of things that were once indifferent and are now irrelevant. One must be constantly aware that the church has done and said many foolish and wicked things as well as many wise and godly things. But the story of the church is the story of the ways in which, despite folly, failure, and downright sin, God's future has already burst in upon what, for our forebears, was the present time, leaving us a legacy of that bit of the past that is full not only of mistakes and culturally conditioned lifestyles but also of patterns of new creation, which have already, from our point of view, been woven into history—bits of God's future, so to speak, which are now already bits of our past.

It is, of course, all-important to discern what, in tradition, is to be seen as an example of this and what is to be seen as an example of the church getting it wrong. But jettisoning tradition just because it is tradition is to capitulate to postmodernity and to a kind of ultra-Protestantism that cuts the tree off at the root because it believes that trees should be entirely visible and obviously fruitful, no part of them buried in dirty soil.

In particular, the gospels (especially John) and the early practice of the church (as in Paul) reflect the very early understanding of the church that *the first day of the week,* the day of Easter, has become a sign within the present world and its temporal sequence that the life of the age to come has already broken in. Sunday, kept as a commemoration of Easter ever since that event itself (a quite remarkable phenomenon when you come to think about it), is not simply a legacy of Victorian values but a perpetual sign, joyfully renewed week by week, that all time belongs to God and stands under the renewing lordship of Jesus Christ.

—Surprised by Hope 261–62

Reading Scripture with an Advent Focus

Scripture—the Old and New Testaments—is the story of creation and new creation. Within that, it is the story of covenant and new

covenant. When we read scripture as Christians, we read it precisely as people of the new covenant and of the new creation. We
do not read it, in other words, as a flat, uniform list of regulations
or doctrines. We read it as the narrative in which we ourselves are
now called to take part. We read it to discover "the story so far" and
also "how it's supposed to end."

As we do this—as groups, churches, and individuals—we must
allow the power of God's promised future to have its way with
us. As we read the gospels, we must remind ourselves again and
again—because the pull of prevailing Western culture is so strong
that if we don't it will suck us back down into dualism—that this
is the story of how God's kingdom was established on earth as in
heaven in and through the work of Jesus, fulfilling Israel's great
story, defeating the power of evil, and launching God's new world.
As we read the letters, we must remind ourselves that these are the
documents designed to shape and direct the community of the new
covenant, the people who were called to take forward the work of
new creation.

As we read Revelation, we must not allow the wonderful heavenly vision in chapters 4 and 5 to lull us into imagining that this is
the *final* scene in the story, as though the narrative were simply to
conclude (as in Charles Wesley's hymn) with the redeemed casting
their crowns before the throne. This is a vision of *present* reality,
seen in its heavenly dimension. We must read on to the end, to the
final vision of Revelation 21–22, the chapters that give final meaning to all that has gone before and indeed to the entire canon.

The Bible as a whole thus does what it does best when read from
the perspective of new creation. And it is designed not only to tell
us *about* that work of new creation, as though from a detached perspective, not only to provide us with true information about God's
fresh, resurrection life, but also to *foster* that work of new creation
in the churches, groups, and individuals who read it, who define
themselves in terms of the Jesus they meet in it, who allow it to

shape their lives. The Bible is thus the *story of* creation and new creation, and it is itself, through the continuing work of the Spirit who inspired it, an *instrument of* new creation in human lives and communities.

—*Surprised by Hope* 281–82

How Will New Creation Come?

The New Testament, true to its Old Testament roots, regularly insists that the major, central, framing question is that of God's purpose of rescue and re-creation for the whole world, the entire cosmos. The destiny of individual human beings must be understood within that context—not simply in the sense that we are only part of a much larger picture but also in the sense that part of the whole point of being saved in the present is so that we can play a vital role (Paul speaks of this role in the shocking terms of being "fellow workers with God") within that larger picture and purpose.

And that in turn makes us realize that the question of our own destiny, in terms of the alternatives of joy or woe, is probably the wrong way of looking at the whole question. The question ought to be, *How will God's new creation come?* and then, *How will we humans contribute to that renewal of creation and to the fresh projects that the creator God will launch in his new world?* The choice before humans would then be framed differently: Are you going to worship the creator God and discover thereby what it means to become fully and gloriously human, reflecting his powerful, healing, transformative love into the world? Or are you going to worship the world as it is, boosting your corruptible humanness by gaining power or pleasure from forces within the world but merely contributing thereby to your own dehumanization and the further corruption of the world itself?

—Surprised by Hope 184–85

Turning the World the Right Way Up

"The kingdom of God is at hand" (Mark 1:15). This announcement was the center of Jesus's public proclamation. He was addressing the world we described at the end of the previous chapter, the world in which the Jewish people were anxious for their God to rescue them from pagan oppression and put the world to rights—in other words, to become king fully and finally. The gospels tell the story in such a way as to hold together the ancient promises and the urgent current context, with Jesus in the middle of it all. There is no good reason to doubt that this was how Jesus himself saw his own work.

But what did he mean? The prophet Isaiah, in line with several Psalms and other biblical passages, had spoken of God's coming kingdom as the time when (a) God's promises and purposes would be fulfilled, (b) Israel would be rescued from pagan oppression, (c) evil (particularly the evil of oppressive empires) would be judged, and (d) God would usher in a new reign of justice and peace. Daniel had envisaged a coming time when the monsters (that is, the pagan empires) would do their worst, and God would vindicate his people to set everything straight. The world was to be turned the right way up at last. To speak of God's kingdom arriving in the present was to summon up that entire narrative, and to declare that it was reaching its climax. God's future was breaking in to the present. Heaven was arriving on earth.

—Simply Christian 99–100

Waiting and Struggle

What on earth does it mean, today, to say that Jesus is king, that he is lord of the world? How can we say such a thing in our confused world? If we do want to say it, what are we saying that Jesus is up to, in our swirling mix of modern, postmodern, and other cultural movements? What is he doing, in the midst of the dangerous clash of the new secularisms and the new fundamentalisms? What does the lordship of Jesus look like in practice in the world where we bail out the big banks when they suddenly run out of cash, but don't lift a finger to help the poorest of the poor who are paying the banks interest so the banks can get rich again?

All this is, of course, the subject for another book, or perhaps several. There are a thousand issues crying out for serious engagement. But part of the problem, I think, is farther back. Most Christians in today's world have not even begun to think how calling Jesus "Lord" might affect the real world. When I said "what on earth" at the start of this chapter, I meant, of course, what Jesus meant in the Lord's Prayer: "Thy kingdom come *on earth* as in heaven." How do we even get to first base in thinking about this today?

—*Simply Jesus* 207

Stewardship Begins Here and Now

When God saves people in this life, by working through his Spirit to bring them to faith and by leading them to follow Jesus in discipleship, prayer, holiness, hope, and love, such people are designed—it isn't too strong a word—to be a sign and foretaste of what God wants to do for the entire cosmos. What's more, such people are not just to be a sign and foretaste of that ultimate salvation; they are to be *part of the means by which* God makes this happen in both the present and the future. That is what Paul insists on when he says that the whole creation is waiting with eager longing not just for its own redemption, its liberation from corruption and decay, but *for God's children to be revealed:* in other words, for the unveiling of those redeemed humans through whose stewardship creation will at last be brought back into that wise order for which it was made. And since Paul makes it quite clear that those who believe in Jesus Christ, who are incorporated into him through baptism, are already God's children, are already themselves saved, this stewardship cannot be something to be postponed for the ultimate future. It must begin here and now.

In other words—to sum up where we've got so far—the work of salvation, in its full sense, is (1) about whole human beings, not merely souls; (2) about the present, not simply the future; and (3) about what God does *through* us, not merely what God does *in and for* us. If we can get this straight, we will rediscover the historic basis for the full-orbed mission of the church.

—Surprised by Hope 200–1

Joining Heaven and Earth with Action and Story

How do you say something so drastic to people who are expecting something quite different? In two ways in particular: by symbols (particularly dramatic actions) and by stories. Jesus used both. His choice of twelve close followers ("disciples"—that is, "learners") was a powerful symbol in itself, speaking of the remaking of the whole people of God, the twelve tribes of Israel descended from the twelve sons of Jacob. That remaking of God's people was at the heart, too, of his remarkable healings. There is no doubt, historically, that he possessed healing powers; that was why he attracted not only crowds but also accusations of being in league with the devil.

But Jesus didn't see his healings simply as a kind of premodern traveling hospital. He wasn't healing the sick just for the sake of it, important though the healing itself was. Nor was it just a way of attracting people to listen to his message. Rather, the healing was a dramatic sign of the message itself. God, the world's creator, was at work through him, to do what he had promised, to open blind eyes and deaf ears, to rescue people, to turn everything right side up. The people who had been at the bottom of the heap would find themselves, to their own great surprise, on top. "Blessed are the meek," he said, "for they shall inherit the earth." And he went about making it happen.

Equally, he told stories—stories which got under the skin of his contemporaries precisely because they both were and were not the stories they were expecting. The ancient prophets had spoken about God replanting Israel after the long winter of exile; Jesus told stories about people sowing seed, about some seed being fruitful but a good deal going to waste, about seeds growing secretly and then a sudden harvest, about tiny seeds producing great shrubs. These "parables" weren't, as has often been supposed, "earthly stories with heavenly meanings." The whole point of Jesus's work was to bring heaven to earth and join them together forever, to bring God's future into the present and make it stick there. But when heaven comes to earth and finds earth unready, when God's future arrives in the present while people are still asleep, there will be explosions. And there were.

—*Simply Christian* 101–2

The Shock of the New

At the heart of Paul's message, teaching, and life was—to use a technical phrase—*radical messianic eschatology.* Eschatology: God's long-awaited new day has arrived. Messianic: Jesus is the true son of David, announced as such in his resurrection, bringing to completion the purposes announced to Abraham and extended in the Psalms to embrace the world. Radical: nothing in Paul's or Barnabas's background had prepared them for this new state of affairs. The fact that they now believed it was what the One God had always planned did not reduce their own sense of awe and astonishment. They knew firsthand that such a program would meet stiff resistance and even violence.

—*Paul: A Biography* 130

A New Day Has Dawned

"Paul, an apostle," he begins, in his letter to the Galatians—and then interrupts himself by adding, in brackets as it were, "my apostleship doesn't derive from human sources . . ." Then he recovers his balance and states the foundation principle. His apostleship derives from God himself, and from Jesus the Messiah, our *Kyrios,*

> who gave himself for our sins, to rescue us from the present
> evil age, according to the will of God our father, to whom
> be glory to the ages of ages. Amen. (1:4–5)

Each element here is vital. The "good news" Paul has announced is what the One God always planned and intended. It is not a sudden afterthought. The message about Jesus may look to Jews in Jerusalem or Galatia as though it's a strange, peculiar eccentricity. But it is, in truth, the leading edge of the long-awaited new creation. This is central and will remain so throughout Paul's work.

The central point concerns the difference between "the present evil age" and the new day that has dawned. Paul here affirms the well-known and widespread ancient Jewish belief that world history is divided into two "ages," the "present age" of sorrow, shame, exile, and death and the "age to come," when all things will be put right. That belief was common for centuries before Paul, and it remained the norm all the way through the much later rabbinic period.

But for Paul something had happened. The living God had acted in person, in the person of Jesus, to rescue people from that "present age" and to launch "the age to come." The two ages were not, as it were, back to back, the first stopping when the second began. The new age had burst upon the scene while the "present age" was still rumbling on. This was the direct effect of the divine plan by which Jesus "gave himself for our sins"; the power of the "present age" was thereby broken, and the new world could begin. There is a sense in which the whole letter, and in a measure all of Paul's work, simply unpacks and explains this opening flourish.

—Paul: A Biography 157–58

Jesus: The Starting Point and the Goal

Why should Paul's ideas and personality be placed on the Procrustean bed of our modern likes and dislikes? He might well have a sharp retort for any such suggestion. Why should *he* not question *our* criteria, our ideas, our preferred personality types? Where does one even start to ask such questions?

For Paul there was no question about the starting point. It was always Jesus: Jesus as the shocking fulfillment of Israel's hopes; Jesus as the genuinely human being, the true "image"; Jesus the embodiment of Israel's God—so that, without leaving Jewish monotheism, one would worship and invoke Jesus as Lord *within*, not alongside, the service of the "living and true God." Jesus, the one for whose sake one would forsake all idols, all rival "lords." Jesus, above all, who had come to his kingdom, the true lordship of the world, in the way that Paul's friends who were starting to write the Jesus story at that time had emphasized: by dying under the weight of the world's sin in order to break the power of the dark forces that had enslaved all humans, Israel included.

Jesus, who had thereby fulfilled the ancient promise, being "handed over because of our trespasses and raised because of our justification." Jesus, who had been bodily raised from the dead on the third day and thereby announced to the world as the true Messiah, the "son of God" in all its senses (Messiah, Israel's representative, embodiment of Israel's God). Jesus, therefore, as the one in whom "all God's promises find their yes," the "goal of the law," the true seed of Abraham, the ultimate "root of Jesse." Jesus, then, the Lord at whose name every knee would bow. Jesus, who would reappear in a great future event that would combine the sense of a true king coming to claim and establish his kingdom and the sense of the long-hidden God at last being made visible.

Jesus, whose powerful message could and did transform lives in the present time ahead of the final moment when he would raise his people from the dead. And, in and with all of this, Jesus not just as the label to put on an idea, a theological fact, if you like, but as the living, inspiring, consoling, warning, and encouraging presence, the one whose love "makes us press on," the one "who

loved me and gave himself for me," the one whom to know, Paul
declared, was worth more than all the privileges that the world, including the ancient biblical world, has to offer. Jesus was the starting point. And the goal.

—*Paul: A Biography* 400–1

The Urgency of Now

What, then, caused the urgent note in Paul's eschatology? The
main point is that the long-awaited event could occur *at any time*,
not that it had to occur within a specific time frame. The event that
was to occur within a generation was not the end of the world but,
according to Mark 13 and the parallels in Matthew and Luke, *the
fall of Jerusalem.* This was woven deep into the structure of early
Christianity in a way that until recently, with the rise of contemporary studies of the Jewish world of the time, was not usually
appreciated. But Jerusalem, and the Temple specifically, had always been seen as the place where heaven and earth met; so much
so that when Isaiah speaks of "new heavens and new earth," some
commentators will now say, without the need for much elaboration,
that this is referring to the ultimate rebuilding of the Temple, the
heaven-and-earth building.

—*Paul: A Biography* 403

Living in the Last Days, and
Living in the First Days

People have often written as if Paul believed himself to be living in the *last* days, and in a sense that was true. God had, in the Messiah, brought the old world of chaos, idolatry, wickedness, and death up short, had taken its horror onto himself, and had launched something else in its place. But that meant that, equally, Paul was conscious of living in the *first* days, the opening scenes of the new drama of world history, with heaven and earth now held together not by Torah and Temple, but by Jesus and the spirit, pointing forward to the time when the divine glory would fill the whole world and transform it from top to bottom. You would not find this vision in the non-Jewish world of Paul's day. It is Jewish through and through, including in the fact that it has been reshaped around the one believed to be Israel's Messiah.

Paul's motivation and mindset, then, was shaped centrally and radically by Jesus himself as crucified and risen Messiah and Lord and by the new shape that the Jewish hope had as a result. This is why his loyalty always appeared contested. And this is where we can understand, in its proper context, what he had to say about human beings, their plight, and their rescue.

—*Paul: A Biography* 405–6

Building for the Kingdom in Advent

The task of the church between ascension and *parousia* is therefore set free both from the self-driven energy that imagines it has to build God's kingdom all by itself and from the despair that supposes it can't do anything until Jesus comes again. We do not "build the kingdom" all by ourselves, but we do build *for* the kingdom. All that we do in faith, hope, and love in the present, in obedience to our ascended Lord and in the power of his Spirit, will be enhanced and transformed at his appearing. This too brings a note of judgment, of course, as Paul makes clear in 1 Corinthians 3:10–17. The "day" will disclose what sort of work each builder has done.

In particular, the present rule of the ascended Jesus Christ and the assurance of his final appearing in judgment should give us—which goodness knows we need today—some clarity and realism in our political discourse. Far too often Christians slide into a vaguely spiritualized version of one or other major political system or party. What would happen if we were to take seriously our stated belief that Jesus Christ is already the Lord of the world and that at his name, one day, every knee would bow?

—Surprised by Hope 143–44

Heaven's Treasure Store

Heaven is actually a reverent way of speaking about God so that "riches in heaven" simply means "riches in God's presence" (as we see when, elsewhere, Jesus talks about someone being or not being "rich toward God"). But then, by derivation from this primary meaning, heaven is the place where *God's purposes for the future are stored up*. It isn't where they are meant to stay so that one would need to go to heaven to enjoy them; it is where they are kept safe against the day when they will become a reality on earth. If I say to a friend, "I've kept some beer in the fridge for you," that doesn't mean that he has to climb into the fridge in order to drink the beer. God's future inheritance, the incorruptible new world and the new bodies that are to inhabit that world, are already kept safe, waiting for us, not so that we can go to heaven and put them on there but so that they can be brought to birth in this world or rather in the new heavens and new earth, the renewed world of which I spoke earlier.

—*Surprised by Hope* 151–52

Frameworks of the Coming King

Here is the larger framework: God calls humans to be his rulers over creation, and though humans have distorted this vocation into ugly parodies, treating God's creation as if it were a mere toy to play with or resource to exploit, God has not rescinded the project or the vocation.

Here is the narrower framework: God calls Israel, a human family, to be his rescue operation for the world, and though Israel has distorted this vocation and used this opportunity to bite the hand that feeds it, and to worship other gods instead of him, God has not rescinded the project or the vocation.

But now, within the sharp focus of both frameworks, God calls David, a human being after God's own heart, the one who will sum up the task and vocation of Israel in himself. It is to David, or more specifically David's son and heir, that the task has now devolved of bringing the nations into submission to Israel's God, the creator.

The psalms we noted before, such as 2, 18, 21, 72, and 110, are not random exaltations of a militaristic monarch. They express, in the language and idiom of the time, the conviction that it is through the coming king (the human one, Israel's anointed representative) that YHWH will establish his rule on earth as in heaven.

—Case for the Psalms 61–62

Ethical Life in Advent Focus

The problems Paul addresses—problems of personality cults in the church, problems of sexual morality, problems about how to live in the wider pagan world, problems about how to organize public worship—most of these problems relate more or less directly to the good news itself. Once people grasp that the events of the Messiah's death and resurrection have transformed everything and that they are now living between that initial explosive event and God's final setting right of the world (when God is "all in all"), then everything will change: belief, behavior, attitudes, expectations, and not least a new love, a real sense of belonging, which springs up among those who share all this. That is what so much of Paul's writing is about. Get the gospel right, and everything else will come right.

—Simply Good News 26–27

A New Life of Transformation
Here and Now

So how might we summarize the good news—both the good news announced by Jesus and the good news that his first followers announced when they talked about him later on? The good news is that *the one true God has now taken charge of the world, in and through Jesus and his death and resurrection.* The ancient hopes have indeed been fulfilled, but in a way nobody imagined. God's plan to put the world right has finally been launched. He has grasped the world in a new way, to sort it out and fill it with his glory and justice, as he always promised. But he has done so in a way beyond the wildest dreams of prophecy. The ancient sickness that had crippled the whole world, and humans with it, has been cured at last, so that new life can rise up in its place. Life has come to life and is pouring out like a mighty river into the world, in the form of a new power, the power of love. The good news was, and is, that all this *has* happened in and through Jesus; that one day it *will* happen, completely and utterly, to all creation; *and that we humans, every single one of us, whoever we are, can be caught up in that transformation here and now.* This is the Christian gospel. Do not allow yourself to be fobbed off with anything less.

—Simply Good News 55

JUSTICE

"That was just ignorance; but the time for it has passed, and God has drawn a veil over it. Now, instead, he commands all people everywhere to repent, because he has established a day on which he intends to call the world to account with full and proper justice by a man whom he has appointed. God has given all people his pledge of this by raising this man from the dead."

—Acts 17:30–31, *The Kingdom New Testament* 276

God's Putting-the-Word-to-Rights Future in the Present

The world has *already* been turned upside down; that's what Easter is all about. It isn't a matter of waiting until God eventually does something different at the end of time. God has brought his future, his putting-the-world-to-rights future, into the present in Jesus of Nazareth, and he wants that future to be implicated more and more in the present. That's what we pray for every time we say the Lord's Prayer: "Thy kingdom come, thy will be done on earth as it is in heaven." And that's why that prayer goes on to pray for bread and forgiveness, which is, I suggest, where the issue of justice comes closest to our global village today.

—Surprised by Hope 215

The Energy for Justice Lies in Resurrection

Precisely because Jesus Christ rose from the dead, God's new world has already broken in to the present and Christian work for justice in the present, for instance, in the ongoing campaigns for debt remission and ecological responsibility, take the shape they do. If Jesus left his body behind in the tomb and if we are going to do the same, as many theologians of the last generation thought, then we are robbed both of the ground and the energy for our work to bring real, bodily, concrete signs of hope to the present world.

—Surprised by Hope 213

Justice "On Earth as It Is in Heaven"

It is important to see, and to say, that those who follow Jesus are committed, as he taught us to pray, to God's will being done "on earth as it is in heaven." And that means that God's passion for justice must become ours, too. When Christians use their belief in Jesus as a way of escaping from that demand and challenge, they are abandoning a central element in their own faith. That way danger lies.

Equally, we should not be shy about telling the stories that many skeptics in the Western world have done their best to forget. When the slave trade was at its height, with many people justifying it on the grounds that slaves are mentioned in the Bible, it was a group of devout Christians, led by the unforgettable William Wilberforce in Britain and John Woolman in America, who got together and made it their life's business to stop it. When, with slavery long dead and buried, racial prejudice still haunted the United States, it was the Christian vision of Martin Luther King Jr. that drove him to peaceful, but highly effective, protest. Wilberforce was grasped by a passion for God's justice on behalf of the slaves, a passion which cost him what might otherwise have been a dazzling political career. Martin Luther King's passion for justice for African Americans cost him his life. Their tireless campaigning grew directly and explicitly out of their loyalty to Jesus.

In the same way, when the apartheid regime in South Africa was at its height (with many people justifying it on the grounds that the Bible speaks of different races living different lives), it was the long campaign of Christian leaders like Desmond Tutu that brought about change with remarkably little bloodshed. (I well remember how, in the 1970s, politicians and news commentators took it for granted that change could only come through massive violence.) Tutu and many others did a lot of praying, a lot of reading the Bible with leaders and government officials, a good deal of risky speaking out against the many evil facets of apartheid, and a large amount of equally risky confrontation with black leaders and followers who believed that only violence would work.

Again and again Tutu was caught in the middle, distrusted and hated by both sides. But under the new postapartheid government, he chaired the most extraordinary commission ever to grace the political scene: the South African Commission for Truth and

Reconciliation, which has begun the long and painful process of healing the memory and imagination of a whole country, of allowing grief to take its proper course and anger to be expressed and dealt with. Who in the 1960s or even the 1980s would have thought such a thing possible? Yet it happened; and all because of people whose passion for justice and loyalty to Jesus combined to bring it about.

—*Simply Christian* 13–14

Justice in Real Life

There are three basic ways of explaining this sense of the echo of a voice, this call to justice, this dream of a world (and all of us within it) put to rights. We can say, if we like, that it is indeed only a dream, a projection of childish fantasies, and that we have to get used to living in the world the way it is. Down that road we find Machiavelli and Nietzsche, the world of naked power and grabbing what you can get, the world where the only sin is to be caught.

Or we can say, if we like, that the dream is of a different world altogether, a world where we really belong, where everything is indeed put to rights, a world into which we can escape in our dreams in the present and hope to escape one day for good—but a world that has little purchase on the present world except that people who live in this one sometimes find themselves dreaming of that one. That approach leaves the unscrupulous bullies running this world, but it consoles us with the thought that things will be better somewhere, sometime, even if there's not much we can do about it here and now.

Or we can say, if we like, that the reason we have these dreams, the reason we have a sense of a memory of the echo of a voice, is that there is someone speaking to us, whispering in our inner ear—someone who cares very much about this present world and our present selves, and who has made us and the world for a purpose which will indeed involve justice, things being put to rights, *ourselves* being put to rights, the world being rescued at last.

Three of the great religious traditions have taken this last option, and not surprisingly they are related; they are, as it were, second cousins. Judaism speaks of a God who made the world and built into it the passion for justice because it was his own passion. Christianity speaks of this same God having brought that passion into play in the life and work of Jesus of Nazareth. Islam draws on some Jewish and some Christian stories and ideas and creates a new synthesis in which the revelation of God's will in the Koran is the ideal that would put the world to rights, if only it were obeyed. There are many differences among these three traditions, but on this point they are agreed: The reason we think we have heard a voice is because we have. It wasn't a dream. There are ways of getting back in touch with that voice and making what it says come true. In real life. In *our* real lives.

This book is written to explain and commend one of those traditions, the Christian one. It's about real life, because Christians believe that in Jesus of Nazareth the voice we thought we heard became human and lived and died as one of us. It's about justice, because Christians not only inherit the Jewish passion for justice but claim that Jesus embodied that passion, and that what he did, and what happened to him, set in motion the Creator's plan to rescue the world and put it back to rights. And it is therefore about us, all of us, because we are all involved in this.

—*Simply Christian* 8–10

The Answer to the Justice Skeptics

How do you answer someone who says, rightly, that the world will not be completely just and right until the new creation and who deduces, wrongly, that there is no point trying to bring justice to the world (or for that matter ecological health, another topic for which there is no space here) until that time? Answer, from everything I have said so far: insist on inaugurated eschatology, on a radical transformation of the way we behave as a worldwide community, *anticipating* the eventual time when God will be all in all even though we all agree things won't be complete until then. There is the challenge. The resurrection of Jesus points us to it and gives us the energy for it. Let us overcome our surprise that such a hope should be set before us and go to the task with prayer and wisdom.

—*Surprised by Hope* 221–22

The Putting-Right People for the World

If the cross is to be interpreted as the coming of the kingdom on earth as in heaven, centering on some kind of messianic victory, with some kind of substitution at its heart, making sense through some kind of representation, then the four gospels leave us with the primary application of the cross not in abstract preaching about "how to have your sins forgiven" or "how to go to heaven," but in an agenda in which the forgiven people are put to work, addressing the evils of the world in the light of the victory of Calvary. Those who are put right with God through the cross are to be putting-right

people for the world. Justification is God's advance putting right of
men and women, against the day when he will put all things right,
and thereby constituting the justified people as the key agents in
that latter project. From this there flows both a new missiology,
including an integrated political theology, and the new ecclesiology
that will be needed to support it, a community whose very heart
will be forgiveness.

—How God Became King 244

The Calling of Justice-Bringers

One of the beautiful things that distinguishes the Christian idea of
justice from others is that it is participatory: *we* are part of bringing
it about. Once Jesus has done what he has to do, he will send the
Spirit upon his followers, so that through our witness a new sort of
justice will be born:

> When [the Spirit] comes, he will prove the world to be in
> the wrong on three counts: sin, justice, and judgment. In
> relation to sin—because they don't believe in me. In relation
> to justice—because I'm going to the father, and you won't see
> me anymore. In relation to judgment—because the ruler of
> this world is judged. (John 16:8–11).

With this astonishing vision, the agenda Jesus has for his followers is *to prove the world in the wrong.* How will we do this? By
following him. By being, for the world, what he was for Israel. "As
the father sent me," he said after his resurrection, "so I'm sending
you" (20:21). His people are sent into the world *as justice bringers,*

to confront the powers that carve up the world with the news that there is a different justice and that it has already won its case.

—Broken Signposts 25–26

Speak Up!

The church is to prove the world wrong about justice. Jesus is to be vindicated by the father in his ascension, and this is the ultimate moment of justice, of putting the world right. The world thinks it knows what justice is, but again and again the world gets it wrong, favoring the rich and powerful, turning a blind eye to wickedness in high places, forgetting the cry of the poor and needy who the Bible insists are the special objects of God's just and right care. So the church, in the power of the Spirit, has to speak up for God's justice, in the light of Jesus's ascension to the throne of the world, and to draw the world's attention to where it's getting this wrong.

This has immediate and urgent application in holding our governments to account concerning justice for the world's poorest, who have been kept poor by the unpayable compound interest owed to Western banks on loans made decades ago to corrupt dictators. The injustice has itself been compounded by our governments' breathtaking bailing out of superrich companies, including banks, when they defaulted: the very rich did for the very rich what they still refuse to do for the very poor.

In the early church, bishops got a reputation for tirelessly championing the needs and rights of the poor. They were a nuisance to the rich and powerful, but they would not shut up. They were doing precisely what Jesus says would happen when the Spirit came and held the world's injustice up to the light of his justice.

As well as investigating obvious injustices, the church has the responsibility to test those causes that claim the words *justice* or *rights* but are, in fact, merely special-interest groups. As Pope Benedict XVI said in his address to the United Nations in April 2008, the language of rights is borrowed from the great Christian tradition, but if you cut off those Christian roots, you get all kinds of abuses, each claiming the postmodern high ground of victimhood but only succeeding in debasing the coinage of rights itself. Part of the task of holding the world to account is thinking and speaking clearly, humbly, and wisely in these areas.

—*Surprised by Scripture* 193–94

Justice in Three Dimensions: Space, Time, and Matter

The church that takes sacred *space* seriously not as a retreat from the world but as a bridgehead into it will go straight from worshipping in the sanctuary to debating in the council chamber—discussing matters of town planning, of harmonizing and humanizing beauty in architecture, in green spaces, in road traffic schemes, and in environmental work. If it is true, as I have argued, that the whole world is now God's holy land, we must not rest as long as that land is spoiled and defaced.

The church that takes seriously the fact that Jesus is Lord of all *time* will not just celebrate quietly every time we write the date on a letter or document, will not just set aside Sunday as far as humanly and socially possible as a celebration of God's new creation (and will point out the human folly of a seven-day working week), will not just seek to order its own life in an appropriate rhythm of worship and work. Such a church will also seek to bring wisdom, and freshly humanizing order, to the rhythms of work in offices and shops, in local government, in civic holidays, and in the shaping of public life. The enormous shifts during my own lifetime, from the whole town observing Good Friday and Easter to those great days being simply more occasions for football matches and yet more televised reruns of old movies are an index of what happens when a society loses its roots and drifts with prevailing social currents.

And, of course, the church that take seriously the fact that in and through Jesus the Creator God has grasped the world of *matter* once more and has transformed it by his own person and presence, and will one day fill it with his knowledge and glory as the waters cover the sea, not only will seek to celebrate the coming of God in Christ in and through the sacramental elements but also will go straight from baptism and the Eucharist to make God's healing, transforming presence a reality in the physical matter of real life. One of the things I have most enjoyed about being a bishop is watching ordinary Christians going straight from worshipping Jesus in church to making a radical difference in the material lives of people down the street by running playgroups for children of single working moms; by organizing credit unions to help people at the bottom of the financial ladder find their way to responsible solvency; by campaigning for better housing, against dangerous roads, for drug rehab centers, for wise laws relating to alcohol, for decent library and sporting facilities, for a thousand other things in which God's sovereign rule extends to hard, concrete reality.

—*Surprised by Hope 265–67*

Justice Is a Manifestation
of God's Love

Although many people know the famous verse in John 3:16 about how God "so loved the world" that he sent his Son to save it, they might not realize that this is followed almost immediately by this powerful statement about justice. God's light will expose the evil deeds done in darkness. Justice is a manifestation of God's love.

So the coming of God's light and love into the world is all about God's putting everything right in the end. It is about that final "passing of judgment" which, in the Jewish world, was the ultimate revelation of "justice."

John's gospel, then, depicts a God who cares deeply about justice. This point is fundamental: although we humans have within ourselves a strong echo of this longing for justice, in God himself that longing is complete and perfected. Part of the hope the Christian faith offers is the knowledge that God will not allow injustice to be the last word. That is a central element in the good news of the gospel.

It is vital, then, to remember that *John's gospel is a book about how the whole world is being put right at last*. It *is* a book about justice. It tells the story of how the creator God himself is passionate about things being sorted out, straightened out. And it tells us what he has done to bring it about. Unless we read the book with this larger story in mind, we won't understand the teaching about love and comfort that we are (rightly and properly) wanting and expecting.

—*Broken Signposts* 15–16

Fighting Force with
Prayer-Led Justice

On the cross the living God took the fury and violence of the world onto himself, suffering massive injustice—the biblical stories are careful to highlight this—and yet refusing to lash out with threats or curses. Part of what Christians have called "atonement theology" is the belief that in some sense or other Jesus exhausted the underlying power of evil when he died under its weight, refusing to pass it on or keep it in circulation. Jesus's resurrection is the beginning of a world in which a new type of justice is possible. Through the hard work of prayer, persuasion, and political action, it is possible to make governments on the one hand and revolutionary groups on the other see that there is a different approach than unremitting violence, than fighting force with force. The (mostly) quiet, prayerful revolutions that overturned eastern European Communism are a wonderful example. The extraordinary work of Desmond Tutu in South Africa is another. The attempts to initiate programs of "restorative justice" within police work and criminal justice systems offer yet another. In each case, onlookers have been tempted to suggest that the way of nonviolence appears weak and ineffectual. The results suggest otherwise.

To work for a healing, restorative justice—whether in individual relationships, in international relations, or anywhere in between—is therefore a primary Christian calling. It determines one whole sphere of Christian behavior. Violence and personal vengeance are ruled out, as the New Testament makes abundantly clear. Every Christian is called to work, at every level of life, for a world in which reconciliation and restoration are put into practice, and so to anticipate that day when God will indeed put everything to rights.

—*Simply Christian* 226

No Compromising on Resurrection Means No Acquiescence to Injustice

It was people who believed robustly in the resurrection, not people who compromised and went in for a mere spiritualized survival, who stood up against Caesar in the first centuries of the Christian era. A piety that sees death as the moment of "going home at last," the time when we are "called to God's eternal peace," has no quarrel with powermongers who want to carve up the world to suit their own ends. Resurrection, by contrast, has always gone with a strong view of God's justice and of God as the good creator. Those twin beliefs give rise not to a meek acquiescence to injustice in the world but to a robust determination to oppose it. English evangelicals gave up believing in the urgent imperative to improve society (such as we find with Wilberforce in the late eighteenth and early nineteenth centuries) about the same time that they gave up believing robustly in resurrection and settled for a disembodied heaven instead. It would take a longer study than this one to see whether the same shift happened at the same time in the United States and elsewhere, but I would not be surprised to find that it did.

—*Surprised by Hope* 26–27

God Is Utterly Determined to Put Everything Right

The wrath of God is simply the shadow side of the love of God for his wonderful creation and his amazing human creatures. Like a great artist appalled at the way his paintings have been defaced by the very people who were supposed to be looking after them, God's implacable rejection of evil is the natural outflowing of his creative love. God's anger against evil is itself the determination to *put things right,* to get rid of the corrupt attitudes and behaviors that have spoiled his world and his human creatures. It is because God loves the glorious world he has made and is utterly determined to put everything right that he is utterly opposed to everything that spoils or destroys that creation, especially the human creatures who were supposed to be the linchpins of his plan for how that creation would flourish. That's why, as Paul's argument progresses in Romans, he frames its central passage not with God's *anger* but with his powerful, rescuing *love* (Rom. 5:1–11; 8:31–39).

Many times, when people preach what they think is the gospel from the letter to the Romans, you would never know that underneath the warning about wrath is the glorious truth of divine love. A poet who had written a wonderful, long poem would be horrified if someone came and tore pages out of it or crossed out some of the best lines and scribbled in bits of doggerel instead. It is because God loves the world he has made, and especially his human creatures, that he hates everything that spoils, wrecks, or defaces it.

—*Simply Good News* 70–71

Time to Unmask the
Principalities and Powers

It is comparatively easy to name yesterday's idolatrous systems. It is much harder to point to the equivalents in today's and tomorrow's world. Here the church needs the wisdom of the serpent as well as the innocence of the dove, and both often seem to be in short supply. But when Christians in non-Western countries look at Europe and America, they see, behind our own much-vaunted "freedoms," another set of idolatries and enslavements. The familiar trio of money, sex, and power are enthroned as securely as ever. A sign in my local charity shop tells me that a quarter of the world's wealth is owned by so few people that they could all fit on an ordinary bus, while millions of desperately poor people save up what little they have to pay people smugglers to ferry them dangerously across the Mediterranean, where, if they make it across the sea, barbed wire and refugee camps await them and local politicians agonize over how to cope.

You don't have to hold a doctorate in global economics to know that something is radically wrong with whatever "systems" we have, or don't have, in place. Western politicians clearly have no ready answers, bent as they are on solving yesterday's problems with pragmatic short-term solutions. We don't have a narrative that could make sense of the problem, let alone one that might solve it. And with a newly militant branch of Islam (disowned, of course, by the vast majority of the world's Muslims) ready to advance its own cause by exploiting the plight of others, we are all aware that things could get worse.

Faced with this situation, churches of all kinds in all countries need the gift of discernment to see where idolatry has resulted in slavery and to understand what it would mean to announce, in those places, the forgiveness of sins and the consequent breaking of the enslaving powers. This will be complicated, contested, and controversial. These things always are. But the attempt must be made. Clearly money is a major factor, and the nations that for centuries have profited from their "enlightened" cultural, technological, and economic status must look at themselves in the mirror and ask the kinds of questions that white South Africans had to face in the 1980s. Clearly too the way in which the Enlightenment had defined "religion" so as to separate it from the rest of real life has turned out to be an apparent luxury whose price is only now being revealed. The principalities and powers have been quite happy to have that discreet veil cast over their steady advance, and it is time for them to be unmasked.

—The Day the Revolution Began 393–94

Calling the World to Account for Sin, Justice, and Judgment

But speak up and speak out we must, because we have not only the clear instruction of Jesus himself, but the clear promise that *this is how he will exercise his sovereignty; this is how he will make his kingdom a reality.* In John's gospel, Jesus tells his followers that the Spirit will call the world to account:

> "When he comes, he will prove the world to be in the wrong on three counts: sin, justice, and judgment. In relation to sin—because they don't believe in me. In relation to justice—because I'm going to the father, and you won't see

me anymore. In relation to judgment—because the ruler of
this world is judged." (16:8–11)

And the point of this dense little promise is worryingly clear: the
Spirit will do all this *through the church*. That is the mandate. That
is how Jesus intends to operate. That is how the victory he won at
Calvary is to be implemented in the world.

—*Simply Jesus* 226–27

The Flabbiness of an Easygoing Tolerance of Everything

The failure of liberal optimism in Western society has been matched
by the obvious failure of the equivalent liberal optimism in theology, driven as it was by the spirit of the age. It is a shame to have
to rerun the story of nearly a hundred years ago, with Karl Barth
furiously rejecting the liberal theology that had created the climate
for World War I, but it does sometimes feel as though that is what
has happened. Faced with the Balkans, Rwanda, the Middle East,
Darfur, and all kinds of other horrors that enlightened Western
thought can neither explain nor alleviate, opinion in many quarters
has, rightly in my view, come to see that there must be such a thing
as judgment.

Judgment—the sovereign declaration that *this* is good and to be
upheld and vindicated, and *that* is evil and to be condemned—is
the only alternative to chaos. There are some things, quite a lot
of them in fact, that one must not tolerate lest one merely collude
with wickedness. We all know this perfectly well, yet we conve-
niently forget it whenever squeamishness or the demands of current

opinion make it easier to go with the flow of social convention. The problem is that much theology, having lived for so long on the convenience food of an easygoing tolerance of everything, an "inclusivity" with as few boundaries as McWorld, has become depressingly flabby, unable to climb even the lower slopes of social and cultural judgment let alone the steep upper reaches of that judgment of which the early Christians spoke and wrote.

But judgment is necessary—unless we were to conclude, absurdly, that nothing much is wrong or, blasphemously, that God doesn't mind very much. In the justly famous phrase of Miroslav Volf, there must be "exclusion" before there can be "embrace": evil must be identified, named, and dealt with before there can be reconciliation. That is the basis on which Desmond Tutu has built his mind-blowing work on the South African Commission for Truth and Reconciliation. And—this is, of course, the crunch—where those who have acted wickedly refuse to see the point, there can be no reconciliation, no embrace.

God is utterly committed to set the world right in the end.

—*Surprised by Hope* 178–79

The Strength of Forgiveness

In many cultures and countries in the world "forgiveness" is seen as a sign of weakness. If someone has wronged you, you should get even! Justice has not been done! You have been robbed of your rights! I have seen people eaten up by that philosophy. It pervades every aspect of their lives. Every thought turns into a grudge, and every grudge clamors for revenge. And I have seen people who have given up that philosophy and discovered the healing power of forgiveness. It can and does happen. This always catches us by surprise, perhaps because it is the true and sure sign of the world still waiting to be fully birthed.

When, in June 2015, relatives of the murder victims in Charleston, South Carolina, came face-to-face with the killer, several of them told him at once that they forgave him. Something similar happened after the Amish school shooting in October 2006. These incidents, widely reported, strike secular journalists and their readers as strange to the point of being almost incredible. Do these people really mean it? It is clear that they do. The forgiveness was unforced. It wasn't said through clenched teeth, in outward conformity to a moral standard, while the heart remained bitter. Forgiveness was already a way of life in these communities. They were merely exemplifying and extending, in horrific circumstances, the character they had already learned and practiced.

In fact, once again, the incredulity of many who heard those stories matches the incredulity of people in the first century, as well as in our own, when hearing the story of Jesus's resurrection. And for the same reason. In both cases, we are witnessing a new world coming to birth. Resurrection and forgiveness belong together. Both are the direct result of the victory won on the cross, because the victory won on the cross was won by dealing with sin and hence with death. Resurrection is the result of death's defeat; forgiveness, the result of sin's defeat. Those who learn to forgive discover that they are not only offering healing to others. They are receiving it in themselves. Resurrection is happening inside them. The wrong done to them is not permitted to twist their lives out of shape. Forgiveness isn't weakness. It was and is a great strength.

—*The Day the Revolution Began* 385–86

God's Justice Overthrows the
Powers of the World

From thence he shall come to judge the quick and the dead.

To the objection that the kingdom seems not to have gotten very far just yet—an objection that actually ignores the massive positive changes in the world and in our own society brought about by faithful and usually unknown Christians—this clause gives the answer: "From thence"! This is a direct allusion to Philippians 3:20–21, in which Jesus comes "from heaven," from his place of utter sovereignty, to complete the work of establishing that sovereignty on earth. The scene here is not so much that of Michelangelo's *Last Judgment*, though it may include elements of that as well. It is more a question of Jesus's last confrontation with the representatives of Caesar and all that he stands for, not to mention the dark powers that stand behind him. As Paul says, Jesus comes as "the savior, the Lord, the king" (Phil. 3:20)—all of them titles for Caesar. The "last judgment" will be the moment when the powers of the world are overthrown by the power of God, the power that was displayed fully in the crucifixion of the Lamb.

—*How God Became King* 269–70

God's Coming Judgment Is
Something to Be Celebrated

The picture of Jesus as the coming judge is the central feature of another absolutely vital and nonnegotiable Christian belief: that there will indeed *be* a judgment in which the creator God will set the world right once and for all. The word *judgment* carries negative overtones for a good many people in our liberal and postliberal world. We need to remind ourselves that throughout the Bible, not least in the Psalms, God's coming judgment is a good thing, something to be celebrated, longed for, yearned over. It causes people to shout for joy and the trees of the field to clap their hands. In a world of systematic injustice, bullying, violence, arrogance, and oppression, the thought that there might come a day when the wicked are firmly put in their place and the poor and weak are given their due is the best news there can be. Faced with a world in rebellion, a world full of exploitation and wickedness, a good God *must* be a God of judgment. The liberal optimism of the nineteenth century had a long run for its money, outlasting some of the more obvious counterarguments provided by the huge systemic evil of the twentieth century. But more recent theology has returned to the theme of judgment, recognizing that the biblical analysis of evil corresponds more closely to reality.

—Surprised by Hope 137–38

Paul Means It When He Talks About Judgment

Paul's speech on the Areopagus in Athens concludes with the statement that God has fixed a day on which he will judge the world by a man whom he has appointed, giving assurance of the fact by raising him from the dead. Paul can refer almost casually (in Rom. 2:16) to the fact that according to the gospel he preaches, God will judge the secrets of all hearts through Jesus the Messiah. Although people often suppose that because Paul taught justification by faith, not works, there can be no room for a future judgment "according to works," this only goes to show how much some have radically misunderstood him. The future judgment according to deeds, a judgment exercised by Jesus at his "judgment seat," is clearly taught in, for instance, Romans 14:9–10, 2 Corinthians 5:10, and elsewhere. Equally important, these are not isolated places where Paul is quoting a tradition that doesn't fully fit with his developed theology. They are fully and tightly integrated into his thinking and preaching. For him, as much as for anyone else in the early church, the final judgment exercised by Jesus the Messiah was a vital element, without which all sorts of other things simply wouldn't stand up.

—Surprised by Hope 139

Humility, Patience, and
Our Deepest Longing

Believing in the second coming itself is anything but arrogant. The whole point of it is to insist, over against not only the wider pagan world, but against all self-delusion or pretension within the church, that Jesus remains sovereign and will return at last to put everything right. This putting right (the biblical word for it is "justice") is the sort of sigh-of-relief event that the whole world, at its best and at many other times too, longs for most deeply. All sorts of things are out of joint, both on a large and a small scale, in the world; and God the creator will put them straight. All sorts of things are still going wrong, corrupting the lives of human beings and the larger life of the environment, the planet itself; God the creator will put them right. All sorts of things are still wrong *with us, Jesus's followers;* Jesus, when he comes, will put us right as well. That may not be comfortable, but it's what we need. Believing he will do it is part of Christian humility. Waiting for it is part of Christian patience:

> When the king is revealed (and he is your life, remember), then you too will be revealed with him in glory. (Col. 3:4)

> Beloved ones, we are now, already, God's children; it hasn't yet been revealed what we are going to be. We know that when he is revealed we shall be like him, because we shall see him as he is. (1 John 3:2)

—Simply Jesus 201

God's "Judgment" Will Perform a Great Act of New Creation

The second coming takes on all the dimensions present in Israel's scriptures, the dimensions of the whole creation singing with delight when Israel's God comes to "judge" the world (Pss. 96; 98). "Judgment" in this sense is like the "judgment" given when a poor widow finally has her case heard, the bullies who have been oppressing her are firmly rebuked, and she is vindicated. "Judgment" is what happens when someone who has been robbed of home and dignity and livelihood is upheld, with everything restored. "Judgment" is what happens when a forest that has been damaged through overzealous logging, on the one hand, and acid rain, on the other, is wisely replanted and the source of pollution identified and stopped. The world is out of joint, and God's "judgment" will perform a great act of new creation through which it will be restored to the way God always intended it to be.

To speak of the second coming is therefore to speak of God's whole new world, the new world envisaged in Revelation 21–22 or Romans 8, and of Jesus at the middle of it, administering God's just, wise, and healing rule. Jesus is the truly human being who will, in the end, take the properly human role (as in Genesis) of reflecting the creator's image of wise and fruitful order into the whole creation. That is what his "coming" and his "judgment" will mean. God will do for the whole cosmos, in the end, what he did for Jesus at Easter; the risen Jesus, remember, is the *prototype* of the new creation. God will do this *through* Jesus himself; the ascended Jesus, remember, is the *ruler* within the new creation as it bursts in upon the old. And God will do it through the *presence* of the risen and ascended Jesus when he comes to heal, to save, and also to judge.

—Simply Jesus 202–3

CHRISTMAS

This is how you should think among yourselves—with the mind that you have because you belong to the Messiah, Jesus:

> *Who, though in God's form, did not*
> *Regard his equality with God*
> *As something he ought to exploit.*
> *Instead, he emptied himself,*
> *And received the form of a slave,*
> *Being born in the likeness of humans.*
> *And then, having human appearance,*
> *He humbled himself, and became*
> *Obedient even to death,*
> *Yes, even the death of the cross.*
> *And so God has greatly exalted him,*
> *And to him in his favor has given*
> *The name which is over all names:*
> *That now at the name of Jesus*
> *Every knee within heaven shall bow—*
> *On earth, too, and under the earth;*
> *And every tongue shall confess*
> *That Jesus, Messiah, is Lord,*
> *To the glory of God, the father.*

—Philippians 2:5–11, *The Kingdom New Testament* 403

Chronological Outline of Jewish History

The whole point of Christmas is that God came into the middle of ordinary, messy, dangerous human history. Here is how that history can be laid out. It encourages us to reflect on ways in which God comes, today, into the ordinary, messy, and often sad history of our own lives.

BABYLONIAN PERIOD: 597–539 BC

597	Jerusalem taken by Nebuchadnezzar II
587	Jerusalem destroyed, people exiled to Babylon
539	Fall of Babylon

PERSIAN/GREEK PERIOD: 538–320 BC

538	Return of (some) exiles; rebuilding of Temple begun (completed 516)
450s/440s	Ezra and Nehemiah in Jerusalem
336	Alexander the Great comes to power
332	Alexander conquers Palestine
323	Alexander dies; empire divided

EGYPTIAN PERIOD: 320–200 BC

Ptolemies of Egypt rule Palestine; local government by high priests

SYRIAN PERIOD: 200–63 BC

200	Antiochus III defeats Egyptians
175	Antiochus IV Epiphanes enthroned

171	Menelaus (high priest) favors Antiochus; Jews revolt
167	Antiochus desecrates Temple, builds altar to Zeus Olympus
166	Judas Maccabeus ("Judah the Hammer") leads revolutionary group
164	Judas cleanses Temple
160	Death of Judas
160–63	Quasi-independent rule of Maccabean (Hasmonean) dynasty

ROMAN PERIOD: 63 BC ONWARD

63	Pompey (Roman general) takes Jerusalem
44	Death of Julius Caesar; Roman civil wars
37	Herod established as "King of Judaea"
31	Octavian (Augustus) wins civil war, transforms Roman republic into an empire
7–4 BC (?)	Birth of Jesus of Nazareth
4 BC	Death of Herod; civil unrest and "messianic" movements
4 BC	Herod's kingdom divided: Antipas rules Galilee; Archelaus, Judaea
AD 6	Archelaus deposed after protests; Judaea ruled by "prefects"
AD 14	Death of Augustus; accession of Tiberius
26–36	Pontius Pilate "prefect" of Judaea
30 (33?)	Crucifixion of Jesus of Nazareth

—*Simply Jesus* 62

Confounding Expectations

Let's put it like this. The Jewish people of the first century were expecting their God to come back in person to rescue them, revealing his glorious presence, defeating their enemies, and reestablishing them as his people once and for all.

They got Jesus.

They were hoping for a new exodus—that is, a repeat performance of what had happened fifteen hundred years earlier, when the Israelites had been enslaved in Egypt and their God (they believed) came to rescue them. He had overcome the powerful Egyptian rulers, liberated his people, and led them in person through the Sinai Desert to bring them to the promised land. Many prophets had said that one day God would do something like this again. Many people were hoping it would be soon.

They got Jesus.

They were hoping for a new age of justice and peace. Ancient scriptures had spoken of a time when the wolf would lie down with the lamb, the mountains would drip sweet wine, and the earth would be full of the knowledge and the glory of the one true God like waters filling the sea.

They got Jesus.

Is it any wonder they were puzzled?

In one story, on the third day after his death, two of his close friends explain sadly to a stranger that they had hoped he was the one who would redeem Israel. The point was, they crucified him, so he can't have been the one to do it after all. We must have been mistaken.

—*Simply Good News* 40–41

Far More Than We Ever Imagined

The reason Jesus wasn't the sort of king people had wanted in his own day is—to anticipate our conclusion—that he *was* the true king, but they had become used to the ordinary, shabby, second-rate sort. They were looking for a builder to construct the home they thought they wanted, but he was the architect, coming with a new plan that would give them everything they needed, but within quite a new framework. They were looking for a singer to sing the song they had been humming for a long time, but he was the composer, bringing them a new song to which the old songs they knew would form, at best, the background music. He was the king, all right, but he had come to redefine kingship itself around his own work, his own mission, his own fate.

—*Simply Jesus* 5

What Christianity Is Not

In other words, Christianity is *not* about a new moral teaching—as though we were morally clueless and in need of some fresh or clearer guidelines. This is not to deny that Jesus, and some of his first followers, gave some wonderfully bracing and intelligent moral teaching. It is merely to insist that we find teaching like that within a larger framework: the story of things that happened through which the world was changed.

Christianity isn't about Jesus offering a wonderful moral example, as though our principal need was to see what a life of utter love and devotion to God and to other people would look like, so that we could try to copy it. If that had been Jesus's main purpose, we could certainly say it had some effect. Some people's lives really have been changed simply by contemplating and imitating the example of Jesus. But observing Jesus's example could equally well simply make a person depressed. Watching Richter play the piano or Tiger Woods hit a golf ball doesn't inspire me to go out and copy them. It makes me realize that I can't come close and never will.

Nor is Christianity about Jesus offering, demonstrating, or even accomplishing a new route by which people can "go to heaven when they die." This is a persistent mistake, based on the medieval notion that the point of all religion—the rule of the game, if you like—was to make sure you ended up at the right side of the stage at the end of the mystery play (that is, in heaven rather than in hell), or on the right side of the painting in the Sistine Chapel. Again, that isn't to deny that our present beliefs and actions have lasting consequences. Rather, it's to deny both that Jesus made this the focus of his work and that this is the "point" of Christianity.

Finally, Christianity isn't about giving the world fresh teaching about God himself—though clearly, if the Christian claim is true, we do indeed learn a great deal about who God is by looking at Jesus. The need that the Christian faith answers is not so much that we are ignorant and need better information, but that we are lost and need someone to come and find us, stuck in the quicksand waiting to be rescued, dying and in need of new life.

—*Simply Christian* 91

So What Is Christianity About, Then?

Christianity is about something that *happened*. Something that happened *to Jesus of Nazareth*. Something that happened *through* Jesus of Nazareth.

Christianity is all about the belief that the living God, in fulfillment of his promises and as the climax of the story of Israel, has accomplished all this—the finding, the saving, the giving of new life—in Jesus. He has done it. With Jesus, God's rescue operation has been put into effect once and for all. A great door has swung open in the cosmos that can never again be shut. It's the door to the prison where we've been kept chained up. We are offered freedom: freedom to experience God's rescue for ourselves, to go through the open door and explore the new world to which we now have access. In particular, we are all invited—summoned, actually—to discover, through following Jesus, that this new world is indeed a place of justice, spirituality, relationship, and beauty, and that we are not only to enjoy it as such but to work at bringing it to birth on earth as in heaven. In listening to Jesus, we discover whose voice it is that has echoed around the hearts and minds of the human race all along.

—*Simply Christian* 91–92

How to Ask the Question: "Who Was Jesus?"

John F. Kennedy is perhaps one of the best-known Americans of the mid-twentieth century. His presidency was, of course, cut short by his sudden and violent death, a death that had, and perhaps still has, iconic significance for many Americans and others around the world. Those of us alive at the time all still remember where we were when we heard the news.

Now suppose we had four books containing very detailed accounts of what Kennedy did and said during his three-year presidency, with only a brief glance at what went before. Suppose it was quite clear that these were put together by people who believed that what Kennedy had done and said had lasting importance for their own day. But suppose as well that, instead of the overwhelming multitude of sources we actually possess for the decades before his day, we simply had a history book written in the early years of the twenty-first century (i.e., forty years after his death) plus a scattering of other material—a few letters, tracts, coins, souvenir artifacts, that kind of thing—to help us reconstruct the world within which what Kennedy did and said made the sense it did at the time, and particularly to get some idea of why some thought him a hero and others thought he had to be killed. One can imagine all the theories—the reconstructions of the Cold War mentality, the social and cultural tensions of the 1960s United States, and so on. There would be plenty of wiggle room for interpretation.

That is more or less our challenge with the historical evidence for Jesus. We have the four "gospels," written later by people who believed passionately that what Jesus had done and said, coupled with his death and what happened afterward, were of massive ongoing significance. The gospels are highly detailed; one of the problems of writing the present book has been trying to decide what to leave out. They are clearly written from particular (pro-Jesus) points of view. But, unlike today's historian studying JFK in his actual context, we have simply a history book written forty or fifty years later (by Josephus, an aristocratic Jew who went over to the Roman side in the war of AD 66–70) and a scattering of other material, bits and pieces, tracts, coins, letters, and so forth. Out of these very disparate sources we have to reconstruct the setting in which what Jesus did and said made the sense it did, so much sense that some thought he was God's Messiah and others thought he had to be killed at once. If we don't make the effort to do this reconstruction, we will, without a shadow of doubt, assume that what Jesus did and said makes the sense it might have made in some other context— perhaps our own. This kind of easy-going anachronism is almost as corrosive to genuine Christian faith as skepticism itself.

—*Simply Jesus* 20–21

What We Mean When We Call Jesus "the Lord"

From very early times (indeed, according to the gospels, since Jesus's own lifetime), Christians have referred to Jesus himself as "the Lord." In early Christian speech, this phrase carried at least three meanings: (a) "the master," "the one whose servants we are," "the one we've promised to obey"; (b) "the true Lord" (as opposed to Caesar, who claimed the same title); and (c) "the LORD"—that is, YHWH—as spoken of in the Old Testament. All these meanings are visible in Paul, the earliest Christian writer we have. The early Christians rejoiced in this flexibility, but for us it has become a source of confusion.

Within contemporary Western culture, under the influence of Deism, the phrase "the Lord" has shifted from referring either to Jesus specifically or to the YHWH of the Old Testament. It has become, instead, a way of referring simply to a rather distant, generalized deity, who might conceivably have something to do with Jesus but equally well might not, and would probably not have much to

do with YHWH either. Thus it has come about that ancient Israelite
scruples, medieval mistranslation, and fuzzy eighteenth-century
thinking have combined to make it hard for us today to recapture
the vital sense of what a first-century Jew would understand when
thinking of YHWH, what an early Christian would be saying when
speaking of Jesus or "the Lord," and how we might now properly
reappropriate this whole tradition.

Still, the effort has to be made. All language about God is ultimately mysterious, but that is no excuse for sloppy or woolly
thinking. And since the title "Lord" was one of the favorite early
Christian ways of speaking about Jesus, it is vital that we get clear
on the point.

—*Simply Christian* 68–69

Confessing the Worldwide
Sovereignty of Jesus

And in Jesus Christ his only son, our Lord . . .

The Christian who is wise as well as "orthodox" will know the two
things we mentioned earlier. First, that "Christ" means "Israel's
Messiah" and that with that title the whole history of Israel is
brought into one place—as Paul says, "when the fullness of time
arrived" (Gal. 4:4). The history, then, of the people who invoke
the one creator God as king of the whole world—that history has
become a person, and that person is called Jesus. Second, when we
call Jesus God's "son," we not only hail him as the second person of
the Trinity, but we celebrate him as the one spoken of in Psalm 2,
the one enthroned over the nations of the world. To call Jesus "son"

is to celebrate him as the agent of the kingdom of God. And to hail him as "Lord" was never, in the canon, a merely honorary word. It was one of the regular imperial titles. It declared that Jesus is Lord of the whole world. The word "our" doesn't restrict the scope of Jesus's sovereignty; it merely indicates that "we," the people saying this creed, are those who acknowledge gladly and openly what the rest of the world doesn't yet know. That worldwide sovereignty of Jesus has been the burden of our song for much of this book.

—*How God Became King* 266–67

King Jesus

The evangelists insist that the kingdom truly was inaugurated by Jesus in his active public career, during the time between his baptism and the cross. That entire narrative is the story of "how God became king in and through Jesus." But note what follows. We in the West, perhaps ever since Chalcedon or even Nicaea, have read as the main text what the gospels treated as presupposition. In all four gospels, Jesus is the embodiment ("incarnation") of Israel's God. But this is not the gospels' main theme. Not even, I think, John's. The main theme is that, in and through Jesus the Messiah, Israel's God reclaims his sovereign rule over Israel and the world.

In musical terms, we have mistaken key for tune. The key in which the gospels are set is that of incarnational Christology. But the melody is that of the kingdom and of "Christology" in the much stricter sense of "Jesus as Messiah." Those whose catechism was based on the great creeds would never guess what their canonical scriptures were trying to tell them. In the messianic life and death of Jesus, Israel's God really did become king of the world. Again and again I read devout works in which this point, utterly central to the New Testament witness to Jesus, is passed over in silence.

—*How God Became King* 240–41

Redefining Incarnation

Jesus, as we have already seen, had been going about saying that this God, Israel's God, was right now becoming king, was taking charge, was establishing his long-awaited saving and healing rule on earth as in heaven. Heaven and earth were being joined up—but no longer in the Temple in Jerusalem. The joining place was visible where the healings were taking place, where the party was going on (remember the angels celebrating in heaven and people joining in on earth?), where forgiveness was happening. In other words, the joining place, the overlapping circle, was taking place *where Jesus was and in what he was doing.* Jesus was, as it were, a walking Temple. A living, breathing place-where-Israel's-God-was-living.

As many people will see at once, this is the very heart of what later theologians would call the doctrine of the incarnation. But it looks quite different from how many people imagine that doctrine to work. Judaism already had a massive "incarnational" symbol, the Temple. Jesus was behaving as if he *were* the Temple, in person. He was talking about Israel's God taking charge. And he was doing things that put that God-in-chargeness into practice. It all starts to make sense. In particular, it answers the old criticism that "Jesus talked about God, but the church talked about Jesus"—as though Jesus would have been shocked to have his pure, God-centered message corrupted in that way. This sneer fails to take account of the fact that, yes, Jesus talked about God, but he talked about God *precisely in order to explain the things that he himself was doing.*

So we shouldn't be surprised at Jesus's action in the Temple. The Temple had, as it were, been a great signpost pointing forward to another reality that had lain unnoticed for generations, like the vital clue in a detective story that is only recognized as such in the final chapter. Remember the promise to David—that God would build him a "house," a family, founded on the son of David who would be the son of God? David had wanted to build a house for God, and God had replied that *he* would build *David* a "house." David's coming son is the ultimate reality; the Temple in Jerusalem is the advance signpost *to* that reality. Now that the reality is here, the signpost isn't needed anymore.

—*Simply Jesus* 133–34

The True King Reclaiming His Kingdom

Jesus was not offering a teaching that could be compared with that of other teachers—though his teaching, as it stands, is truly remarkable. He was not offering a moral example, though if we want such a thing he remains outstanding. He was claiming to do things *through which the world would be healed, transformed, rescued, and renewed.* He was, in short, announcing good news, for Israel and the whole world.

His world, at least, was waiting for good news. The Jewish world of Jesus's day buzzed with speculation. Their great traditions told the story of the childless nomad Abraham, called by God to start a family through which the world would be rescued. This people would learn firsthand what rescue meant, since they would be enslaved in Egypt before being delivered by God in the Passover. God himself would lead them through the Red Sea, through years of wandering in the desert, until they finally inherited their promised land. That event (the exodus) remained central to Jewish life and thought. It shaped, and continues to shape, how Jews saw and see the world. It speaks of the one true God making himself known in power, defeating the powers of evil, and rescuing his people. It speaks of what, in later scriptures, came to be called the kingdom of God. In other words, it speaks of God *becoming* king of the world in a whole new way. The one true God was always the rightful ruler of the world, but he needed to reclaim his kingdom after the power of evil had usurped it.

Many people in Jesus's day believed that the time had come for this dream to turn into reality. This was the backstory for the good news they were eager to hear.

The exodus shaped Jesus, too. He shared the belief of his contemporaries (that the one God would finally rescue his people and the world through a new exodus) but with one big difference. He believed it was his own job to make it happen. This was his vocation, his special calling. People used to be bothered by the fact that Jesus talked about God but his followers talked later about Jesus himself—as though the early Christians were doing something Jesus never intended. That is nonsense. Yes, Jesus talked about God. Of course. But he did so precisely *to explain what he himself was up to.* "If I'm casting out demons because I'm in league with God's spirit," he said when challenged, "well, then, God's kingdom has arrived on your doorstep!" (Matt. 12:28). He was claiming, in effect, to *be* the good news in person.

—*Simply Good News 36–37*

How Heaven and Earth
Are Brought Together

The four gospels, completely in line with Genesis, the Psalms, Isaiah, and the rest, tell of *how God became king:* how the creator God, in and through Jesus of Nazareth, launched his new-creation project for the world. On every page, what we are looking at is precisely new *creation:* not just a new spirituality, certainly not a system for rescuing people *from* this world, but a movement of God's creative spirit, anointing Jesus but also breathed out by him, through which humans are called to become genuine humans at last, rescued from all that thwarts that, and so equipped to carry forward God's plan of new creation. Once again, God is remaking the world not by an intervention that drowns out everything else, as some supernatural schemes would have it, nor by allowing natural causes to take their course, as some evolutionary schemes—including some would-be Christian evolutionary schemes!—would have it, but by the act of redemptive new creation through which humans are able once more to reflect God into his world and the world back, in worship, to God. The whole project of Jesus is a *new-temple* project, which is why the Jerusalem temple and then the pagan temples become so problematic in the gospels and Acts; it is the project, in other words, in which *heaven and earth are brought together at last,* with God's sovereign rule extending *on earth as in heaven* through the mission of Jesus, climactically in his death and resurrection, and then through the similarly shaped and spirit-driven mission of his followers.

—Surprised by Scripture 23–24

A Love Partnership

I do not think that Jesus "knew he was divine" in the same way that we know we are cold or hot, happy or sad, male or female. It was more like the kind of "knowledge" we associate with vocation, where people *know*, in the very depths of their being, that they are called to be an artist, a mechanic, a philosopher. For Jesus, this seems to have been a deep "knowledge" of that kind, a powerful and all-consuming belief that Israel's God was more mysterious than most people had supposed; that within the very being of this God there was a give-and-take, a to-and-fro, a love given and received. Jesus seems to have believed that he, the fully human prophet from Nazareth, was one of those partners in love. He was called, in obedience to the Father, to follow through the project to which that love would give itself freely and fully.

This has brought us to the borders of language as well as theology. But the conclusion I have reached as a historian is that such an analysis best explains why Jesus did what he did, and why his followers, so soon after his death and resurrection, came to believe and do what they believed and did. And the conclusion I reach as a Christian is that this understanding of Jesus and his role explains, in turn, why it is that I and millions of others have discovered Jesus to be personally present and active in the world and in our lives, our rescuer and our Lord.

—*Simply Christian* 119

The Royal Purpose

Yes, Jesus was and is fully divine and fully human. But the *point* of his divinity in the gospels is that in him and *as* him the living God is becoming king. And the point of his humanity in the gospels is that, in him and as him, human beings are at last taking up again their God-given vocation of being the royal priesthood through which God brings his wise, redemptive ordering to the garden. And yes, the good news is good news of salvation. But in the Bible we are saved not simply so we can go to heaven and enjoy fellowship with God but so that we can be his truly human royal priesthood in his world. "You were slaughtered," sings the great crowd in Revelation 5 in praise of the Lamb, "and with your own blood you purchased a people for God, . . . *and made them a kingdom and priests to serve our God, and they will reign on the earth.*"

—Surprised by Scripture 32

The Climax of the Real Project

Who was conceived by the Holy Ghost, born of
the virgin Mary, suffered under Pontius Pilate,
was crucified, died, and was buried . . .

The "incarnation" of the second person of the Trinity, in the strange and mysterious birth reported in Matthew and Luke, is, as we saw earlier, a highly political moment when Herod (in Matthew) and Caesar (in Luke) are both caught napping. Both even collude unwittingly with the event, Herod by sending the wise men to Bethlehem, Augustus Caesar by sending Joseph and Mary there. The virginal conception of Jesus thus speaks of the living God coming precisely to establish his sovereignty, dependent on no human agency; the attempt to make Mary's "Fiat" ("Let it be") into a kind of equal and opposite contribution to that of God misses the point entirely and makes another that leads us a long way off track.

Wise readers of the creed already know at this point, then, that the one who is thus born to Mary is the one who has come to establish the kingdom of the one true God. To make "virgin birth" mean "miraculous divinity" and thereby to screen out "inaugurating God's kingdom" is to falsify it—however "orthodox" it may sound. What it means is the launching of God's kingdom purposes by the one who is, precisely, the sovereign of all.

This means that we must now read the statement of Jesus's suffering, death, and burial as the climax of *this* project, rather than some other. "For us men, and for our salvation," says the Nicene Creed at this point. Yes, indeed, but that "salvation" is not a rescue *from* the earth, from God's creation, but in and *for* the earth, and for us as creatures of earth. The mention of Pilate in the creed (a remarkable enough point at the best of times, scarcely to be explained by some early Christians thinking, in their misguided enthusiasm, that Pilate was actually a hero, perhaps even a saint, for facilitating Jesus's saving death!) is no mere historical marker, though it is important in that respect as well.

The mention of Pilate and of Jesus's suffering at his command speaks loudly and clearly into the world of early Christianity, after those three initial centuries of persecution, of Jesus as the one who won the great initial victory over the dark powers of which Caesar's rule (and Pilate's subrule) were the immediate instrument. "Suffered under Pontius Pilate." Yes, we think, because that is how the great scene in John 18–19 comes to its close, with Jesus speaking of kingdom, truth, and power and going to the cross to make them all happen!

—How God Became King 267–68

The Remaking of Creation

If you tell this story from the point of view of the good creation, the coming of Jesus emerges as the moment all creation had been waiting for. Humans were made to be God's stewards over creation, so the one through whom all things were made, the eternal son, the eternal wisdom, becomes human so that he might truly become God's steward, ruler over all his world. Equally, if you tell the story from the point of view of human rebellion and the consequent sin and death that have engulfed the world, this again emerges as the moment all creation had been waiting for: the eternal expression of the father's love became the incarnate expression of the father's love so that by his self-giving to death, even the death of the cross, the whole creation can be reconciled to God. If you put these two ways of telling the story together and cast them into poetry, you will find you have rewritten Colossians 1:15–20. This is the real cosmic Christology of the New Testament: not a kind of pantheism, running under its own steam and cut off from the real Jesus, but a retelling of the Jewish story of wisdom in terms of Jesus himself, focusing on the cross as the act whereby the good creation is brought back into harmony with the wise creator.

The balance of the clauses in the poem in Colossians 1 shows the extent to which Paul insists on holding together creation and redemption. Redemption is not simply making creation a bit better, as the optimistic evolutionist would try to suggest. Nor is it rescuing spirits and souls from an evil material world, as the Gnostic would want to say. It is the remaking of creation, having dealt with the evil that is defacing and distorting it. And it is accomplished by the same God, now known in Jesus Christ, through whom it was made in the first place.

—*Surprised by Hope* 96–97

In Jesus, All God's Promises Find Their "Yes"

According to the prophets, Israel's story (from Abraham all the way through to exile and beyond) would narrow down to a remnant, but would also focus on a coming king, so that the king himself would be Israel personified. But second, there was *God's* story—the story of what the One God had done, was doing, and had promised to do. (The idea of God having a story, making plans, and putting them into operation seems to be part of what Jews and early Christians meant by speaking of this God as being "alive.") And this story too would likewise narrow down to one point. Israel's God would return, visibly and powerfully, to rescue his people from their ultimate enemies and to set up a kingdom that could not be shaken. "All God's promises," Paul would later write, "find their yes in him."

Saul came to see that these two stories, Israel's story and God's story, had, shockingly, merged together. Both narratives were fulfilled in Jesus. Jesus was Israel personified; but he was also Israel's God in person.

—*Paul: A Biography* 71

A Paean of Praise

The "mind of the Messiah" is then the subject of one of the greatest Jesus-focused poems of all time. Echoing Genesis, the Psalms, and Isaiah in particular, Philippians 2:6–11 tells the story of Jesus going down to the lowest depths and then being exalted as Lord of the whole world. The poem works at several levels. It expresses many things Paul believed about Jesus himself—the truly human one, the ultimate Israelite, the Servant of the Lord, the embodiment of Israel's God in person, the reality of which Caesar was a shallow parody.

This is the story of Adam (everyone), of Israel, of the One God—all in the form of a perfectly balanced poem about Jesus. The poem is cast in the idiom of a Hellenistic paean of praise for a great man, but the content is, of course, deeply Jewish and scriptural. It is, in fact, a poem that sums up a great deal of what Paul believed: that Jesus is the messianic fulfillment of Israel's story, the embodiment of Israel's One God, and hence the appointed Lord of the whole world. Its careful structure, giving full weight to the cross in the very center, encapsulates exactly what Paul most deeply believed about the gospel. It is *because* of the cross—the defeat of the powers—that Jesus has been exalted as Lord and that every knee shall bow at his name.

—Paul: A Biography 272–74

Shot Through with the Life of Heaven

Our minds are so conditioned, I'm afraid, by Greek philosophy, whether or not we've ever read any of it, that we think of heaven as by definition nonmaterial and earth by definition as nonspiritual or nonheavenly. But that won't do. Part of the central achievement of the incarnation, which is then celebrated in the resurrection and ascension, is that heaven and earth are now joined together with an unbreakable bond and that we too are by rights citizens of both together. We can, if we choose, screen out the heavenly dimension and live as flatlanders, materialists. If we do that, we will be buying in to a system that will go bad, and will wither and die, because earth gets its vital life from heaven.

But if we focus our attention on the heavenly dimension, all sorts of positive and practical results will follow. In Colossians 3:11, Paul sees the unity of the church across cultural and ethnic boundaries as one of the first of these results. In the passage that follows, he lists all kinds of other things that ought to appear in the life of anyone who really sets his or her mind on the world that is now Jesus's primary home, the world that is designed to heal and restore our present one. In each case, what he's talking about *is actual current physical reality, shot through now with the life of heaven.*

—*Surprised by Hope* 251

An Extraordinary, Breathtaking, Ridiculous Truth

Paul's letter to Colossae carries an explosive charge in inverse proportion to its short length. Paul wrote it from prison. When he makes his sweeping and all-embracing statements about Jesus, he knows he is flying in the face of the apparent reality. And yet he doesn't hold back:

He is the image of god, the invisible one,
The firstborn of all creation.
For in him all things were created,
In the heavens and here on the earth.
Things we can see and things we cannot—
Thrones and lordships and rulers and powers—
All things were created both through him and for him.
(Col. 1:15–16)

And so on. We need to let Paul remind us, precisely when major cultural change is upon us, that our confidence is not in the solidity of Western culture or the basic goodness of modern democracy. Our confidence is in Jesus and him alone. We need this message with every fiber of our beings. And we need to generate and sustain communities and educational institutions where this extraordinary, breathtaking, ridiculous truth is woven into the very fabric of all we do.

Some might see this great claim as shutting down all academic inquiry: If Christ is the answer, what's the point of asking the question? I see it exactly the other way around: Jesus is lord of the world, so all truth is his truth; let's go and explore it with reverence and delight. Whether you look through the telescope or the microscope, whether you study texts or traditions, whether it's oceanography or paleography, you are thinking Jesus's thoughts after him.

In particular, Paul declares—despite languishing in prison!—that all rulers and authorities were created through and for Jesus the Messiah. We are called today to think afresh what that might mean in terms of modern Western democracy.

—*Surprised by Scripture* 184–85

Uncovering Multiple Layers of Meaning

What matters, I have become convinced, is that we need to under-stand how *worldviews* work. If you have been born and bred within a culture that tells certain stories, observes certain customs and festivals, practices particular domestic habits, and sings particular songs, and if these things all go together and reinforce one another, a single phrase or action may well carry multiple layers of mean-ing. Imagine a visiting Martian landing in the middle of a game of baseball or cricket. Those of us who have played those games appreciate the subtleties, the nuances, the finely balanced match, the implications of how the ball is pitched or bowled, of who it is that's coming up to bat next. We know what it means when people, attending those games, sing particular songs. You or I would take all of that in at a glance, but it might take us an hour or more to explain it, in all its detail, to our alien guest. That doesn't mean it's horribly theoretical or abstract. It only means that most people, most of the time, live more complex lives than we often realize.

That complexity is likely to increase when you go to a place like first-century Jerusalem at Passover-time, with pilgrims sing-ing those psalms again and families getting ready to tell one an-other the story they already know, the story of God and Moses and Pharaoh and the Red Sea and the hope of freedom at last, while the Roman soldiers are looking down from their watchtowers and while an excited procession comes over the Mount of Olives, led by a man on a donkey, and starts to sing about the kingdom that is going to appear at any minute . . .

—Simply Jesus 23

The Real Challenge

Plenty of Christians, alas, have imagined that a "divine Jesus" had come to earth simply to reveal his divinity and save people away from earth for a distant "heaven." (Some have even imagined, absurdly, that the point of "proving that Jesus really did all those things" is to show that the Bible is true—as though Jesus came to witness to the Bible rather than the other way around.) It has been all too possible to use the doctrine of the incarnation or even the doctrine of the inspiration of scripture as a way of protecting oneself and one's worldview and political agenda against having to face the far greater challenge of God taking charge, of God becoming king, on earth as in heaven. But that is what the stories in the Bible are all about. That's what the story of Jesus was, and is, all about. That is the real challenge, and skeptics aren't the only ones who find clever ways to avoid it.

Once we begin to see beyond these three distracting angles of vision, then, and grasp the story in its own terms, we find ourselves compelled forward into the narrative again. If the time is fulfilled, what will happen to bring even this fulfilled-time moment to its proper conclusion? If Jesus is behaving as though he were the Temple in person, what will this mean both for the existing Temple and for his followers? And if, through his work, new creation is breaking into the world, how is it going to make any headway against the apparently still all-powerful forces of corruption, evil, and death itself?

—*Simply Jesus* 149–50

A New Time Has Been Launched

Now, and only now, do we see what Jesus meant when he said *the time is fulfilled.* That was part of his announcement right at the start of his public career (Mark 1:15). Only this, I believe, will enable us to understand his extraordinary behavior immediately afterward. He seems to have gone out of his way to flout the normal sabbath regulations. Most people in the modern church have imagined that this was because the sabbath had become "legalistic," a kind of observance designed to boost one's sense of moral achievement, and that Jesus had come to sweep all that away in a burst of libertarian, antilegalistic enthusiasm. That, though commonplace, is a trivial misunderstanding. It is too "modern" by half. Rather, the sabbath was the regular signpost pointing forward to God's promised future, *and Jesus was announcing that the future to which the signpost had been pointing had now arrived in the present.* In his own career. He was doing the "God's-in-charge" things. He was explaining what *he* was doing by talking about what *God* was doing. The time was fulfilled, and God's kingdom was arriving.

In particular, Jesus came to Nazareth and announced the jubilee. This was the time—the *time!*—when all the sevens, all the sabbaths, would rush together. This was the moment Israel and the world had been waiting for. When you reach your destination, you don't expect to see signposts anymore. Nobody puts up a sign on Capitol Hill pointing to "Washington." Nobody needs a signpost saying "London" in Piccadilly Circus. You don't need the sabbath when the time is fulfilled. It was completely consistent with Jesus's vision of his own vocation that he would do things that said, again and again from one angle after another, that the time had arrived, that the future, the new creation, was already here, and that one no longer needed the sabbath. The sabbath law was not, then, a stupid rule that could now be abolished (though some of the detailed sabbath regulations, as Jesus pointed out, had led to absurd extremes, so that you were allowed to pull a donkey out of a well on the sabbath, but not to heal the sick). It was a signpost whose purpose had now been accomplished. It was a marker of time pointing forward to the time when time would be fulfilled; and that was now happening.

Something new is happening; a new time has been launched; different things are now appropriate. Jesus has a sense of a rhythm to his work, a short rhythm in which he will launch God's kingdom, the God's-in-charge project, and complete it in the most shocking and dramatic symbolic act of all.

—Simply Jesus 137–38

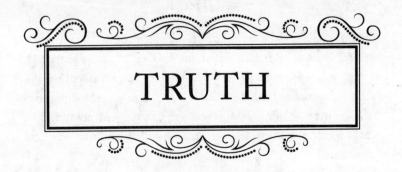

TRUTH

"So!" said Pilate. "You are a king, are you?"

"You're the one who's calling me a king," replied Jesus. "I was born for this; I've come into the world for this: to give evidence about the truth. Everyone who belongs to the truth listens to my voice."

"Truth!" said Pilate. "What's that?"

—John 18:37–38, *The Kingdom New Testament* 216

Truth Stands Before You

Though Pilate would never understand it, Truth was standing before him, the truth of creation rescued and renewed, truth turned into flesh, Truth loving his own who were in the world and now loving them to the uttermost, Truth leading the way through death and out the other side into God's new world, giving his followers the Spirit of truth, so that they could come after him and speak the creative truth that will bring that world into being. Part of the challenge of following Jesus is to learn the difficult, dangerous but beautiful art of speaking fresh, healing truth into the world that often still seems to be ruled by Caesar's agents.

—*Broken Signposts* 154

The Love of Truth

The sort of thing we could and should mean by "truth" will vary according to what we're talking about. If I want to go into town, it matters whether the person who has told me to take the number 53 bus is speaking the truth or not. But by no means all truth is of that kind, or testable in the same way. If there's any truth lying behind the quest for justice, it is that the world isn't meant to be morally chaotic; but what do we mean by "meant," and how would we know? If there's any truth in the thirst for spirituality, it could be simply that humans find satisfaction in exploring a "spiritual" dimension to their lives, or it could be that we are made for relationship with another Being who can only be known that way. And, talking of relationships, the "truth" of a relationship is in the relationship itself, in being "true to" one another, which is considerably more than (though presumably it includes) telling each other the truth about the number 53 bus. As for beauty, we cannot collapse "truth" into "beauty" without running the risk of deconstructing truth by pointing out, as we did earlier, the fragility and ambiguity of the beauty we know here and now.

What we mean by "know" is likewise in need of further investigation. To "know" the deeper kinds of truth we have been hinting at is much more like "knowing" a person—something which takes a long time, a lot of trust, and a good deal of trial and error—and less like "knowing" about the right bus to take into town. It's a kind of knowing in which the subject and the object are intertwined, so that you could never say that it was either purely subjective or purely objective.

One good word for this deeper and richer kind of knowing, the kind that goes with the deeper and richer kind of truth, is "love."

—*Simply Christian* 50–51

The Freedom in Seeking the Truth

"We deceive ourselves," says the old prayer book, "and the truth is not in us" (1 John 1:8). And yet we know that we are called to be truth-telling creatures. We certainly want everyone else to tell the truth, and we are cross when they don't—especially the politicians and businesspeople who cook the books for profit while the people they are supposed to be serving pick up the tab.

And yet we deceive ourselves very easily, including telling lies about telling lies ("It wasn't really a lie"). Our highly selective memories pick out and highlight the tiny number of facts from the millions available to back up the picture we have of ourselves, our lives, and our behavior. This can, of course, itself go a different route. People who are inclined to depression or feelings of guilt may only remember the "facts" that fuel their sense of despair and shame. Truth itself seems as far away as the farthest star. But we still gaze at it in wonder. It is a thing of beauty—or so it seems.

The Christian gospel, however, offers a deeper approach to truth than the world is able to provide. In a world where it is suggested that truth itself is an illusion—where truth itself seems like a broken signpost, leading us around in self-defeating circles—the followers of Jesus ought to respond that to proclaim the absence of truth is itself a lie. There is such a thing as truth, even if it's more elusive and strange than we sometimes imagine. What's more, it is the truth that will set us free—free to live as new creations and free to become truth tellers in our own right.

—Broken Signposts 104–5

Jesus's Exclusive Truth Claim

"I am the way," replies Jesus, "and the truth and the life!" (John 14:6). Some have read this as a Jewish way of saying "I am the true and living way," and that may be right as well. But the emphasis seems to me to fall equally on all three nouns, "way," "truth," and "life."

This extraordinary claim should not be heard so much within the sounding chamber of our modern world, where "truth" is the arrogant claim of the powerful. Truth here is the strange, gentle yet also powerful truth of new creation, the new creation that fulfills the old by taking the shame and death of the old into itself and overcoming it. Truth is the reality of love, divine love, Jesus's love, the Love made flesh.

This is not a claim to be measured alongside others, as though Jesus and half a dozen other teachers or leaders were being weighed against some arbitrary modern standard of "religion." Either Israel is the people of the creator God, or Israel is not; either Jesus is Israel's Messiah, or he is not. Either the creator God launched his new creation in and through Jesus as Israel's Messiah, or he did not. John's gospel is written to affirm all three propositions: Israel is God's people, Jesus is Israel's Messiah, and through him God has set in motion his new creation.

—Broken Signposts 143

Questions and Answers and Puzzles

There is a crescendo of questions to which in the end there can be only one answer.

Why are you speaking like this? Are you the one who is to come? Can anything good come out of Nazareth? What sign can you show us? Why does he eat with tax-collectors and sinners? Where did this man get all this wisdom? How can this man give us his flesh to eat? Who are you? Why do you not follow the traditions? Do the authorities think he's the Messiah? Can the Messiah come from Galilee? Why are you behaving unlawfully? Who then is this? Aren't we right to say that you're a Samaritan and have a demon? What do you say about him? By what right are you doing these things? Who is this Son of Man? Should we pay tribute to Caesar? And climactically: Are you the king of the Jews? What is truth? Where are you from? *Are you the Messiah, the son of the Blessed One?* Then finally, too late for answers, but not too late for irony: Aren't you the Messiah? Save yourself and us! If you're the Messiah, why don't you come down from that cross?

Whatever we say about Jesus, there can be no doubt that his actions and his teaching raised these questions wherever he went. And Jesus had his own questions. Who do you say I am? Do you believe in the Son of Man? Can you drink the cup I'm going to drink? How do the scribes say that the Messiah is David's son? Couldn't you keep watch with me for a single hour? And finally and horribly: My God, my God, why did you abandon me?

The answers come too in more or less equal profusion. But, like all the best answers to the hardest questions, they come themselves as a set of sparkling puzzles, as though to remind people both ancient and modern that the questions are questions precisely because something is going on that demands a collapse of categories, a breaking of boundaries, a widening of worldview to the point where the new thing, whatever it is, will make the sense it does. The reason there were so many questions, in both directions, was that—as historians have concluded for many years now—Jesus fitted no ready-made categories.

—*Simply Jesus* 167–68

God's Truth

So what might be said, from different angles, about the reasons for the surprising long-term success of Paul's work? To go a step further, helping us to get a sense of the significance of the apostle's work, let's ask: How might Paul himself assess this success if he could have seen it?

Paul would probably begin with a theological answer. There is One God, and this God has overcome the powers of darkness through his son; we should expect that by his spirit he will cause the light of the knowledge of his glory to spread throughout the world—through the faithful, suffering, and prayerful witness of Jesus's followers. Or, to put it another way, the One God has already built his new Temple, his new *microcosmos;* the Jew-plus-Gentile church is the place where the divine spirit already lives in our midst, already reveals his glory as a sign of what will happen one day throughout the whole world. So, sooner or later, this movement is bound to thrive.

—*Paul: A Biography* 414–15

The Necessary Self-Sacrificing Victory

Part of John's meaning of the cross is that it is not only what happens, purely pragmatically, when God's kingdom challenges Caesar's kingdom. It is also *what has to happen* if God's kingdom, which makes its way (as Jesus insists) by nonviolence rather than by violence, is to win the day. This is the "truth" to which Jesus has come to bear witness, the "truth" for which Pilate's worldview has no possible space (18:38). It is at once exemplified, dramatically, by Jesus taking the place of Barabbas the brigand (18:38–40). This is the "truth" to which Jesus bears witness—the truth of a kingdom accomplished by the innocent dying in place of the guilty.

—*How God Became King* 230

We Can *Change the World*

I am convinced that the climate of skepticism, which for the last two hundred years has made it unfashionable and even embarrassing to suggest that Jesus's resurrection really happened, was never and is not now itself a neutral thing, sociologically or politically. The intellectual coup d'état by which the Enlightenment convinced so many that "we now know that dead people don't rise," as though this was a modern discovery rather than simply the reaffirmation of what Homer and Aeschylus had taken for granted, goes hand in hand with the Enlightenment's other proposals, not least that we have now come of age, that God can be kicked upstairs, that we can get on with running the world however we want to, carving it up to our advantage without outside interference. To that extent, the totalitarianisms of the last century were simply among the varied manifestations of a larger totalitarianism of thought and culture against which postmodernity has now, and rightly in my view, rebelled.

Who, after all, was it who didn't want the dead to be raised? Not simply the intellectually timid or the rationalists. It was, and is, those in power, the social and intellectual tyrants and bullies; the Caesars who would be threatened by a Lord of the world who had defeated the tyrant's last weapon, death itself; the Herods who would be horrified at the postmortem validation of the true King of the Jews. *And this is the point where believing in the resurrection of Jesus suddenly ceases to be a matter of inquiring about an odd event in the first century and becomes a matter of rediscovering hope in the twenty-first century.* Hope is what you get when you suddenly realize that a different worldview is possible, a worldview in which the rich, the powerful, and the unscrupulous do not after all have the last word. The same worldview shift that is demanded by the resurrection of Jesus is the shift that will enable us to transform the world.

—Surprised by Hope 74–75

We Have a New Ruler, so Watch What Happens Next

When Jesus went around saying that God was now in charge, he wasn't walking (as it were) into virgin territory. He wasn't making his announcement in a vacuum. Imagine what it would be like, in Britain or the United States today, if, without an election or any other official mechanism for changing the government, someone were to go on national radio and television and announce that there was now a new prime minister or president. "From today onward," says the announcer, "we have a new ruler! We're under new government! It's all going to be different!" That's not only exciting talk. It's fighting talk. It's treason! It's sedition! By what right is this man saying this? How does he think he'll get away with it? What exactly does he mean, anyway? An announcement like this isn't simply a proclamation. *It's the start of a campaign.* When a regime is already in power and is simply transferring that power to the next person in line, you just announce that it's happening. But if you make that announcement while someone else appears to be in charge, you are saying, in effect, "The campaign starts here."

So what *did* Jesus mean? What sort of a campaign could this have been? Those were the questions, we can be sure, in his hearers' minds. Frustratingly, for us and for them, Jesus's answer to, "What exactly does he mean?" seems to have been partly, "Wait and see." But in the meantime he was still demonstrating what it meant, up close and personal. His healings and celebrations were part of the meaning of God becoming king. This is what it looked like.

—*Simply Jesus* 69

The Knowing Subject and the Fear of the Lord

There are three steps to biblical wisdom. They are all summarized in a much-repeated shorthand that may sound forbidding to us: "The fear of the Lord," say the writers, "is the beginning of wisdom" (Ps. 111:10). Our problem with that is that we've forgotten who "the Lord" is, mistaking him for a distant, faceless bureaucrat.

Consequently, we've forgotten that fear does not mean a cringing, nervous, slavish state, but rather the reverence and awe properly due the creator and sustainer of all things. In other words, just as the concept of faith changes with its object—if you put your faith in a being rather like an amorphous and characterless gas, it will be a very different thing from a faith placed in the father of Jesus Christ—so fear changes depending on whether the God you imagine is a celestial bully or the God of faithful love. My point is this: in the biblical traditions and the later traditions that reflect them, the human subject is imagined not as a lonely, isolated individual who can work things out for himself (it was always a "he"), but as someone who is located in relation to three other coordinates.

First, the knowing subject is made in the image of the creator, meaning that the subject is called to *reflect* the creator's wisdom and care into the world and to reflect the praises of creation back to the creator.

Second, the knowing that goes with wisdom in the biblical sense sees the object of study not as an isolated entity to be manipulated or exploited but as part of a much larger world of interlocking connections and mutual relationships.

Third, the knower never knows in isolation. True wisdom is both bold and humble. It is never afraid to say what it thinks it has seen but always covets other angles of vision.

—*Surprised by Scripture* 157–58

Whose Authority?

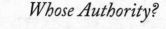

The risen Jesus, at the end of Matthew's gospel, does not say, "All authority in heaven and on earth is given to the books you are all going to write," but "All authority in heaven and on earth is given to me" (28:18). This ought to tell us, precisely if we are taking the Bible itself as seriously as we should, that we need to think carefully what it might mean to think that the authority of Jesus is somehow exercised through the Bible.

—*Scripture and the Authority of God* xi

Read in Context

We must be committed to a *totally contextual* reading of scripture. Each word must be understood within its own verse, each verse within its own chapter, each chapter within its own book, and each book within its own historical, cultural, and indeed canonical setting. All scripture is "culturally conditioned." It is naive to pretend that some parts are not, and can therefore be treated as in some sense "primary" or "universal," while other parts are, and can therefore safely be set aside.

—*Scripture and the Authority of God* 128

The Work to Better Understand Scripture Never Stops

What does it mean, within this setting, to appeal to "the authority of scripture"? This phrase is sometimes used as a way of saying, "A plague on all your scholarship; we just believe the Bible." This is simply unsustainable. Without scholars to provide Greek lexicons and translations based on them, few today could read the New Testament. Without scholarship to explain the world of the first century, few today could begin to understand it (as often becomes painfully evident when people without such explanations try to read it aloud, let alone expound it).

Scholarship of some sort is always assumed; what the protest often means, unfortunately, is that the speakers prefer the scholarship implicit in their early training, which is now simply taken for granted as common knowledge, to the bother of having to wake up mentally and think fresh thoughts. Again and again, such older scholarship, and such older traditions of reading, turn out to be flawed or in need of supplementing. Today's and tomorrow's will be just the same, of course, but this does not absolve us from constantly trying to do better, from the never-ending attempt to understand scripture more fully.

It is my own experience that such attempts regularly result in real advances (measured not least in terms of the deep and many-sided sense that is made of the text), and that even making the effort almost always results in fresh pastoral and homiletic insights. To affirm "the authority of scripture" is precisely *not* to say, "We know what scripture means and don't need to raise any more questions." It is always a way of saying that the church in each generation must make fresh and rejuvenated efforts to understand scripture more fully and live by it more thoroughly, even if that means cutting across cherished traditions.

—*Scripture and the Authority of God* 90–91

Understanding Scripture's
Authority Through the Trinity

The gospel by which individuals come to personal faith, and so to that radical transformation of life spoken of so often in the New Testament, is the personalizing of the larger challenge just mentioned: the call to every child, woman, and man to submit in faith to the lordship of the crucified and risen Jesus and so to become, through baptism and membership in the body of Christ, a living, breathing anticipation of the final new creation itself (see Gal. 6:15; 2 Cor. 5:17). The power of God, which acts through the gospel message to accomplish this end, is regularly unleashed, as we saw, through the combination of the power of the Spirit and the spoken or written word; and, throughout the history of the Christian mission, that word is normally the word of scripture, read, preached, explained, and applied.

"The authority of scripture" refers not least to God's work *through* scripture to reveal Jesus, to speak in life-changing power to the hearts and minds of individuals, and to transform them by the Spirit's healing love. Though this can happen in the supposed "desert island" situation, where an individual reads the Bible all alone, it normally comes about through the work of God's people, from those who translated and published the Bible itself (even on a desert island, one is dependent on others!) to those who, like Philip with the Ethiopian eunuch in Acts 8, helped others to understand it and apply it to their own lives.

"The authority of scripture" thus makes the sense it does within the work of God's kingdom, at every level from the cosmic and political through to the personal. Only when that all-inclusive authority is put in first place might we discover what the phrase could

mean in terms of the ordering of the church's own life to enable it
to be the agent of God's mission, and in terms of its challenge to
every Christian to live under the authority of God in all depart-
ments of life.

—Scripture and the Authority of God 116–17

The Church Goes to Work with the Bible in Its Hand, Its Head, and Its Heart

The shorthand phrase "the authority of scripture," when unpacked,
offers a picture of God's sovereign and saving plan for the entire
cosmos, dramatically inaugurated by Jesus himself, and now to be
implemented through the Spirit-led life of the church *precisely as the
scripture-reading community.* "Reading" in that last phrase is itself a
shorthand for a whole complex of tasks to which we shall return.
But the emphasis I want to insist on is that we discover what the
shape and the inner life of the church ought to be only when we
look first at the church's mission, and that we discover what the
church's mission is only when we look first at God's purpose for
the entire world, as indicated in, for instance, Genesis 1–2, Genesis 12, Isaiah 40–55, Romans 8, 1 Corinthians 15, Ephesians 1 and
Revelation 21–22. We read scripture in order to be refreshed in our
memory and understanding of the story within which we ourselves
are actors, to be reminded where it has come from and where it is
going to, and hence what our own part within it ought to be.

This means that "the authority of scripture" is most truly put
into operation as the church goes to work in the world on behalf of
the gospel, the good news that in Jesus Christ the living God has

defeated the powers of evil and begun the work of new creation. It
is with the Bible in its hand, its head, and its heart—not merely
with the newspaper and the latest political fashion or scheme—
that the church can go to work in the world, confident that Jesus
is Lord and Caesar is not. The wisdom commended in scripture
itself (e.g., Col. 4:5–6; 1 Pet. 3:15) suggests that we will not go
about this work simply by telling people what the Bible says. In
the power and wisdom of the Spirit, we must so understand the
priorities of the gospel and the way in which they work to pull
down strongholds (2 Cor. 10:3–6) that we can articulate for ourselves, addressing particular contexts and settings, the challenge
of the God who loves the world so much that he longs to rescue
it from folly, oppression, and wickedness. Scripture's authority is
thus seen to best advantage in its formation of the mind of the
church, and its stiffening of our resolve, as we work to implement
the resurrection of Jesus, and so to anticipate the day when God
will make all things new, and justice, joy, and peace will triumph
(Eph. 1:3–23).

—*Scripture and the Authority of God* 114–15

Scripture, Tradition, Reason, and Experience

"Scripture, tradition, and reason" were never the same *kind* of
thing. The image of the stool with three matching legs is itself misleading. They are not so much like apples, pears, and oranges as
like apples, elephants, and screwdrivers. As we have seen, a long
line of theologians from Aquinas through Hooker to many writers
today would insist that "tradition" is the legacy of what the church

has said when reflecting on scripture, and "reason" is the rule of discourse by which such reflection is saved from random nonsense and integrated into a holistic view of God and the world. This too, however, can only be part of the story, and might imply a more solid and fixed form for "tradition" and "reason" than the story of the church warrants.

To change the picture, scripture, tradition, and reason are not like three different bookshelves, each of which can be ransacked for answers to key questions. Rather, scripture is the bookshelf; tradition is the memory of what people in the house have read and understood (or perhaps misunderstood) from that shelf; and reason is the set of spectacles that people wear in order to make sense of what they read—though, worryingly, the spectacles have varied over time, and there are signs that some readers, using the "reason" available to them, have severely distorted the texts they were reading. "Experience" is something different again, referring to the effect on readers of what they read, and/or the worldview, the life experience, the political circumstances, and so on, within which that reading takes place.

This can be seen—in "experience"!—by the chaos that results if "experience" is allowed to be the final arbiter. Whether in official statistics or in anecdotal evidence, the "experience" of Christians, and of everyone else for that matter, always and inevitably comes up with several simultaneous and incompatible stories. "Experience" is far too slippery for the concept to stand any chance of providing a stable basis sufficient to serve as an "authority," unless what is meant is that, as the book of Judges wryly puts it, everyone should simply do that which is right in their own eyes. And that, of course, means that there is no authority at all. Indeed, the stress on "experience" has contributed materially to that form of pluralism, verging on anarchy, which we now see across the Western world.

—*Scripture and the Authority of God* 101–2

Theology Is the Backbone of a Healthy Church

Although the thinkers were seldom the people who made the gospel spread—that accolade belongs to the local communities that were living out the gospel imperatives, often under the threat or the reality of persecution—the church would not have survived or thrived without their work. Theology is the backbone of a healthy church. The body still needs limbs and organs, joints and tissue. Paul, with his own image of the Messiah's body, would have been the first to insist on that. But without a backbone the body will not survive. The survival and flourishing of the church of subsequent centuries look back to Paul's achievement in teaching his followers not only what to think, but how to think. He knew only too well what that would cost, but he believed it was the genuinely human way, a way that would win out precisely by the power of that genuine humanness.

—*Paul: A Biography* 428–29

Easter Hope Is Different from Constant Progress and Constant Decay

The early Christians did not believe in progress. They did not think the world was getting better and better under its own steam—or even under the steady influence of God. They knew God had to do something fresh to put it to rights.

But neither did they believe that the world was getting worse and worse and that their task was to escape it altogether. They were not dualists.

Since most people who think about these things today tend toward one or other of those two points of view, it comes as something of a surprise to discover that the early Christians held a quite different view. They believed that God was going to do for the whole cosmos what he had done for Jesus at Easter.

—Surprised by Hope 93

Confronting Big Lies

In the light of that larger story, truth must be told that will confront lies and hold them up to shame. Only so will people be set free from the grip of the lie. But how? The greatest crimes of the twentieth century—the Turkish massacre of Armenians, the Nazi massacre of Jews, and Pol Pot's massacre of his political opponents and anyone else in the way—were able to happen because people who knew about them didn't speak up. Many politicians have discovered that people will detect and confront a small lie, but if you tell a really big lie (think of Hitler telling the German people that Winston Churchill was aiming at world domination), people will either not notice or assume it must somehow be true, despite appearances.

So Jesus confronts his opponents as they are confronting him. (Their response, not for the first time, is to accuse him of being demon-possessed.) The truth he is telling simply won't fit into their models of how the world works. They are frantically shoring up the world the way they see it.

The sign that their agenda is driven by the dark anticreation power is that they too want to use violence. John 8 begins with the threat to stone the adulterous woman, and it ends with the attempt to stone Jesus (8:59). This is all part of the buildup to the climax of the gospel, when again the question of truth and falsehood stands right beside the question of life and death. Gradually the point emerges. *The reason truth is such a paradox in the present time is that the ultimate truth is the new creation, which fulfills the present creation by abolishing death, which has corrupted it.* No wonder the forces of darkness, of anticreation, the diabolical, accusing forces, shriek and snarl and throw stones.

—*Broken Signposts* 148

The Quest for Truth

I once heard a great contemporary scientist say that whether we are looking into a microscope at the smallest objects we can discern, or gazing through a telescope at the vast recesses of outer space, the most interesting thing in the world remains that which is two inches or so on the near side of the lens—in other words, the human brain, including mind, imagination, memory, will, personality, and the thousand other things which we think of as separate faculties but which all, in their different ways, interlock as functions of our complex personal identity. We should expect the world and our relation to it to be at least as complex as we are. If there is a God, we should expect such a being to be at least as complex again.

I say this because people often grumble as soon as a discussion about the meaning of human life, or the possibility of God, moves away from quite simple ideas and becomes more complicated. Any world in which there are such things as music and sex, laughter and tears, mountains and mathematics, eagles and earthworms, statues and symphonies, and snowflakes and sunsets—and in which we humans find ourselves in the middle of it all—is bound to be a world in which the quest for truth, for reality, for what we can be sure of, is infinitely more complicated than simple yes-and-no questions will allow. There is appropriate complexity along with appropriate simplicity. The more we learn, the more we discover that we humans are fantastically complicated creatures. Yet, on the other hand, human life is full of moments when we know that things are also very, very simple.

Think about it. The moment of birth; the moment of death; the joy of love; the discovery of vocation; the onset of life-threatening illness; the overwhelming pain and anger that sometimes sweep us off our feet. At such times, the multiple complexities of our human-ness gather themselves together and form one simple great excla-mation mark, or (as it may be) one simple great question mark—a shout of joy or a cry of pain, a burst of laughter or a bursting into tears. Suddenly, the rich harmony of our genetic package seems to sing in unison, and say, for good or ill, *This is it.*

We honor and celebrate our complexity and our simplicity by continually doing five things. We tell stories. We act out rituals. We create beauty. We work in communities. We think out beliefs. In and through all these things run the threads of love and pain, fear and faith, worship and doubt, the quest for justice, the thirst for spirituality, and the promise and problem of human relation-ship. And if there's any such thing as "truth," in some absolute sense, it must relate to, and make sense of, all this and more.

—*Simply Christian* 48–49

Stop Giving Nineteenth-Century Answers to Sixteenth-Century Questions

The root problem we face as Christians is that in articulating a Christian vision of the cosmos the way we want to do, we find ourselves hamstrung because it is assumed that to be Christian is to be anti-intellectual, antiscience, obscurantist, and so forth. This constitutes a wake-up call to us in this form: though the Western tradition and particularly the Protestant and evangelical traditions have claimed to be based on the Bible and rooted in scripture, they have by and large developed long-lasting and subtle strategies for not listening to what the Bible is, in fact, saying. We must stop giving nineteenth-century answers to sixteenth-century questions and try to give twenty-first-century answers to first-century questions. Our concern is for the truth and beyond that for our love of the God of truth and our strong, biblically rooted sense that this God calls us to celebrate the wonder of his creation and to work for his glory within it.

—Surprised by Scripture 26

When Was the Turning Point of History?

The reason the Enlightenment has taught us to trash our own history, to say that Christianity is part of the problem, is that it has had a rival eschatology to promote. It couldn't allow Christianity to claim that world history turned its great corner when Jesus of Nazareth died and rose again, because it wanted to claim that world history turned its great corner *in Europe in the eighteenth century*. "All that went before," it says, "is superstition and mumbo-jumbo. We have now seen the great light, and our modern science, technology, philosophy, and politics have ushered in the new order of the ages." That was believed and expounded in America and France, and it has soaked into our popular culture and imagination. (George Washington contrasted the "gloomy age of ignorance and superstition" up to that point with the new epoch ushered in by the great revolutions of the late eighteenth century, when "the rights of mankind were better understood and more clearly defined.")

So of course Christianity is reduced from an eschatology ("This is where history was meant to be going, despite appearances!") to a religion ("here is a way of being spiritual"), because world history can't have *two* great turning points. If the enlightenment is the great, dramatic, all-important corner of world history, Jesus can't have been. He is still wanted on board, of course, as a figure through whom people can try to approach the incomprehensible mystery of the "divine" and as a teacher of moral truths that might, if applied, actually strengthen the fabric of the brave new post-enlightenment society. But when Christianity is made "just a religion," it first muzzles and then silences altogether the message the gospels were eager to get across. When that happens, the gospel message is substantially neutralized as a force in the world beyond the realm of private spirituality and an escapist heaven. That, indeed, was the intention. And the churches have, by and large, gone along for the ride.

—*How God Became King* 163–64

Faith, History, and Science

What I am suggesting is that faith in Jesus risen from the dead *transcends but includes* what we call history and what we call science. Faith of this sort is not blind belief that rejects all history and science. Nor is it simply—which would be much safer!—a belief that inhabits a totally different sphere, discontinuous from either, in a separate watertight compartment. Rather, this kind of faith, which is like all modes of knowledge defined by the nature of its object, is faith in the creator God, the God who has promised to put all things to rights at the end, the God who (as the sharp point where those two come together) has raised Jesus from the dead *within* history, leaving, as I said, evidence that demands an explanation from the scientist as well as anybody else. Insofar as I understand scientific method, when something turns up that doesn't fit the paradigm you're working with, one option at least, perhaps when all others have failed, is to change the paradigm, not to exclude everything you've known to that point but to include it within a larger whole. That is, if you like, the Thomas challenge.

If Thomas represents an epistemology of faith, which transcends but also includes historical and scientific knowing, we might suggest that Paul represents at this point an epistemology of hope. In 1 Corinthians 15, he sketches his argument that there will be a future resurrection, as part of God's new creation, the redemption of the entire cosmos as in Romans 8. Hope, for the Christian, is not wishful thinking or mere blind optimism. It is a mode of knowing, a mode within which new things are possible, options are not shut down, and new creation can happen.

—*Surprised by Scripture* 61

Take the Risk!

That is why, although the historical arguments for Jesus's bodily resurrection are truly strong, we must never suppose that they will do more than bring people to the questions faced by Thomas and Peter, the questions of faith and love. We cannot use a supposedly objective historical epistemology as the ultimate ground for the truth of Easter. To do so would be to be like someone who lit a candle to see whether the sun had risen. What the candles of historical scholarship will do is show that the room has been disturbed, that it doesn't look like it did last night, and that would-be normal explanations for this won't do. Maybe, we think after the historical arguments have done their work, morning has come and the world has woken up. But to find out whether this is so, we must take the risk and open the curtains to the rising sun. When we do so, we won't rely on candles anymore, not because we don't believe in evidence and argument, not because we don't believe in history or science, but because they will have been overtaken by the larger reality from which they borrow, to which they point, and in which they will find a new and larger home. All knowing is a gift from God, historical and scientific knowing no less than that of faith, hope, and love; but the greatest of these is love.

—*Surprised by Scripture* 63

The Truth of Genesis 1

Our modern culture has become so hung up on how to interpret the six days of Genesis 1 that it has forgotten three things about that chapter. First, it has forgotten that the sixfold sequence was a way, in that culture, of describing the construction of a *temple:* the creation was designed to be a place where the living God would dwell. The two spheres of created order, called in the Bible "heaven" and "earth," were not separate, detached from one another, as in Epicureanism ancient and modern. Nor was it the case that heaven was good and earth bad, as in Platonism; nor was earth important and heaven irrelevant, as in secularism. Heaven and earth were the twin halves of the good creation, made to overlap and interlock, so that the God who lived in heaven would also be present, though mysteriously so, here on earth, and the dwellers on earth would always be within arm's length of heaven. The whole world, heaven and earth together, was the diverse-but-united home where God and his creatures would live in harmony.

The second thing people forget about creation, and about the worldview it gives us, is that instead of a man-made temple with the statue of a god inside it, we have a heaven-and-earth world with the image of God within it—in other words, with male and female human beings as the way in which the invisible God becomes present to his world, the sovereign God becomes the caretaker, the "taking-care-person," the steward of his world. This at once removes human beings from any possibility of being mere detached, fly-on-the-wall observers, such as is often dreamed of in the quest for objective science, and they become instead responsible participants in God's plans for his world. This has enormously significant consequences for study of the natural world. We are indeed summoned, as human beings, to become as familiar as we can, each through his or her own gifts, with God's world. But this is never so that we can report back to one another on the curious things we have discovered. It is so that we can worship God the creator and be wise stewards of his world.

But there is a third thing as well. Genesis offers us, right up front, not one creation story but two. Genesis 1 and 2 are not strictly compatible—at least, not if you try to take them as left-brain, rationalistic narratives about what happened. They are not, and are not intended to be, what we would call scientific accounts. Part of the point of there being two of them is to alert the reader—and sadly many readers in the last two centuries have not taken the hint!—to the fact that they are poetic images, narratives replete with metaphor, stories designed to help us grasp with our right brains what creation is *for*.

—*Surprised by Scripture* 141–42

Truth Telling by Truthfully Telling the Story of Jesus

Jesus's followers will be commissioned to be people of the truth. This will be immensely costly for them, as it was for him. But they will be directed into this vocation by the Spirit himself, now designated precisely as "the spirit of truth."

This new Spirit, Jesus's own Spirit, will come and enable them to tell the truth, particularly to tell the world the truth about Jesus himself, the truth that doesn't fit into the old world but that makes ultimate, radical, and renewing sense of that old world.

In other words, *truth itself will come to birth as Jesus's followers speak the words that bring the new creation into existence.* This is the exciting new vocation that makes sense of our puzzles about truth in philosophy and culture. The truth of new creation, which flows outward from the truth of Jesus, his kingdom, his death, and his resurrection, makes its way not least through the truth telling of Jesus's followers. This cannot collapse back into the rationalism or modernism of some Christian expressions of "truth," the brittle attempts to "prove" the gospel through arguments that (apparently) only a fool would deny. What Jesus is talking about will include the telling of his own story, of course, but that storytelling, like Jesus's own storytelling, will be the inner explanation for the larger goal of truth *living*, bringing the healing and hope of new creation in all directions.

This means, as we would have guessed from the commissioning in John 20:19–23, that the Spirit will enable Jesus's followers to be for the world what Jesus was for Israel. And this in turn will mean that, far from leaving behind the story of who precisely he was and what he did in his public career, that must remain central. At the heart of the church's truth telling will be its true telling of the story of Jesus himself. The Spirit will help the church to go on telling this story and telling it properly.

And this is in keeping with the prayer Jesus prays at the conclusion of the discourses. *Set them apart for yourself in the truth; your word is truth* (17:15–19).

The word for "set apart" is the same as the word for "sanctify"; here Jesus's followers are being set apart for God's special use, like the vessels in the Tabernacle.

—*Broken Signposts* 151–53

LENT

We implore people on the Messiah's behalf to be reconciled to God. The Messiah did not know sin, but God made him to be sin on our behalf, so that in him we might embody God's faithfulness to the covenant.

So, as we work together with God, we appeal to you in particular: when you accept God's grace, don't let it go to waste! This is what he says: I listened to you when the time was right; I came to your aid on the day of salvation. Look! The right time is now! Look! The day of salvation is here!

We put no obstacles in anybody's way, so that nobody will say abusive things about our ministry. Instead, we recommend ourselves as God's servants: with much patience, with sufferings, difficulties, hardships, beatings, imprisonments, riots, hard work, sleepless nights, going without food, with purity, knowledge, great-heartedness, kindness, the holy spirit, genuine love, by speaking the truth, by God's power, with weapons for God's faithful work in left and right hand alike, through glory and shame, through slander and praise; as deceivers, and yet true; as unknown, yet very well known; as dying, and look—we are alive; as punished, yet not killed; as sad, yet always celebrating; as poor, yet bringing riches to many; as having nothing, yet possessing everything.

—2 Corinthians 5:20b–6:10, *The Kingdom New Testament* 371

The Cost of Discipleship

When I was growing up, all the local towns and villages had their own war memorials from World Wars I and II. I knew many families (including my own) who had lost one, two, or more members in those conflicts, and we solemnly remembered them year after year. In ancient Galilee, even without stone memorials to the rebels who had died, the towns and villages in which Jesus announced God's kingdom would have had similar memories of people known, loved, and lost to Roman brutality. When he told his followers to pick up their own crosses and follow him, they would not have heard this as a metaphor.

—*The Day the Revolution Began* 58

The Line Between Good and Evil
Runs Down the Middle of Each of Us

The line between good and evil does not lie between "us" and "them," between the West and the rest, between Left and Right, between rich and poor. That fateful line runs down the middle of each of us, every human society, every individual. This is not to say that all humans, and all societies, are equally good or bad; far from it. Merely that we are all infected and that all easy attempts to see the problem in terms of "us" and "them" are fatally flawed.

—*Surprised by Scripture* 115

The Nailed Vocation of
Crucifixion Revolutionaries

Those who are working for justice and beauty, just like those who are working to bring a fresh new articulation of the good news so that people may believe, must themselves have the same things etched, perhaps nailed, into their own lives. It will be painful. That is part of the point, not that we seek the pain, but that we seek to follow Jesus. Holiness and mission are two sides of the same coin. Both involve bringing the reign of Jesus to bear in places where up to now the powers have held sway. The powers will not give in without a fight. But, exactly as with Jesus himself and exactly as he told his first followers, the fight itself and the suffering it involves (of whatever sort) are not incidental. The insight at the heart of Jesus's own vocation was that suffering would not simply be the dark tunnel through which Israel would pass to God's future. It would somehow be the means by which that future would be achieved. Most Christians today do not see things like this. Once we realize that we are part of the revolutionary movement that began at the cross, it may become clear once again, as it was to the first generation of Jesus's followers.

—*The Day the Revolution Began* 406

Identifying Evil

Without the perspective that sees evil as a dark force that stands *behind* human reality, the issue of "good" and "bad" in our world is easy to decipher. It is fatally easy, and I mean fatally easy, to typecast "people like us" as basically good and "people like them" as basically evil. This is a danger we in our day should be aware of, after the disastrous attempts by some Western leaders to speak about an "axis of evil" and then to go to war to obliterate it. We turn ourselves into angels and "the other lot" into demons; we "demonize" our opponents. This is a convenient tool for avoiding having to think, but it is disastrous for both our thinking and our behavior.

But when you take seriously the existence and malevolence of nonhuman forces that are capable of using "us" as well as "them" in the service of evil, the focus shifts. As the hazy and shadowy realities come into view, what we thought was clear and straightforward becomes blurred. Life becomes more complex, but arguably more realistic. The traditional lines of friend and foe are not so easy to draw. You can no longer assume that "that lot" are simply agents of the devil and "this lot"—us and our friends—are automatically on God's side. If there is an enemy at work, it is a subtle, cunning enemy, much too clever to allow itself to be identified simply with one person, one group, or one nation. Only twice in the gospel story does Jesus address "the satan" directly by that title: once when rebuking him in the temptation narrative (Matt. 4:10), and again when he is rebuking his closest associate (Mark 8:33) for resisting God's strange plan. The line between good and evil is clear at the level of God, on the one hand, and the satan, on the other. It is much, much less clear as it passes through human beings, individually and collectively.

This is precisely the kind of redefinition that was going on in Jesus's Nazareth manifesto. Traditional enemies were suddenly brought, at least in principle, within the reach of the blessing of God's great jubilee. And traditional friends—those who might have thought that they were automatically on the right side—had to be looked at again. Perhaps one can no longer simply identify "our people" as on the side of the angels and "those people" as agents of the satan. That's why Jesus was run out of town and nearly killed. He had suggested that foes could become friends and by implication was warning that the "good people"—Israel as the people of God—might become enemies. Ironically, his own townsfolk proceeded to prove the point by their reaction.

—Simply Jesus 122–23

A Suffering That Transforms

The gospel story of Jesus seen as the launching of the renewed people of God includes, as a central element, the incomprehension, failure, and rebellion of that people, until they are stunned into new faith by the resurrection and energized into new obedience by the Spirit. The themes of kingdom and cross are not simply theological themes that the disciples have to learn, abstract ideas on their way to constituting a creedal "orthodoxy." They are the pattern of their life, both as they follow Jesus around Galilee, despite not understanding what he's up to, and as they then follow him, in the power of the Spirit, to the ends of the earth.

We should not be surprised, then—though many in the church down through the years would be very surprised to hear this—that the early Christians understood their vocation as Jesus's followers to include, as a central and load-bearing element, their own suffering, misunderstanding, and likely death. It isn't just that, as followers of a misunderstood Messiah, they themselves would naturally expect misunderstanding and persecution, though that is certainly part of it. It is, rather—and it will take the later books of the New Testament and indeed much of the Christian writing of the second century to explore this—that the suffering of Jesus's followers is actually, like Jesus's own suffering, not just the inevitable accompaniment to the accomplishing of the divine purpose, but actually itself part of the *means* by which that purpose is to be fulfilled.

—*How God Became King* 198–99

Temptation and Handing Over Your God-Given Power

Holiness will always be shaped by the cross. Paul speaks of "putting to death" the impulses and deeds that bubble up from within us and distort our genuine human vocation. His letters are full of sharp practical counsel of this sort. Financial corruption, sexual immorality, evil and malicious speaking—all must be killed off (see, for instance, Col. 3:1–11). Easier said than done, of course, but once more the victory of the cross is central. And note carefully: this is not a matter of saying, "Now that you're a Christian, you must follow the rules." Rules matter, but they matter because they are one of the guardrails within the much larger vocation, to worship the true God and work for his kingdom.

Every time you are tempted to sin, you are being asked to hand over to some alien force a little bit of your own God-given power, which is supposed to be exercised over yourself, your life, and the parts of the world you touch. You are being drawn into the sphere in which some "power" is at work, under the control of the satan. At that moment, you are also being called (did you but know it) to exercise your true power as a genuine human being, to practice your vocation as part of the royal priesthood. Sin is a distraction from our true tasks, a distortion (at best) of our true vocation. It keeps the powers in power. Resisting it—especially when we have allowed habit to take us effortlessly in that direction—will be difficult, sometimes painful, sometimes profoundly depressing. That is part of taking up the cross.

—The Day the Revolution Began 403–4

What Is Success?

Yes, it will mean taking up our own cross. Jesus warned us of exactly that (Mark 8:34–38). It will mean denying ourselves—a phrase we used to hear in hymns and sermons, but for some reason don't hear quite so much today. How remarkable it is that the Western church so easily embraces self-discovery, self-fulfillment, and self-realization as though they were the heart of the "gospel"—as though Mark 8 didn't exist! Yes, following Jesus will mean disappointment, failure, frustration, muddle, misunderstanding, pain, and sorrow—and those are just the "first-world problems." As I have already said, some Christians, even while I have been working on this book, have been beheaded for their faith; others have seen their homes bombed, their livelihoods taken away, their health ruined. Their witness is extraordinary, and we in the comfortable West can only ponder the ways in which our own unseen compromises—perhaps because of our platonic eschatology—have shielded us from the worst things that are happening to our true family only a short plane ride away.

But the first generations of Christians, with the New Testament writers at their head, would remind us that these are not simply horrible things that may happen to us despite our belief in the victory of Jesus. They are things that may come, in different ways and at different times, because this is how the kingdom comes. We are always tempted to turn the kingdom of God into the instrument of our own worldly "success" or "comfort." Some in our own day have forgotten the warnings of 1 Timothy 6:5–10, warnings against attempting to use the gospel as a way to get rich. Many have ignored the fact that for every word of Jesus against sins of the body there are a dozen against sins of the bank-book. Yes, there are also promises of great blessings. There will be seasons of apparent "success" and times of great "comfort." But both those words get redefined by the gospel, redefined according to the revolutionary victory won on the cross. And this applies as much to ministry in the church as it does to individual lives. It is all too easy to equate "success" with increasing congregations and growing budgets. Church history teaches otherwise.

—*The Day the Revolution Began* 409–10

The Prayer That Invites You to
Look Beyond Your Concerns

> May your kingdom come,
> May your will be done
> As in heaven, so on earth.
> (Matt. 6:10)

The traditional words go so well with everything Jesus did and said—everything Jesus *was*—that simply to repeat them appears to sum up his whole agenda. "Your kingdom come! Your will be done, on earth as in heaven!" And with this, we sense—if we have our wits about us—that we have turned a corner. Up to this point, working back through the prayer, we have focused on our own needs. Now we look up and see a larger plan. *It's time for God to become king—here and now.*

Granted, the theme of God's kingdom was also often seen by people in Jesus's day as being specifically about their own needs. Many Jews of Jesus's time, as we have seen, spoke of God becoming king to refer to social and political liberation from Rome, establishment of a free and independent Jewish state, and peace and prosperity for all God's people. Some might even have envisaged the pagan nations coming to learn about this remarkable, unique God; this was important in some biblical prophecies. Thus many Jews of Jesus's day had, as it were, their own meaning for "give us bread" (we want peace and prosperity), "forgive us our sins" (whatever we did to deserve this mess, please wipe it out), "don't test us to breaking point" (if things go on this way, we're all doomed), and "help!" (we're in a mess—do something!). When they heard people talking about God's kingdom, they had various natural ways of understanding this, mainly in terms of the later petitions in the prayer. We often find ourselves doing the same if we're not careful.

God's kingdom does indeed address all these issues. But the way Jesus announced God's kingdom—and the way he both *enacted* and *explained* it—meant that he was telling people to look up, beyond their concerns, beyond the way they thought everything ought to work out. This is why his good news both was and wasn't what people expected or hoped for. That's the same for us, too. That is why Jesus told his followers that if they wanted to continue in his company, they had to "take up their cross and follow him," and that only those who were prepared to lose their lives would actually save them.

—*Simply Good News* 161–62

Set Aside What You Normally Assume for Human Flourishing

The deepest revolution in virtue that we find at the heart of the gospel—and of the gospels—is found just here. Jesus shouldered the burden, not so much of "sin" in the abstract, in a kind of transaction which took place away from the actual events that led to his death, but rather of the actual weight—the power and results—of human sin and rebellion, the accumulation of the actual human pride, sin, folly, and shame that, at that moment in history, concentrated themselves in the arrogance of Rome, the self-seeking of the Jewish leaders, and the distorted dreams of the Jewish revolutionaries—and, indeed, the failures of Jesus's own followers. I have quoted before, and I quote here again, a matchless sentence from my teacher, Professor George Caird: "Thus in literal historic truth, not simply in theological interpretation, the one bore the sins of the many."

Some theories of "atonement" detach themselves from the actual events and superimpose on (or even substitute for) the gospel narrative a theological scheme of interpretation culled from elsewhere, in order to "explain" how sinners may ultimately leave this world and go to heaven. Such theories are no better, at the level of a proper theological method, than theories of the kingdom that ignore the cross. Kingdom and cross belong together. The whole story is the whole story. And it is within that whole story, not within some truncated version, that Jesus's call to a new-creation kind of virtue makes the sense which it does.

Jesus's call to follow him, to discover in the present time the habits of life that point forward to the coming kingdom and already, in a measure, share in its life, only makes sense when it is couched in the terms made famous by Dietrich Bonhoeffer: "Come and die." Jesus didn't say, as do some modern evangelists, "God loves you and has a wonderful plan for your life." Nor did he say, "I accept you as you are, so you can now happily do whatever comes naturally." He said, "If you want to become my followers, deny yourself, take up your cross, and follow me" (Mark 8:34). He spoke of losing one's life in order to gain it, as opposed to clinging to it and so losing it. He spoke of this in direct relation to himself and his own forthcoming humiliation and death, followed by resurrection and exaltation. Exactly in line with the Beatitudes, he was describing, and inviting his followers to enter, an upside-down world, an inside-out world, a world where all the things people normally assume about human flourishing, including human virtue, are set aside and a new order is established.

—*After You Believe* 114–15

A Thousand Small Changes

Virtue, in this sense, isn't simply another way of saying "goodness." The word has sometimes been flattened out like that (perhaps because we instinctively want to escape its challenge), but that isn't its strict meaning. Virtue, in this strict sense, is what happens when someone has made a thousand small choices, requiring effort and concentration, to do something that is good and right but doesn't "come naturally"—and then, on the thousand and first time, when it really matters, they find that they do what's required "automatically," as we say. On that thousand and first occasion, it does indeed look as if it "just happens"; but reflection tells us that it doesn't "just happen" as easily as that.

—After You Believe 20–21

Colluding with Indolence

Look at it like this. If someone came to you and said he or she was having real trouble resisting temptation and was always falling helplessly into sin, but that it didn't matter because one day God would provide a new body that wouldn't be capable of sinning, so why not wait for that, I hope that you would respond with a sharp dose of inaugurated eschatology. God, you would say, has *already* begun that ultimate, final work of new creation; by baptism and faith you have left behind the old order of sin and death, and by God's spirit within you, you have God's own resurrection power to enable you, even in the present, to resist sin and live as a fully human being at last; you must therefore live, in the present, as far as possible like you will live in the future.

—*Surprised by Scripture* 94–95

Humility in Lent

What's more, if we try to put God in our debt by trying to make ourselves "good enough for him" (whatever that might mean), we are prone to make matters worse. One of the horrid truths that we are all too aware of in our own day is that some of the nastiest, most callous and brutal deeds are done by people in the name of "religion." The fact that this is often, manifestly, an excuse for violence whose real causes and motivations lie elsewhere simply proves my point. Saying, in effect, "and, by the way, God is on my side," means that all further moral restraint is unnecessary. And even if nobody else is involved, someone who is determinedly trying to show God how good he or she is is likely to become an insufferable prig. We would all prefer to live with people who knew perfectly well that they weren't good enough for God, but were humbly grateful that God loved them anyway, than with people who were convinced that they had made it to God's standard and could look down on the rest of us from a lofty moral mountaintop.

—*After You Believe* 61

We Are Not Defined by Whatever Longings Come Out of Our Hearts

A sinning Christian is like someone walking on stage and reciting the lines that belonged in yesterday's play. We have been given new lines for the new play, the great drama in which the royal priesthood takes up its new duties, including, of course, the renewed vision of holiness, but going far beyond into the life of worship and witness where the "rules" are a small, if still vital, element in a much larger vocation. And part of that vocation is precisely to celebrate Jesus as Lord *on the territory where other gods have been worshipped.*

When it comes to Mammon, we need to know how to use money, particularly how to give it away. When it comes to Aphrodite, we need to know how to celebrate and sustain marriage, how to celebrate and sustain celibacy, and how to counsel and comfort those who, in either state, find themselves overwhelmed with conflicting and contrary desires. We are not, after all, defined by whatever longings and aspirations come out of our hearts, despite the remarkable rhetoric of our times. In the area of human well-being, that is the road to radical instability; in the area of theological beliefs, it leads to Gnosticism (where you try to discern the hidden divine spark within yourself and then be true to it). Jesus himself was quite clear, following in the prophetic tradition: the human heart is deceitful, and out of it come all kinds of things that defile people, that is, that make them unable to function as genuine human beings, as the royal priesthood they were called to be. The gospel Jesus announced was not about getting in touch with your deepest feelings or accepting yourself as you really are. It was about taking up your cross and following him. That is tough, and it doesn't stop being tough when you've done it for a year, or a decade, or a lifetime. The victory won through suffering on the cross is implemented, here as elsewhere, through the suffering of Jesus's followers, most of whom will continue to be troubled from time to time by temptation in relation to money and sex and many other things beside.

—*The Day the Revolution Began* 397–98

The False Promises of Idols

When someone sins, Jesus is saying, this isn't just a moral glitch. It is not simply about an occasional lapse or mistake. It is a sign that someone or something else is calling the shots. You may still have to agree to the impulses, but your resistance has been weakened. Your slave master has given the orders, and you find yourself driven helplessly down the wrong path. At a certain point you may even have convinced yourself that it is the right path, just as George Orwell's hero in *Nineteen Eighty-Four*, Winston Smith, eventually gave up the unequal struggle and simply loved Big Brother. That is what Jesus is talking about.

So what is this dark power that takes over people, that Jesus could see had taken over his own people, the people who prided themselves on being "children of Abraham"? The larger category in the scriptures that explains what is going on here is idolatry. Idols, all the more powerful when not recognized as such, are anything at all that humans place above and give their ultimate allegiance to other than the One God himself.

Why do we do this? Because idols always promise a bit extra—or perhaps a lot extra. An idol starts off as something good, a good part of God's good creation. But when it attracts attention and begins to offer more than it can appropriately deliver, it starts to demand sacrifices. You have to abandon part of your proper allegiance to God—and often to your neighbors, your family, your other duties—in order to give fresh and inappropriate attention to the new idol, whatever it is.

Idols are addictive. We know a good deal in our generation about the forms of addiction that are rife in our society. Far fewer people are addicted to cigarettes than was the case fifty years ago, but the same kind of compulsive behavior, and often the same kind of *destructive* behavior, is now associated not only with alcohol, cannabis, and other drugs, but with our electronic systems: smartphones, social media, Facebook, and so on. These, as is well known, can become *self*-destructive when people portray themselves in a particular light and then struggle to live up to the image they have created. These forms of addiction can become a classic example of Luther's definition of sin: "Humans turned in upon themselves." Technology can, of course, be a blessing, bringing people together in all sorts of ways, but in the last analysis real relationships with real people are a form of freedom. Half-relationships with a screen personality can be a step toward slavery.

—*Broken Signposts* 126–27

Misdirected Worship and Its Distortion of Our Humanity

When human beings give their heartfelt allegiance to and worship that which is not God, they progressively cease to reflect the image of God. One of the primary laws of human life is that you become like what you worship; what's more, you *reflect* what you worship not only back to the object itself but also outward to the world around. Those who worship money increasingly define themselves in terms of it and increasingly treat other people as creditors, debtors, partners, or customers rather than as human beings. Those who worship sex define themselves in terms of it (their preferences, their practices, their past histories) and increasingly treat other people as actual or potential sexual objects. Those who worship power define themselves in terms of it and treat other people as either collaborators, competitors, or pawns. These and many other forms of idolatry combine in a thousand ways, all of them damaging to the image-bearing quality of the people concerned and of those whose lives they touch. My suggestion is that it is possible for human beings so to continue down this road, so to refuse all whisperings of good news, all glimmers of the true light, all promptings to turn and go the other way, all signposts to the love of God, that after death they become at last, by their own effective choice, *beings that once were human but now are not,* creatures that have ceased to bear the divine image at all. With the death of that body in which they inhabited God's good world, in which the flickering flame of goodness had not been completely snuffed out, they pass simultaneously not only beyond hope but also beyond pity. There is no concentration camp in the beautiful countryside, no torture chamber in the palace of delight. Those creatures that still exist in an ex-human state, no longer reflecting their maker in any meaningful sense, can no longer excite in themselves or others the natural sympathy some feel even for the hardened criminal.

—*Surprised by Hope* 182–83

The Cross and the Throne

Luke's consistent emphasis is on the divine plan that "must" be fulfilled, the plan that would send Jesus not to a throne, but to a cross—or, rather, as all four gospel writers insist, a cross that is to be seen as a throne. This, they all say, is how Jesus is enthroned as "King of the Jews." *Jesus's vocation to be Israel's Messiah and his vocation to suffer and die belong intimately together.*

What is more, they are *together* the means by which, he believed, Israel's God would decisively launch his kingdom on earth as in heaven. The disciples wanted a kingdom without a cross. Many would-be "orthodox" or "conservative" Christians in our world have wanted a cross without a kingdom, an abstract "atonement" that would have nothing to do with this world except to provide the means of escaping it. Many too have wanted a "divine" Jesus as a kind of "super-man" figure, a heavenly hero come to rescue them, but not to act as Israel's Messiah, establishing God's kingdom on earth as in heaven. Jesus's shocking combination of scriptural models into a single vocation makes excellent historical sense; that is, it explains at a stroke why he did and said what he did and said. But it remains as challenging in our world, and indeed in our churches, as it was in Jesus's own day.

—*Simply Jesus* 173–74

Choosing Death, Not Life

So what happens if we understand the human vocation as bearing God's image, of reflecting God's wise authority into the world and the glad praises of creation back to God? What happens if we see "sin" in *that* context?

Within that story, "sin" becomes the refusal of humans to play their part in God's purposes for creation as a whole. It is a *vocational* failure as much as what we call a *moral* failure. This vocational failure, choosing to worship the creature rather than the Creator, is the choice of death over life. This is why "sin" and "death" are so inextricably intertwined in biblical thinking. The former is not the breaking of arbitrary rules; the latter is not the inflicting of arbitrary punishment. To be sure, they can often be spoken of, not least in the prophets, as a legal code to which appropriate penalties are attached. That is a natural way, on the surface, to refer to the whole sorry state of affairs. But deep down underneath there is nothing arbitrary about sin or death. Choose the one, and you choose the other. Worship idols, and you'll go into exile. Obey the serpent's voice, and you will forfeit the right to the Tree of Life. You can't have it both ways.

—The Day the Revolution Began 103

Learn the Language of Heaven

In the new heavens and new earth, there will be new vocations and new tasks, the ultimate fulfillment of those given to Human in the first place. Once we glimpse this, we will be in a position to see how the New Testament's vision of Christian behavior has to do, not with struggling to keep a bunch of ancient and apparently arbitrary rules, nor with "going with the flow" or "doing what comes naturally," but with the learning of the language, in the present, which will equip us to speak it fluently in God's new world.

—*After You Believe* 78

Set Free to Be In-Between People

According to that original revolution, rescued humans are set free to be what they were made to be. "Forgiveness," achieved through God's Son's "giving himself for our sins," is the key to the liberating victory. Sin matters, and forgiveness of sins matters, but they matter because sin, flowing from idolatry, corrupts, distorts, and disables the image-bearing vocation, which is much more than simply "getting ready for heaven." An overconcentration on "sin" and how God deals with it means that we see things only with regard to "works," even if we confess that we have no "works" of our own and that we have to rely on Jesus to supply them for us. (Equally, an underemphasis on "sin" and how God deals with it is an attempt to claim some kind of victory without seeing the heart of the problem.)

The biblical vision of what it means to be human, the "royal priesthood" vocation, is more multidimensional than either of the regular alternatives. To reflect the divine image means standing between heaven and earth, even in the present time, adoring the Creator and bringing his purposes into reality on earth, ahead of the time when God completes the task and makes all things new. The "royal priesthood" is the company of rescued humans who, being part of "earth," worship the God of heaven and are thereby equipped, with the breath of heaven in their renewed lungs, to work for his kingdom on earth. The revolution of the cross sets us free to be in-between people, caught up in the rhythm of worship and mission.

Expressing the missional vocation in this way and basing it like this on the revolutionary victory of the cross help us to avoid some obvious dangers. Without the sense of the victory being already won, we might easily lurch from arrogance (thinking that we had to win that victory ourselves) to fear (thinking that the world was too powerful and that we should escape it or at least hunker down and wait for Jesus to return and sort everything out himself). The initial victory gives us the platform for work that is both confident and humble. However, without the sense that the victory is won *through* the forgiveness of sins, "mission" could easily detach itself from the calling to be people who themselves have been rescued from the grip of the powers, people who themselves know what it means to live as grateful forgiven sinners.

—*The Day the Revolution Began* 363–64

The Rescue Mission by a People Who Needed Rescuing

When humans take up their divinely appointed role, looking after God's world on his behalf, this is not a Promethean attempt to usurp God's role. It is the humble, obedient carrying out of the role that has been assigned. The real arrogance would be to refuse the vocation, imagining that we knew better than God the purpose for which we have been put here.

But there is then a further vocation, one that has routinely been forgotten throughout much of church history. In the Bible, God not only called human beings to look after creation. He also called Israel to be the means of rescuing the world from the plight into which it had fallen.

God's call of Abraham echoes the vocation of Adam: "Be fruitful and multiply" in Genesis 1:28 turns into "I will make you exceedingly . . . I will make you exceedingly fruitful" in Genesis 17:2, 6. And whereas the story of Genesis 3–11 is one of disaster, curse, and continuing human arrogance, the story that begins in Genesis 12 with God's call of Abraham has for its motto the promise, "in you all the families of the earth shall be blessed" (v. 3). This theme continues in one way or another in many parts of the Old Testament.

The significance of this cannot be overestimated. God created the world in such a way that it was to be looked after by humans who reflect his image. When the humans rebelled, he did not rescind that project. Instead, he called a human family in order that they might reflect not simply his wise ordering and stewardship into the world but now also his rescuing love into that same world, disastrously flawed as it now was. Here is the ecstasy and the agony of the Old Testament: the rich, breathtaking vocation of Israel and the dark, tragic fact that this vocation, this rescue mission, was to be undertaken by a people who were themselves in sore need of the very same rescue.

—*The Case for the Psalms* 51–53

FREEDOM

So Jesus spoke to the Judaeans who had believed in him. "If you remain in my word," he said, "you will truly be my disciples, and you will know the truth, and the truth will make you free."

"We are Abraham's descendants!" they replied. "We've never been anyone's slaves! How can you say, 'You'll become free'?"

"I'm telling you the solemn truth," Jesus replied. "Everyone who commits sin is a slave of sin. The slave doesn't live in the house forever; the son lives there forever. So, you see, if the son makes you free, you will be truly free."

—John 8:31–36, *The Kingdom New Testament* 192

What Freedom Means

Freedom itself must be generated, protected, and celebrated. But thinkers from St. Paul in the middle of the first century to Bob Dylan in the middle of the twentieth, and beyond, are still asking what "freedom" actually means. In a Christian sense, it clearly doesn't mean the random whizzing about of the subatomic particle, however much some eager political or psychological rhetoric may go on about the total removal of constraints. For an actor to be "free" to play Hamlet, other actors must be involved, each of whom will curtail their own "freedom" in search of the higher "freedom" of being constrained by, but finding new meaning again and again within, Shakespeare's play. For musicians to be free to play the blues, the guitar must be in tune, the pianist must be practiced if not perfect, serious if not necessarily completely sober, and the drummer and bass player must discover their "freedom" within the quite severe constraints of a time signature. And for the ordinary citizen to be "free" politically, there must be forces of law and order that can hold back chaos and riot, defend property and life, and prevent the malicious and the violent from doing whatever they fancy.

We willingly accept constraints like these. We recognize that a "freedom" which consists merely of random or spontaneous activity is not necessarily genuine freedom, but may be merely chaos. We seek a freedom which consists in a glad, integrated, thought-out choice of a life-path and which includes taking responsibility for working that path out, paying its way, and living with its consequences. And the Christian, called to reflect God's generous and creative love into the world, must develop the civic as well as personal virtues that will support and sustain this freedom, this giving to human beings the chance to be genuinely human. Like all the great slogans, "Freedom!" raises a question rather than providing answers. But it is a Christian slogan as well, and those called to be royal priests must work at the virtues required to create conditions for it and enable it to flourish where and when it can.

Freedom, like authenticity, is what we are promised when our desires and longings completely coincide with God's designs and plans for us as fully human beings. God's service, says the ancient prayer, is "perfect freedom." And, as with authenticity, freedom grasped too soon becomes an over-realized eschatology, a failure to realize how much work virtue still has to do to bring it to the goal. But the point of virtue is to work at anticipating the future in the present, and glimpsing and grasping the true freedom we are offered in Jesus Christ is a vital element within that. Otherwise, the slogan of "Freedom!" becomes just an excuse for license, as Paul saw already in Galatians 5. To accept appropriate moral constraints is not to curtail true freedom, but to create the conditions for it to flourish.

—*After You Believe* 232–34

The Freedom of Salvation

Salvation is not "going to heaven" but "being raised to life in God's new heaven and new earth." But as soon as we put it like this we realize that the New Testament is full of hints, indications, and downright assertions that this salvation isn't just something we have to wait for in the long-distance future. We can enjoy it here and now (always partially, of course, since we all still have to die), genuinely anticipating in the present what is to come in the future. "We were saved," says Paul in Romans 8:24, "in hope." The verb "we were saved" indicates a past action, something that has already taken place, referring obviously to the complex of faith and baptism of which Paul has been speaking in the letter so far. But this remains "in hope" because we still look forward to the ultimate future salvation of which he speaks in (for instance) Romans 5:9–10.

—*Surprised by Hope* 198

The Freedom of Jesus's Passover

For John, as for all the early Christians, what Jesus did in going to the cross and what the Father was declaring when he raised him from the dead, was a *Passover-shaped message*, the news that true freedom was being won at last, that the great Pharaoh had been overthrown, and that now it was time for the true Tabernacle to be built, for the true Torah to be kept, and for the ultimate inheritance to be claimed. All of that is going on underneath John's sequence of Passovers in his gospel, and the third one in particular.

—*Broken Signposts* 123

Freedom for All Nations

Now comes the judgment of this world!
Now this world's ruler is going to be thrown out!
And when I've been lifted up from the earth,
I will draw all people to myself.
(John 12:31–32)

In other words, Jesus will die on the cross; this will be the way in which his glory is fully revealed (a major theme in the gospel); and it will also be the victory over "this world's ruler," the dark power that has held the nations captive. This is Jesus's answer to the arrival of the Greeks. Once he has died on the cross, "all people" will be free to come to him and so discover the living and true God.

This is the secret of the "Gentile mission," which began with Peter's visit to Cornelius in Acts 10 and continued spectacularly, in practice and also in theory, in the work of Paul. People have often imagined that Paul's mission to the non-Jewish world was undertaken simply because, finding his Jewish contemporaries unwilling to stomach such an odd message, he was desperate to win a few followers, so he went to non-Jews instead, offering them a less demanding message. That demeaning analysis misses the point. The Gentile mission was neither a pragmatic reaction to supposed Jewish intransigence nor a mere opportunistic attempt to boost recruitment for a strange new sect. From the earliest writings we have, it was seen as the direct and necessary result of the creator God overthrowing on the cross the powers that had kept the nations captive. Up to now the nations had been enslaved; the cross had opened the gates to freedom.

—The Day the Revolution Began 388

Setting Free Because of Love

Paul stands between Philemon and Onesimus, joining them together in his own person and appeal. "Here," he says (stretching out one arm), "is Onesimus, my son, my own heart, who has been looking after me here in prison, on your behalf as it were!" And (stretching out the other arm) to Philemon, he says, "Your love gives me so much comfort. You are my partner in the gospel. You owe me, after all, your own very self. You have the chance now to refresh me, even here in prison." Paul stands metaphorically between the two men, reaching out in the shape of the cross. "Oh, and by the way," he says ("not counting their transgressions against them"), "if he's wronged you, put it down on my account. I'll make it good." And then he adds, "One more thing. Get a guest room ready for me. Keep praying, and I will be out of here soon. Then I'll be coming to visit."

This would demand humility and trust on both sides. Onesimus was not going to set off to Colossae with a spring in his step, imagining everything was going to be easy. There had been reasons why he ran away, and those reasons, whatever they were, would have to be confronted. Philemon would be astonished and quite possibly angry to see him return; he would also realize the delicate balance both of what Paul had said and of what he was being asked to do. As a policy statement about slavery, the letter falls short of what we would want. As an experiment in a one-off, down-to-earth pastoral strategy, it is brilliant. And it seems to have worked. Fifty years later, the bishop of Ephesus is a man called Onesimus. The young slave, now an elderly Christian leader? Or a name already respected within the early community?

—*Paul: A Biography* 283–84

Forgiveness of Sins, Reinclusion,
and Reinstatement

"This is what is written," he said. "The Messiah
must suffer and rise from the dead on the third day,
and in his name repentance, for the forgiveness of sins,
must be announced to all the nations, beginning from
Jerusalem. You are the witnesses for all this. Now
look: I'm sending upon you what my father has
promised. But stay in the city until you are
clothed with power from on high."
(Luke 24:44–49)

"Forgiveness of sins," in other words, is to be seen *both* as the sum-
mary of the redemptive blessings promised to Israel *and* as the key
blessing that will enable non-Jews to be welcomed into the one
family. As Deuteronomy 30, Jeremiah 31, Daniel 9, and many other
passages had indicated, "forgiveness of sins" was the key thing that
Israel needed for the long years of desolation to be over at last. And
if the non-Jewish nations were to escape from their slavery to idolatry and all that went with it, "forgiveness of sins" would summarize
what it meant for them to leave that past behind—for, in the words
of the Psalm, the "princes of the people" to "gather as the people of
the God of Abraham" (47:9).

This would become one of the main foundations of Paul's argument for the equal status, in the Messiah's family, of believing Gentiles alongside believing Jews. The latter, turning back as
Deuteronomy had indicated to their true God, were experiencing
through the Messiah's death and resurrection the "forgiveness of
sins" in the ancient biblical sense of the long-awaited covenant re-

newal and "end of exile." The former, turning from their idols to serve the living God, were experiencing the "forgiveness of sins" through the divine amnesty that all along had been aimed at their full inclusion.

—*The Day the Revolution Began* 150–51

The Larger Reality of Forgiveness

Being faithful to the biblical overtones of "forgiveness of sins," means we must insist that the larger reality really matters. The smaller reality—that I, as a sinner, need to know the forgiving love of God in my own life—is vital for each person, one by one. But, as history shows, that reality can all too easily be understood within the Platonized version of the gospel in which the whole emphasis falls on a detached spirituality in the present and a detached future salvation in which the created order is abandoned altogether.

Once again, that is how to domesticate the revolution. The larger reality is that *something has happened within the actual world of space, time, and matter, as a result of which everything is different.* By six o'clock on the Friday evening Jesus died, something had changed, and changed radically. Heaven and earth were brought together, creating the cosmic "new temple": "God was reconciling the world to himself in the Messiah" (2 Cor. 5:19).

This was totally unexpected. No Jews prior to Jesus were walking around with this kind of messianic narrative in their heads. But when the resurrection compelled the disciples to rethink their original and natural reaction to the death of Jesus—a reaction we see graphically portrayed in Luke's picture of the two on the road to Emmaus—we find them grappling with the fresh belief that these events were seen as the dramatic, unexpected, but nevertheless appropriate fulfillment of the ancient prophecies and therefore as the events through which *the long-awaited new age was being ushered in at last*. This was not about inventing a new kind of religion. It had nothing to do with getting rid of the earthbound hopes of the ancient Jews and embracing a "spiritual" reality instead. It was far more revolutionary. It was about the kingdom of God coming "on earth as in heaven."

—*The Day the Revolution Began* 155–56

Forgiveness and Repentance Go Hand in Hand

If we believe that on the cross Jesus won the victory over all the powers that hold people captive, we must take courage and proceed. In particular, we must reaffirm that the heart of that victory is the forgiveness of sins. This too can be misunderstood. "Don't you believe in forgiveness?" people will ask when someone is caught in bad behavior—as though "forgiveness" meant "tolerance" or the declaration of a general "anything goes" kind of amnesty. It does not. In the New Testament, "forgiveness" goes closely with "repentance"; and "repentance" doesn't just mean feeling sorry (perhaps because one has been caught!), but is an active turning away from the idols one had been worshipping.

—*The Day the Revolution Began* 396

The Slavery of Unforgiveness

Forgiveness and healing! The two go so closely together, personally and socially. Whole societies can be crippled by ancient grudges that turn into feuds and then into forms of civil war. Families can be torn apart by a single incident or one person's behavior that is never faced and so never forgiven. Equally, societies and families as well as individuals can be reconciled, can find new hope and new love, through forgiveness. Jesus was tapping into something extremely deep in human life.

—*Simply Jesus* 72

Three Ways
Forgiveness Sets Us Free

1.

Free to Worship

First, the restoration of true worship. Acts describes the new-Temple reality of the coming together of heaven and earth, just as Ephesians 1:10 said: Jesus, the risen human being, is taken up into heaven, thereby joining together in his own person the two spheres of God's good creation. But if heaven and earth are already joined in the ascension, with part of "earth"—the human body of Jesus—now fully and thoroughly at home in "heaven," then they are joined again in the opposite direction, as it were, in

Acts 2, when the powerful wind of the divine Spirit comes upon the disciples. *This is one of the New Testament equivalents of the filling of the tabernacle with the cloud and fire or of Solomon's Temple with the glorious divine Presence.*

Here is the foundation of the belief that with Jesus and the Spirit a new creation has come into being. Instead of the "microcosmos" of the Jerusalem Temple, Jesus himself and his Spirit-filled people constitute the new Temple, the start of the new world. Only by dwelling in and living out of this new reality could it make any sense for the first disciples to speak as they did of the ways in which the kingdom was in the most important sense already present, even though in another sense, with Herod and Caesar still on their thrones, it was also obviously future. The first followers of Jesus were thereby constituted as new-Temple people, which is why, of course, most of the controversies in the book of Acts focus on temples: the charges against Stephen (and his answer to them) in chapters 6–7 and Paul's clashes with the local cult (Acts 14), with the temples in Athens and Ephesus (chaps. 17–19), and then with the Temple in Jerusalem itself (21:28–29; 24:6; 25:8).

And the new life of this new community was itself anchored in worship, declaring "the powerful things God has done" (2:11), establishing a new pattern of life centered upon "the teaching of the apostles and the common life," "the breaking of bread and the prayers" (2:42), a life that, to begin with at least, tried to hold together the ancient Temple and the ordinary domestic sphere:

> Day by day they were all together attending the Temple. They broke bread in their various houses, and ate their food with glad and sincere hearts, praising God and standing in favor with all the people. (2:46–47)

—*The Day the Revolution Began* 161–65

2.

Free to Announce the New Epoch

Second, then, there is the hope for the worldwide rule of this God. Out of worship and prayer there grows witness; and the "witness" is not simply about people saying, "I've had this experience; perhaps you might like it too," but about people announcing that a new state of affairs has come into being. This too begins from the day of Pentecost, as we have seen, when the disciples announced to the startled crowds that the ancient prophecies had been fulfilled, that "forgiveness of sins" had *happened as an event in real space and time*, and that the whole world was now called to order in the name of its creator and restorer. To announce Jesus as Israel's Messiah is to say that this is now happening and "forgiveness of sins" is the key to it all. This witness continues through the many different scenes of gospel announcement: Philip to the Ethiopian eunuch in Acts 8, Peter to Cornelius in Acts 10, and so on. It reaches a first decisive climax in chapter 12, when Herod Agrippa I begins a serious attack on the church but is forestalled, first by Peter's angelic release from prison and then by his own sudden death. Luke's comment makes the position clear: Herod died, "but God's word grew and multiplied" (Acts 12:24). Here is the vital note of *kingdom:* The kingdoms of the world turn out to be, in ultimate terms, powerless against the kingdom of God. They can persecute and kill Jesus's followers, but this—as other New Testament writers were quick to emphasize, following Jesus himself—only strengthened the kingdom of God, since that kingdom was accomplished precisely through Jesus's death and then implemented through the suffering of his followers.

—*The Day the Revolution Began* 161–65

3.

Free to Hope for Rescue

Third, therefore, after worship (acclaiming the returned and reigning God of Israel) and witness (announcing to the world its rightful and rescuing Lord), there is the hope that Israel will be rescued from pagan rule. One might imagine that this had been left behind in the flurry of events taking place on a different plane, but it is important to see that this is not so. When Jesus himself, Israel's Messiah, was raised from the dead, Israel-in-person was set free from death and, with that, from the ultimate weapon of every tyrant, the ultimate exile imposed by every Babylon. In the excitement of the Gentile mission, the reflex for ancient Israel is not forgotten. The death of Jesus, going ahead of Israel into the mouth of the pagan lion, has created a breathing space in which Peter can urge his hearers, "Let God rescue you from this wicked generation" (Acts 2:40). "The whole house of Israel must know this for a fact: God has made him Lord and Messiah" (2:36). Thousands of Jews, including a great many priests, believed this message and became part of the renewed community (2:41, 47; 4:4; 5:14; 6:7; 11:24; 21:21). We should be in no doubt that Luke, like most other early Christian writers, saw the messianic community focused on Jesus as the liberated, redeemed people, those in and for whom the long-awaited promise of rescue from pagan overlords had been fulfilled.

—*The Day the Revolution Began* 161–65

Platonized Eschatology, Moralized Anthropology, Paganized Soteriology

There are two questions as follows. First, what is the calling of humans in this promised new world? Second, granted human failure ("sin"), how are humans to be rescued so that they can fulfill that calling?

The common view has been that the ultimate state ("heaven") is a place where "good" people end up, so that human life is gauged in relation to moral achievement or lack thereof. This sets up a "works contract." Then, this usual view goes on, humans all fail the moral test and so need to be rescued, and this is the effect of Jesus's death. This leads, in some very popular schemes of thought, to a view of "salvation" in which the "punishment" for moral failure is meted out elsewhere while the "moral achievement" that was lacking in everyone else is supplied by Jesus himself. Some versions of this, I have suggested, are closer to the pagan idea of an angry deity being pacified by a human death than they are to anything in either Israel's scriptures or the New Testament.

In other words, in much popular modern Christian thought, we have made a three-layered mistake. We have *Platonized* our eschatology (substituting "souls going to heaven" for the promised new creation) and have therefore *moralized* our anthropology (substituting a qualifying examination of moral performance for the biblical notion of the human vocation), with the result that we have *paganized* our soteriology, our understanding of "salvation" (substituting the idea of "God killing Jesus to satisfy his wrath" for the genuinely biblical notions we are about to explore).

This is a fairly drastic set of charges. Some will no doubt accuse me of caricature, but long experience of what people in churches think they have been taught suggests otherwise. Others will perhaps accuse me of pulling the house down on top of myself, denying things that are basic to the faith. However, it seems to me—and I hope the rest of the book will demonstrate this—that, once the new way of looking at things is grasped, all that was best in the old way will be retained, but in a new framework through which it loses its frankly unbiblical elements.

The new creation will indeed be "heavenly," possessing in complete measure that heaven/earth overlap we sense fitfully in prayer, in scripture study, in the sacraments, and in working for God's kingdom in the world. The human vocation certainly includes a strong and nonnegotiable moral element, which is enhanced rather than eliminated when placed within the larger category of the "image-bearing" *vocation*. And the means of salvation, as we shall see throughout this part of the book, does indeed involve the death of Jesus as the *representative* and then the *substitute* for his people, though not in the sense that many have understood those rather abstract categories.

—*The Day the Revolution Began* 147–48

Freed to a New Humanity

What emerges, as the positive side of the point about the dark forces being overthrown, is the idea of a *new humanity*, a different model of the human race. If Jesus had defeated the powers of the world in his death, his resurrection meant the launching of a new creation, a whole new world. Those who found themselves caught up in the "good news" that Paul was announcing were drawn into that new world and were themselves, Paul taught, to become small working models of the same thing. As I think of Paul launching this new venture, the image of the tightrope over the volcano doesn't seem to go far enough. He was inventing, and must have known that he was inventing, a new way of being human. It must have been a bit like the first person to realize that notes sounded in sequence created melody, that notes sounded together created harmony, and that ordering the sequence created rhythm. If we can think of a world without music and then imagine it being invented, offering a hitherto undreamed-of depth and power to space, time, and matter, then we may have a sense of the crazy magnitude of Paul's vocation.

—*Paul: A Biography* 109

The Rules That Celebrate New Creation

To return to 1 Corinthians, it is the resurrection—both that of Jesus and that of ourselves—that provides, in passages like chapters 5 and 6, the ultimate rationale for Christian behavior. It isn't the case that Christian ethics consists of a few odd regulations and restrictions that Christians are supposed to follow while still living in exactly the same world as everyone else, just as it isn't the case that the resurrection of Jesus was simply a very strange miracle within the world of old creation. The resurrection was the full bursting in to this world of the life of God's new creation; Christian ethics is the lifestyle that celebrates and embodies that new creation. Living out a life of Christian holiness makes sense, perfect sense, *within God's new world*, the world into which we are brought at baptism, the world where we are nourished by the Eucharist. Of course, if you try to live a Christian lifestyle outside this framework, you will find it as difficult, indeed nonsensical, as it would be for an orchestral performer to play his or her part separated from the rest of the players amid the crashes and metallic screeching of an automobile factory. Not that we aren't called, of course, to practice our discipleship in the hard, outside world, which rumbles on as though Easter had never happened. But if we are to be true to our risen Lord, we will need, again and again, to retune our instruments and practice once more alongside our fellow musicians.

—*Surprised by Hope* 284

Our Hope Is the Glory of God

The result is this: since we have been declared "in the right" on the basis of faith, we have peace with God through our Lord Jesus the Messiah. Through him we have been allowed to approach, by faith, into this grace in which we stand; and we celebrate the hope of the glory of God.

That's not all. We also celebrate in our sufferings, because we know that suffering produces patience, patience produces a well-formed character [*dokimē*], and a character like that produces hope.

Hope, in its turn, does not make us ashamed, because the love of God has been poured out in our hearts through the holy spirit who has been given to us.
(Rom. 5:1–5)

There are two key things here for our present purposes: hope and character construction.

The hope is, as Paul states clearly, "the glory of God." We have spoken of this already in terms of two interlocking themes: the sovereign stewardship over creation entrusted by God to human-kind, and the return of the divine glory to dwell amidst God's people after the long years of the Exile. This latter theme seems to be in the back of Paul's mind in several of his writings, but not least here in Romans 5 and in the continuation of the same theme in chapter 8, where the Spirit "dwells within" believers, evoking the theme of God "dwelling in the Temple" in the Old Testament (8:4–11). Frustratingly, the word "glory" is so often used in Christian circles as a vague word for "going to heaven" that these important overtones to the concept of "the glory of God"—overtones that would have been audible to Paul and his first hearers—are often ignored altogether.

What Paul is saying—and it is of central importance for this whole book—is that the hope to which we press, the *telos* or goal of all our pilgrimage, is "the glory of God." When this is explained, it means on the one hand the "royal priesthood" we studied earlier, the vocation of genuine humanness, and on the other hand the place where the living God himself comes to dwell in fulfillment of his ancient promise.

Both parts of this were realized by Jesus himself, as we saw. Paul's point, throughout Romans 5–8 but particularly in chapter 8, is that both are also realized, through the presence and power of the Holy Spirit, in and through God's people. Some people say that the early Christians had no trinitarian theology, but that position can be sustained only by carefully putting the telescope to the blind eye.

—*After You Believe* 175–76

Think Things Through

God wants us to be people, not puppets; real human beings who think things out and make actual decisions, not straws in the wind to be blown this way and that. You need to "figure out properly things that differ," says Paul—and the word he uses for "figure out properly" is our old friend *dokimazein*, as in the *dokimos* root in Romans 5:4 and 12:2. Part of the problem in contemporary Christianity, I believe, is that talk about the freedom of the Spirit, about the grace that sweeps us off our feet and heals and transforms our lives, has been taken over surreptitiously by a kind of low-grade romanticism, colluding with an anti-intellectual streak in our culture, generating the assumption that the more spiritual you are, the less you need to think.

I cannot stress too strongly that this is a mistake. The more genuinely spiritual you are, according to Romans 12 and Philippians 1, the more clearly and accurately and carefully you will think, particularly about *what the completed goal of your Christian journey will be and hence what steps you should be taking, what habits you should be acquiring, as part of the journey toward that goal, right now.* Thinking clearly and Christianly is thus both a key element within the total rehumanizing process (you won't be fully human if you leave your thinking and reasoning behind) and a vital part of the motor which drives the rest of that process.

Once again, none of this can be seen in an individualistic sense. Of course, those who have particular gifts of mind and intellect must use them in God's service. But, as Romans 12 goes on at once to say, we should not think of ourselves more highly than we ought, but should think with sober judgment, since God made us members one of another in Christ, within the one body (Rom. 12:3–5). But even here, stressing the corporate nature of Christian discipleship and hence the absolute requirement of appropriate humility, Paul also stresses that each person must think this out individually: "I am saying this," he writes, "to every single one of you." And again what matters is *thinking:* he's saying, in effect, "Don't *overthink* what you ought to *think*, but *think* with *reasonable thinking*." Paul's wordplay here (*hyperphronein*, *phronein*, and *sōphronein*) climaxes in a word which readers might well recognize as cognate with *sōphrosynē*, "reasonableness" or "moderation," well-known in classical discussions of virtue. All Christians are called to think things through—indeed, to think through the way in which thinking through things makes a radical difference to the life of the body of Christ.

—*After You Believe* 157–59

Come Alive!

In Ephesians, we find the bracing instruction, taken perhaps from an early Christian poem or hymn: "Awake, sleeper, rise from the dead, and the Messiah will give you light!" (5:14).

In other words, it's time to wake up! Living at the level of the nonheavenly world around you is like being asleep; worse, it's like that for which sleep is a metaphor—being dead. Lying, stealing, sexual immorality, bad temper, and so on (Paul lists them all in a devastating short passage) are forms of death, both for the person who commits them and for all whose lives are touched by their actions. They are ways of sleeping a deadly sleep. It's time to wake up, he says. Come alive to the real world, the world where Jesus is Lord, the world into which your baptism brings you, the world you claim to belong to when you say in the creed that Jesus is Lord and that God raised him from the dead. What we all need from time to time is for someone (a friend, a spiritual director, a stranger, a sermon, a verse of scripture, or simply the inner prompting of the Spirit) to say, "It's time to wake up! You've been asleep long enough! The sun is shining and there's a wonderful day out there! Wake up and get a life!"

—*Surprised by Hope* 252

Free for Love

Widespread human experience suggests that freedom often emerges *through* a pathway that seems anything but "free." The freedom to improvise musically or to compose music of your own will only come when the disciplines of learning the scales and the technique for the instrument have been mastered. People sometimes imagine that when musicians improvise, as in jazz and other forms, they are just making up *anything*, playing the first thing that comes into their heads. They couldn't be more wrong. Jazz depends, just as much as classical music does, on the musicians knowing exactly what's going on, listening intently to one another, and making sure that even the most apparently daring riffs and outlandish extra passages come in to land at the right moment, in the right key. The music may sound strange to those unused to the idiom, but it has its own deep coherence. There is the difference between freedom and chaos.

So if we all know that freedom is important, socially and personally, but we all find it harder than we expected to figure out what it actually means, where do we go for help? The Bible shows us that our instinct for freedom has everything to do with the sense of the presence of God. Freedom, we find, is the central story God wants for his people—including both freedom *from* things like sin and idolatry and freedom *for* being loved.

—*Broken Signposts* 119

The Freed Ones Bring Freedom to Others

Free people, then, become agents of freedom in the world, at every level: counselors who help others to shake off the shackles of the past and live in genuine freedom, diplomats who confront bullying and tyrannical rulers with the news that there is a better way to run countries or systems, politicians who craft legislation that sets ordinary people free from clever bullies, and so on. In all this we are once again coming around the corner to the theological point. The desire for freedom is a God-given instinct implanted in all image-bearers. The God who made us *wants us to be free.*

Of course, in many systems—tragically, in many would-be Christian systems and churches—that message has been totally squelched under a large, heavy pile of regulations and expectations. Many people will find any association of "freedom" with "church" like yet another of Sartre's sick jokes. But it isn't. The church at its best—and I have been privileged to glimpse some of that "best"—is in the freedom business, at every level.

This shows, yet again, that the call of freedom, though it appears to run into the sand in so many contexts, was always a genuine call from the creator God. The instinct that causes even tyrants to claim that they are offering people "freedom," the instinct that tells people to break out of their straitjackets and find a new liberty—this instinct is part of the genuine, God-given kit for human life. That remains true however much we abuse it, however much we take the promise of freedom and twist it into new forms of slavery.

—*Broken Signposts* 131

God Loves Us as We Are

I know a choir director who took on the running of a village church choir that hadn't had much help for years. They had struggled valiantly to sing the hymns, to give the congregation a bit of a lead, and on special occasions to try a simple anthem. But, frankly, the results weren't impressive. When the congregation thanked the singers, it was as much out of sympathy for their apparent hard work as out of any appreciation of a genuinely musical sound. However long they practiced, they didn't seem to get any better; they were probably merely reinforcing their existing bad habits. So when the new choir director arrived and took them on, gently finding out what they could and couldn't do, it was in a sense an act of grace. He didn't tell them they were rubbish, or shout at them to sing in tune. That wouldn't have done any good. It would have been simply depressing. He accepted them as they were and began to work with them. But the point of doing so was not so that they could carry on as before, only now with someone waving his arms in front of them. The point of his taking them on as they were was so that they could . . . really learn to sing! And now, remarkably, they can. A friend of mine who went to that church just a few weeks ago reported that the choir had been transformed. Same people, new sound. Now when they practiced they knew what they were doing, and thus they could learn how to sound better.

That is a picture of how God's grace works. God loves us as we are, as he finds us, which is (more or less) messy, muddy, and singing out of tune. Even when we've tried to be good, we have often only made matters worse, adding (short-lived) pride to our other failures. And the never-ending wonder at the heart of genuine Christian living is that God has come to meet us right there, in our confusion of pride and fear, of mess and muddle and downright rebellion and sin.

—After You Believe 62–63

The Freedom in Receiving

When St. Paul says that "if righteousness came by the Law, the Messiah died in vain" (Gal. 2:21), he was stating a foundational principle. Whatever language or terminology we use to talk about the great gift that the one true God has given to his people in and through Jesus Christ ("salvation," "eternal life," and so on), it remains precisely a *gift*. It is never something we can earn. We can never put God into our debt; we always remain in his. Everything I'm going to say about the moral life, about moral effort, about the conscious shaping of our patterns of behavior, takes place simply and solely within the framework of grace—the grace that was embodied in Jesus and his death and resurrection, the grace that is active in the Spirit-filled preaching of the gospel, the grace that continues to be active by the Spirit in the lives of believers. It is simply not the case that God does some of the work of our salvation and we have to do the rest. It is not the case that we begin by

being justified by grace through faith and then have to go to work
all by ourselves to complete the job by struggling, unaided, to live
a holy life.

—After You Believe 60

Free to Form Habits of Mind

When people consistently make choices about their patterns of behavior, physical changes take place within the brain itself. Some
might regard this as common sense, but for many it will come as a
fascinating and perhaps frightening reality. There is a great deal of
work still to be done in this field. Neuroscience is still in compar-
ative infancy. But already the clear indications are that significant
events in your life, including significant choices you make about
how you behave, create new information pathways and patterns
within your brain. Neuroscientists often use the metaphor of the
"wiring" of the brain, which is not inappropriate since, though of
course, there are no wires as such involved, information is indeed
passed here and there within the brain by what are basically electric
currents.

It isn't just that new patterns of wiring are being put down all
the time, corresponding to the choices we make and the behaviors
we adopt—though behavior is, of course, massively habit-forming.
Parts of the brain actually become physically enlarged when an
individual's behavior regularly exercises them. For example, violin
players develop not only their left hand, but also the section of the
brain that controls the left hand. "These regions [of the brain],"
writes John Medina in his fascinating book *Brain Rules*, "are enlarged, swollen and crisscrossed with complex associations." As

Medina stresses, "The brain acts like a muscle. The more activity you do, the larger and more complex it can become." What's more, he says, "Our brains are so sensitive to external inputs that their physical wiring depends upon the culture in which they find themselves." As a result, "learning results in physical changes in the brain, and these changes are unique to each individual."

In other words, as we learn to connect various things in new ways, our brain records those connections. The result is rather like a gardener's discovery that a patch that has been dug over before is much easier to dig a second time. A particular set of associations in the brain, especially if it is connected with intense emotions or physical reactions, whether pleasurable or painful, will make it much easier for those associations to be triggered a second time. Contemporary neuroscience is thus actually able to study and map the way in which lifelong habits come to be formed.

—*After You Believe* 37–38

Rules Matter but Are Not the Center

The real difficulty with rules is not only that we don't keep them very well, though that's true. Nor that there always seem to be troubling exceptions: When we've been taught always to tell the truth, what do we say to the would-be murderer who asks where his intended victim is hiding? Nor, yet, is the real problem that systems of rules differ markedly from one another: in some cultures, you are under a solemn obligation to kill the person who rapes your daughter, and in others you are under a solemn obligation *not* to do so. These are indeed problems. But the biggest problem lies elsewhere.

The real problem is that rules always appear to be, and are indeed designed to be, restrictive. But we know, deep down, that some of the key things that make us human are being creative, celebrating life and beauty and love and laughter. You can't get those by legislation. Rules matter, but they aren't the center of it all. You can tell people that they must obey the rule always to be generous. But if someone gives you a present merely because he is obeying a rule or doing his duty, the glory of gift-giving has slipped through your fingers. If rules are taken as the main thing, then the *truly* main thing seems to be missing. What happened to *character*?

—After You Believe 47

Formed Through God's Promised Future

"Being true to yourself," then, is important, but it isn't the principal thing. If you take it as a framework or as a starting point, you will be sadly deceived. Over against all these frameworks, which I suspect have conditioned in various ways the thinking and behaving of many of my readers, we urgently need to recapture the New Testament's vision of a genuinely "good" human life as a life of *character formed by God's promised future*, as a life with that future-shaped character *lived within the ongoing story of God's people*, and, with that, a freshly worked notion of virtue. This is what we need if we are to answer the question of what happens after you believe.

—After You Believe 57

Grace in Becoming

From a Christian point of view, virtue cannot be conceived solely in terms of the individual journey from a standing start to a future destination. It belongs within an end that has already begun, an eschatology that has already been inaugurated. Virtue, in the great philosophical tradition, has always said, "Become what you will be." Christian virtue says, "What you will be is what you already are in Christ." This is the whole point of saying, as wise Christian theologians always have, that all is of grace. Once that adjustment has been made, we find that the inner dynamic of virtue, the sense of a character that must be shaped by its future prospect and formed by careful thought, hard choices, and moral effort, is not undermined but rather enhanced. This is the whole point of saying, as wise Christian theologians always have, that the way grace works is by the Holy Spirit enabling us to become, at last, truly human. Hence the overlap with Aristotle—and the radical difference.

—*After You Believe* 117–18

Renewed According to the Image of the Creator

When the Messiah is revealed, the one who is your life,
then you also will be revealed with him in glory.
So put to death the earthly parts . . . since you have
put off the Old Human with its deeds, and have put
on the New Human, which is being renewed in knowledge
according to the image of the one who created it.
(Col. 3:4–5, 9–10).

There is Paul's understanding of virtue. Interestingly, it is also John's:

> Now, children, abide in him, so that when he is revealed we
> may have boldness and not be ashamed before him at his
> royal appearing. . . . Beloved, we are now God's children,
> and it has not yet been revealed what we shall be. But we
> know that when he is revealed, we shall be like him, because
> we shall see him as he is. And everyone who possesses this
> hope in him purifies themselves, just as he is pure.
> (1 John 2:28, 3:2–3)

The future event will demonstrate our true, ultimate existence:
we must therefore do the hard work in the present of becoming the
people we are destined to be. In each case, in both Paul and John,
this future destiny (to stress the point once more) is already given
in Jesus Christ and in our membership in him. We are not starting
with raw human material and working it up from scratch. We are
starting with a human character already in Christ, "risen with him"
(Col. 3:1) and "abiding in him" (1 John 2:28); we are greatly beloved
and marked out as "children of God" (1 John 3:1; Gal. 4:1–7).

—*After You Believe* 139–40

The Freedom of Christian Virtue

Looking at Christian behavior in terms of virtue—virtue as anticipating-the-life-of-the-age-to-come—does three things. First, it helps followers of Jesus Christ to understand how Christian behavior "works." That is, it provides a framework within which one may grasp the organic connection between what we are called to do and become in the present and what we are promised as full, genuine human life in the future.

As a result, second, it also ought to provide massive encouragement to all those starting to think seriously about following Jesus. Yes, declares Virtue, this is going to be tough, especially at first. It's an acquired taste. It's a new language with its own alphabet and grammar. But the more you practice, the more "natural" it will become. This is particularly important, because many Christians, finding it difficult (say) to forgive people, just assume, "This is impossible; I'm never going to manage it." Some may even conclude that rules which they find difficult and "unnatural" don't apply to them, or that those particular rules belong in a bygone age when people saw things differently. That misses the point. Did you think you could sit down at the piano and play a Beethoven sonata straight off? Did you think you could just fly to Moscow, get off the plane, and start speaking fluent Russian? Did you think, as a "normal" young person growing up in today's sex-soaked Western world, that you could attain chastity of heart, mind, and body just through praying one prayer about it? But here are the lessons; here is how to practice; here is the path to the goal. And here—to extend the metaphor to correspond to Christian behavior—the spirit of Beethoven, or the spirit of Russia, will inhabit you and give you the help you will need.

Third, looking at Christian behavior in this way means that we approach "ethical" questions—particular questions about what to do and what not to do—through the larger category of the divine purpose for the entire human life. "Ethics" tends to provide a very restrictive view of what human life is about. Even those people with a well-developed conscience don't normally spend every minute of every day wrestling with moral questions about what to do the next minute, and the one after that. But when we look at Christian behavior in terms of the whole of life, seen from the perspective of the Creator's purpose for humans, ethics can be seen as contained within, and hopefully shaped by, that larger vision. The question of content, of how to know what to do, is not then confined to particular "ethical" dilemmas, but opens up as a vocation to the whole of one's life.

—*After You Believe* 67–69

PASSIONTIDE

So they took Jesus away. He carried his own cross, and went to the spot called "Skull Place" (in Hebrew, "Golgotha"). That was where they crucified him. They also crucified two others, one on either side of him, with Jesus in the middle.

Pilate wrote a notice and had it placed on the cross:

JESUS OF NAZARETH
THE KING OF THE JEWS

Lots of the Judaeans read this notice, because the place where Jesus was crucified was close to the city. it was written in Hebrew, Latin, and Greek. So the chief priests said to Pilate, "Don't write 'The king of the Jews'! Write that he said, 'I am the king of the Jews'!"

"What I've written," replied Pilate, "I've written."

When the soldiers had crucified Jesus, they took his clothes and divided them into four parts, giving each soldier one part. When they came to his tunic, they found that it was a single piece of cloth, woven from top to bottom.

"Let's not tear it," they said to each other. "Let's throw lots for it, to see who's going to have it."

This was so that the Bible would be fulfilled, when it says,

They took my clothes and divided them up, They threw the dice to decide on my garments.

And that's what the soldiers did.

Jesus's mother was standing beside his cross. So was her sister, Mary the wife of Clopas, with Mary Magdalene too. Jesus saw his mother, and the disciple he specially loved, standing there.

"Mother," he said. "Look! There's your son."

Then he spoke to the disciple.

"Look!" he said. "There's your mother."

From that time, the disciple welcomed her into his own home. After this, Jesus knew that everything had at last been completed. "I'm thirsty," he said (fulfilling what the Bible had said). There was a jar there full of sour wine. So they put a sponge filled with the sour wine on a hyssop rod and lifted it to his mouth. Jesus drank it.

"It's all done!" he said.

Then he let his head drop, and gave up his spirit.

—John 19:16b–30, *The Kingdom New Testament* 218–19

A Window into the
Meaning of the World

Whether we believe in Jesus, whether we approve of his teaching, let alone whether we like the look of the movement that still claims to follow him, we are bound to see his crucifixion as one of the pivotal moments in human history. Like the assassination of Julius Caesar around seventy years earlier, it marks the end of one era and the start of another.

And Jesus's first followers saw it as something more. They saw it as the vital moment not just in human history, but in the entire story of God and the world. Indeed, they believed it had opened a new and shocking window onto the meaning of the word "God" itself. They believed that with this event the one true God had suddenly and dramatically put into operation his plan for the rescue of the world.

They saw it as the day the revolution began.

It wasn't just that they believed Jesus had been raised from the dead. They did believe that, of course, and that too was scandalous nonsense in their day as it is in ours. But they quickly came to see his resurrection not simply as an astonishing new beginning in itself, but as *the result of what had happened three days earlier.* The resurrection was the first visible sign that the revolution was already under way. More signs would follow.

—The Day the Revolution Began 4

The Vast and Dangerous Ocean
of the Gospel Story

We lift up our eyes and realize that when the New Testament tells us the meaning of the cross, it gives us not a system, but a story; not a theory, but a meal and an act of humble service; not a celestial mechanism for punishing sin and taking people to heaven, but an earthly story of a human Messiah who embodies and incarnates Israel's God and who unveils his glory in bringing his kingdom to earth as in heaven.

The Western church—and we've all gone along with this—has been so concerned with getting to heaven, with sin as the problem blocking the way, and therefore with how to remove sin and its punishment, that it has jumped straight to passages in Paul that can be made to serve that purpose. It has forgotten that the gospels are replete with atonement theology, through and through—only they give it to us not as a neat little system, but as a powerful, sprawling, many-sided, richly revelatory narrative in which we are invited to find ourselves, or rather to lose ourselves and to be found again the other side. We have gone wading in the shallow and stagnant waters of medieval questions and answers, taking care to put on the right footwear and not lose our balance, when only a few yards away is the vast and dangerous ocean of the gospel story, inviting us to plunge in and let the wild waves of dark glory wash us, wash over us, wash us through and through, and land us on the shores of God's new creation.

The cross itself, in short, stands at the center of the Christian message, the Christian story, and the Christian life and mission. It has lost none of its revolutionary and transformative power down through the centuries. The cross is where the great story of God and creation, focused on the strange story of God and Israel and then focused still more sharply on the personal story of God and Jesus, came into terrible but life-giving clarity. The crucifixion of Jesus of Nazareth was a one-off event, the one on behalf of the many, the one *moment in history* on behalf of all others through which sins would be forgiven, the powers robbed of their power, and humans redeemed to take their place as worshippers and stewards, celebrating the powerful victory of God in his Messiah and so gaining the Spirit's power to make his kingdom effective in the world.

—*The Day the Revolution Began* 415–16

The Fulcrum

The meaning of the story is found in every detail, as well as in the broad narrative. The pain and tears of all the years were met together on Calvary. The sorrow of heaven joined with the anguish of earth; the forgiving love stored up in God's future was poured out into the present; the voices that echo in a million human hearts, crying for justice, longing for spirituality, eager for relationship, yearning for beauty, drew themselves together into a final scream of desolation.

Nothing in all the history of paganism comes anywhere near this combination of event, intention, and meaning. Nothing in Judaism had prepared for it, except in puzzling, shadowy prophecy. The death of Jesus of Nazareth as the king of the Jews, the bearer of Israel's destiny, the fulfillment of God's promises to his people of old, is either the most stupid, senseless waste and misunderstanding the world has ever seen, or it is the fulcrum around which world history turns.

Christianity is based on the belief that it was and is the latter.

—*Simply Christian* III

The Unique Story of the Creator God

In the story of Jesus, and particularly his death, cosmic and global evil, in its suprapersonal as well as personal forms, is met by the sovereign, saving love of Israel's God, YHWH, the creator of the world. The gospels intentionally draw the Old Testament narrative to its climax, framing that narrative as the story of God's strange and dark solution to the problem of evil from Genesis 3 on. What the gospels offer is not a philosophical explanation of evil—what it is or why it's there—but the story of an *event* in which the living God *deals with it*. Like the Exodus from Egypt or the return from Babylon, only now with fully cosmic reach, God has rescued his people from the dark powers of chaos. The sea monsters have done their worst, but God has vindicated his people and put creation to rights.

And he has done so *through* the suffering of Israel's representative, the Messiah. This is what it looks like when YHWH says, as in Exodus 3:7–8, "I have observed the misery of my people. . . . I have heard their cry . . . and I have come down to deliver them." This is what it looks like when YHWH says "here is my servant" (Isa. 42:1). As Isaiah says later (chap. 59), it was no messenger, no angel, but his own presence that saved them; in all their affliction, he was afflicted. God chose the appropriate and necessarily deeply ambiguous route of acting from *within* his creation, from *within* his chosen people, to take the full force of evil upon himself and so exhaust it. And the result is that the covenant is renewed. Sins are forgiven; the long night of sorrow, exile, and death is over and the new day has dawned. New creation has begun, the new world in which violence will be overcome and the sea will be no more.

The gospels thus tell a story unique in the world's great literature, religious theories, and philosophies: the story of the creator God taking responsibility for what's happened to creation, bearing the weight of its problems on his own shoulders.

—*Surprised by Scripture* 122–23

The Victory

The way we have normally listed options in atonement theology simply won't do. Our questions have been wrongly put, because they haven't been about the kingdom. They haven't been about God's sovereign, saving rule coming on earth as in heaven. Instead, our questions have been about a "salvation" that rescues people *from* the world, instead of *for* the world. "Going to heaven" has been the object (ever since the Middle Ages at least, in the Western church); "sin" is what stops us from getting there; so the cross must deal with sin, so that we can leave this world and go to the much better one in the sky, or in "eternity," or wherever.

But this is simply untrue to the story the gospels are telling—which, again, explains why we've all misread these wonderful texts. Whatever the cross achieves must be articulated, if we are to take the four gospels seriously, within the context of the kingdom-bringing victory. This is the ultimate redefinition-in-action of the messianic task, the kingdom-bringing messianic vocation. In all four gospels, not only in John, the cross is the victory that overcomes the world. I am wary of describing this simply as a "Christus Victor" interpretation, because historically that has been associated with other kinds of development and has often been set over against other atonement theologies. But the idea of messianic victory as a fresh interpretation of an ancient Jewish theme is precisely what the four gospels have in mind.

—How God Became King 242–43

A New Way of Being Human

The case I have been putting forward in this book is not just a thinker's puzzle for theologians to argue over in dusty seminar rooms. It is immediately and urgently practical. The "victory" is achieved *because* Jesus "gave himself for our sins," rescuing and forgiving humans and so breaking the deadly grip of the powers they had been worshipping. A mission based on a supposed "victory" that does not have "forgiveness of sins" at its heart will go seriously wrong in one direction. That was the danger of the first view I outlined: triumphalism without forgiveness at its core. A mission based on "forgiveness of sins" where we see things only in terms of "saving souls for heaven" will go wrong in the other direction. That was the danger of the second view: a message of forgiveness that left the powers to rule the world unchallenged. The New Testament insists on both and in their proper relation. That has been my case. When we get this right, the church's true vocation emerges once more.

Notice what then happens. When we see the victory of Jesus in relation to the biblical Passover tradition, reshaped through the Jewish longing for the "forgiveness of sins" *as a liberating event within history,* we see the early Christian movement not as a "religion" in the modern sense at all, but as a complete new way of being human in the world and for the world. People talk glibly of the "rise of Christianity" or even of Jesus as the "founder of Christianity" without realizing that to give Jesus's movement a name like that (an "-ity" alongside all the "-isms") is at once to diminish it, to make it one example of a category, one species within a genus. That is not how it appeared to Jesus's contemporaries. To think of his revolutionary movement in that way is at once to distort its sense of mission.

—*The Day the Revolution Began* 362

Gathering at the Foot of the Cross

Jesus's death was seen by Jesus himself, and then by those who told and ultimately wrote his story, as the ultimate means by which God's kingdom was established. The crucifixion was the shocking answer to the prayer that God's kingdom would come on earth as in heaven. It was the ultimate exodus event through which the tyrant was defeated, God's people were set free and given their fresh vocation, and God's presence was established in their midst in a completely new way for which the Temple itself was just an advance pointer. That is why, in John's gospel, the "glory of God"—with all the echoes of the anticipated return of YHWH to Zion—is revealed in and through Jesus, throughout his public career, in the "signs" he performed, but fully and finally as he is "lifted up" on the cross.

How can this be? How can the horrible, ugly, and brutal execution of a young prophet be the means of establishing God's kingdom? What does it mean to say that the point of the story is that God is now in charge, if the means by which that is accomplished is the death of the one who had gone about making it happen?

—*Simply Jesus* 185

The Enemy, the Accusations, and the Cross

I think we can and must say at least this. In Jesus's own understanding of the battle he was fighting, Rome was not the real enemy. The real enemy, to be met head-on by the power and love of God, was the anti-creation power, the power of death and destruction, the force of accusation, the Accuser who lays a charge against the whole human race and the world itself that all are corrupt and decaying, that all humans have contributed to this by their own idolatry and sin. The terrible thing is that this charge is true. All humans have indeed worshipped what is not divine and so have failed to reflect God's image into the world. They, and creation, are therefore subject to corruption and death. At this level, the Accuser is absolutely right.

But the Accuser is wrong to imagine that this is the creator's last word. What we see throughout Jesus's public career is that he himself is being accused—accused of being a blasphemer by the self-appointed thought police, accused of being out of his mind by his own family, even accused by his followers of taking his vocation in the wrong direction. All the strands of evil throughout human history, throughout the ancient biblical story, come rushing together as the gospels tell the story of Jesus, from the demons shrieking at him in the synagogue to the sneering misunderstanding of the power brokers to the frailty and folly of his own friends and followers.

Finally, of course—and this is the point in the story to which the evangelists are drawing our attention—he is accused in front of the chief priests and the council and in the end by the high priest himself. He is accused of plotting against the Temple; he is accused of forbidding the giving of tribute to Caesar (a standard ploy of revolutionaries); he is accused of claiming to be king of the Jews, a rebel leader; he is accused of blasphemy, of claiming to be God's son. Accusations come rushing together from all sides, as the leaders accuse Jesus before Pilate; and Pilate finally does what all the accusations throughout the gospel have been demanding and has him crucified. Jesus, in other words, has taken the accusations that were outstanding against the world and against the whole human

race and has borne them in himself. That is the point of the story
the way the evangelists tell it.

—Simply Jesus 186–87

The Strength of Love

The powers that put Jesus on the cross didn't realize that by doing
so they were, in fact, serving God's purposes, unveiling the "wisdom" that lies at the heart of the universe. Paul puts it even more
positively, seeing the cross as the weapon with which God stripped
the armor from the rulers and authorities, as soldiers would do with
beaten enemies:

> He stripped the rulers and authorities of their armor, and
> displayed them contemptuously to public view, celebrating
> his triumph over them in him. (Col. 2:15).

That is to say, when Jesus died on the cross he was winning the
victory over "the rulers and authorities" who have carved up this
world in their own violent and destructive way. The establishment
of God's kingdom means the dethroning of the world's kingdoms,
not in order to replace them with another one of basically the same
sort (one that makes its way through superior force of arms), but in
order to replace it with one whose power is the power of the servant
and whose strength is the strength of love.

—How God Became King 205

The Meaning of Jesus's Death
Is Found in a Meal

All four evangelists make it abundantly clear that we are to understand both Jesus's kingdom and his death in relation to the Temple—or rather, in relation to the fulfillment of the Temple's role
in Jesus himself (this is a major theme throughout John) and his
upstaging of it in his last great symbolic actions. It is now becoming more widely recognized, I think, that the synoptic evangelists
present the Last Supper as a "new Temple" moment. Jesus, having
pronounced God's judgment on the old Temple in his dramatic
action and then his discourse on the Mount of Olives, now gathers
his friends around him to celebrate a "Passover meal with a difference," a meal that not only looked back, like all Passover meals,
to the exodus itself, but forward to the new exodus that Jesus was
about to accomplish. Like all Passover meals, it was not just a signpost, but a means, through the sharing of food and wine, of par-
taking in that event about to be accomplished. When Jesus wanted
to explain to his followers the meaning of his death, he didn't give
them a theory; he gave them a meal. The synoptics draw this out in
one way, John in another (with the foot washing, chapter 13).

—*How God Became King* 238

Doing It Declares It

Jesus used his final meal with his followers not only as a way of explaining what his forthcoming death would mean, but as a way of enabling them to share in that death, making it quite literally part of their life through eating the bread and drinking the wine. Paul addresses the situation in Corinth, where, as he says in 1 Corinthians 8:5, there were "many gods and many lords," all doing their best to lure the young Christians away from Jesus. "Whenever you eat this bread and drink this cup," he says, "you are announcing the Lord's death until he comes" (11:26). He doesn't mean that the ceremony of the Lord's Supper is a good occasion for a sermon on the meaning of Jesus's death, though no doubt that will sometimes be true as well. He means that *doing it declares it*.

Think how this works. The actual event—the breaking of bread, the pouring of wine, and the sharing of both all in Jesus's name, which recall his last meal before his death—effectively makes a public announcement. This may have seemed odd to the Corinthians, who were used to sharing the bread and the wine in private, not in front of their pagan neighbors or the wider world. But the word Paul uses for "announce" (*katangello*) is a word regularly used in his culture to describe the announcement of a public decree. If a message came from Rome with a new imperial decree to be read out in the public forum in Corinth with all citizens paying attention, *katangello* might well be the word you'd use to describe what was going on.

So what does Paul mean here? *Doing it declares it:* Breaking the bread and sharing the cup in Jesus's name *declares* his victory to the principalities and powers. It states the new, authorized Fact about the world. It confronts the shadowy forces that usurp control over God's good creation and over human lives with the news of their defeat. It shames the dark powers that stand in the wings, waiting for people to give them even a small bit of worship so that they can use that power, sucking it out of the humans who ought to have been exercising it themselves, to enslave people and render them powerless to resist the temptations that the powers have within their repertoire. The bread-breaking meal, the Jesus feast, announces to the forces of evil like a public decree read out by a herald in the marketplace that Jesus is Lord, that he has faced the powers of sin and death and beaten them, and that he has been raised again to launch the new world in which death itself will have no authority.

—*The Day the Revolution Began* 379–80

The Terror of the Cross

We in the modern West, who wear jeweled crosses around our necks, stamp them on Bibles and prayer books, and carry them in cheerful processions, need regularly to be reminded that the very word "cross" was a word you would most likely not utter in polite society. The thought of it would not only put you off your dinner; it could give you sleepless nights. And if you had actually seen a crucifixion or two, as many in the Roman world would have, your sleep itself would have been invaded by nightmares as the memories came flooding back unbidden, memories of humans half alive and half dead, lingering on perhaps for days on end, covered in blood and flies, nibbled by rats, pecked at by crows, with weeping but helpless relatives still keeping watch, and with hostile or mocking crowds adding their insults to the terrible injuries. All this explains

Cicero's statement that everything to do with crucifixion, including the word *crux* itself,

> should be far removed not only from the person of a Roman citizen but from his thoughts, his eyes, and his ears. For it is not only the actual occurrence of these things, or the endurance of them, but liability to them, the expectation, indeed the very mention of them, that is unworthy of a Roman citizen and a free man. (*In Verrem* 16)
>
> —*The Day the Revolution Began* 54

Jesus's Vocation Leads to the Cross

The cross constitutes Golgotha as the new holy mountain. This is where the nations will now come to pay homage to the world's true Lord. The one enthroned there, with "King of the Jews" above his head, is to have the nations as his inheritance, the uttermost parts of the earth as his possession. His victory over them will not be the victory of swords and guns and bombs, but the victory of his people and of their derivative suffering and testimony. That is how, for the four evangelists, the kingdom and the cross come together at last. That is how the darkest of the "powers" are to be overthrown. For God to become king, the usurping rulers must be ousted.

Throughout his public career, Jesus was engaged in launching that project. But it was on the cross that it came to its triumphant conclusion. That is why, when Peter tried to turn Jesus away from his vocation to suffer, Jesus called him "satan." That is why the mocking voices urging Jesus to come down from the cross echo so disconcertingly the mocking voices in the temptation narratives (cf. Matt. 27:39–43; 4:1–10). Without the cross, the satanic rule remains in place. That is why the cross is, for all four gospels (and, as I have argued elsewhere, for Jesus himself) the ultimate messianic task, the last battle. The evangelists do not suppose that the cross is a defeat, with the resurrection as the surprising over-time victory. The point of the resurrection is that it is the immediate result of the fact that the victory has already been won. Sin has been dealt with. The "accuser" has nothing more to say. The creator can now launch his new creation.

—How God Became King 208–9

"King of the Jews"

The Latin word *titulus* was used to describe the public notice that would be attached to the cross of a condemned criminal, indicating the charge that had led to this extreme verdict. (The practice was well known in European countries until at least the nineteenth century.) Though skeptics have challenged many features of the gospel narratives, this one is generally regarded as very well established, because it fits with normal Roman practice, it is recorded in all four gospels, and it is hardly the sort of thing someone would make up (Jesus's execution was a very public affair, and many people would have seen the notice for themselves).

The point for our present purpose is that, in all four gospels, readers are strongly urged to see Jesus's death as explicitly "royal," explicitly "messianic"—in other words, explicitly to do with the coming of the "kingdom." Jesus has, all along, been announcing that God's kingdom was coming. His followers might well have expected that this announcement would lead to a march on

Jerusalem, where Jesus would do whatever it took to complete what he had begun. And they were right—but not at all in the sense they expected or wanted. That is what the evangelists are saying through this particular moment in the story. This is how the kingdom is to come, the kingdom of God, which Jesus has been announcing and, as Messiah, inaugurating.

—How God Became King 218–19

The Foolishness of the Message of the Cross

In other words, every time Paul came into a new town or city and opened his mouth, he knew perfectly well that what he was saying would make no sense. As with Jesus himself, the kind of "signs" that were on offer were not the sort of thing that the Jewish world was wanting or expecting. A crucified Messiah was a contradiction in terms.

As for the non-Jewish world—well, the suggestion that a *Jew* might be the new "Lord" over all other Lords was bad enough, but a *crucified* man? Everybody knew that was the most shameful and horrible death imaginable. How could such a person then be hailed as *Kyrios*? And if the answer was (as it would be for Paul) that God had raised this man from the dead, that would merely convince his hearers that he was indeed out of his mind. (A Roman governor would accuse him of that later on, but Paul must have been quite used to people saying it.) Everybody knew resurrection didn't happen. A nice dream, perhaps—though many would have said they'd prefer to leave the body behind for good, thank you very much. Anyway, there's no point living in fantasy land.

—Paul: A Biography 213–14

Rescued to Resume the Genuine
Human Existence

The death of Jesus, as explained in Romans 8:1–4, is certainly *penal*. It has to do with the punishment on Sin—not, to say it again, on Jesus—but it is punishment nonetheless. Equally, it is certainly *substitutionary:* God condemned Sin (in the flesh of the Messiah), and therefore sinners who are "in the Messiah" are not condemned. The one dies, and the many do not. All those narrative fragments we saw in Luke and John come into their own. "This man has done nothing wrong." "Let one man die for the people, rather than the whole nation being wiped out." But this substitution finds its true meaning not within the normal "works contract," but within the God-and-Israel narrative, the vocational narrative, the story *in accordance with the Bible.* Once we rescue this substitution from its pagan captivity, it can resume its rightful place at the heart of the Jewish and then the messianic narrative, the story through which—in Romans 8:4 as elsewhere—humans are rescued not so they can "go to heaven," but so that "the right and proper verdict of the law could be fulfilled in us, as we live not according to the flesh but according to the spirit." Humans are rescued in order to be "glorified," that is, so that they may resume the genuine human existence, bearing the divine image, reflecting God's wisdom and love into the world.

What Paul has done is to locate the dealing-with-Sin within the larger kingdom-of-God narrative—just as, in their own way, the gospels did. The new Passover (rescue from the enslaving power) is accomplished by dealing with sins; only now, with "sins" growing to their full extent as "Sin," the two stories finally fuse together into one. To put it another way, Paul has told the long, sad story of Israel and arrived at last at the "slavery" of "exile" as in Deuteronomy 28.

Israel needed a fresh start, such as is described in Deuteronomy 30, which Paul quotes in exactly this sense in Romans 10. But for that, as the prophets insisted, Israel's sins needed to be dealt with so that "exile" could be undone. Paul has now shown, through the complex but carefully consistent narrative he has told, how this joins up with the larger expectation of the "new Exodus." At the heart of this conjoined double story, he has told the story of the Messiah, the one who represents Israel and who therefore becomes the "place" where Sin does its worst. Again, this resonates with the narrative of the four gospels, in which, as we saw, evil of every sort was building up like a thunderstorm as Jesus went about announcing the kingdom. It gathered itself together and finally unleashed its full fury upon him.

—*The Day the Revolution Began* 287–88

Ask Better Questions Before Giving Biblical Answers

Two polemical targets—purgatory and the Mass—ensured that when the Reformers were developing their own ways of explaining what the death of Jesus achieved, they were understandably eager to ward off what they saw as ecclesial abuse. It does seem to me that in general terms the Reformers and their successors were thus *trying to give biblical answers to medieval questions.* They were wrestling with the question of how the angry God of the late medieval period might be pacified, both here (through the Mass?) and hereafter (in purgatory?). To both questions, they replied: no, God's wrath was already pacified through the death of Jesus. Not only does this not need to be done again; if we were to try to do it again, we would be implying that the death of Jesus was somehow after all inadequate. They did not challenge the underlying idea that the gospel was all about pacifying divine wrath. It was simply assumed that this was the problem Paul was addressing in Romans 1:18–32 or indeed 1 Thessalonians 1:10 or 5:9.

If, of course, you are faced with the medieval questions, it is better to give them biblical answers than nonbiblical ones. But the biblical texts themselves might suggest that there were better questions to be asking, which are actually screened out by concentrating on the wrong ones. As I have sometimes remarked in reading the gospels, it is possible to check all the correct boxes, but still end up with the wrong result, like a child doing a connect-the-dots puzzle who doesn't realize the significance of the numbers and ends up with an elephant instead of a donkey; or perhaps, writing from Scotland, I should say a Saltire instead of a Union Jack.

I should also add that these last two or three paragraphs, taken by themselves, could give a very lopsided view of the Reformers. Luther and his colleagues were energetic biblical expositors, excited about the New Testament message of the grace and love of God, which they had not heard taught in the days of their youth. In particular, they went back again and again to grace, love, faith, hope, freedom, and joy as the ultimate reasons for everything, and certainly the ultimate reasons for their own excitement and energy. That, for them, was what it was all about. However, in their insistence on certain particular ways of understanding the biblical teaching on Jesus's death, the two factors I have highlighted—purgatory and the Mass—remained extremely influential. Even when they were gazing in gratitude on the cross as the effective sign of God's love, these concerns and the need to consolidate a Reformation in which abuses would not return to a half-taught church remained powerful.

—*The Day the Revolution Began* 32–33

A Confusing Gospel?

It isn't just those outside the Christian faith who have found the cross a symbol of fear. Many inside the church too have shrunk back from one particular interpretation that, in some form or other, has dominated much Western Christianity over the last half millennium. One recent hymn puts it like this:

> And on the cross, when Jesus died,
> The wrath of God was satisfied—

(This makes it sound like hunger that is satisfied by a good meal.) The line of thought goes like this, usually based on a particular arrangement of biblical texts:

A. All humans sinned, causing God to be angry and to want to kill them, to burn them forever in "hell."

B. Jesus somehow got in the way and took the punishment instead (it helped, it seems, that he was innocent—oh, and that he was God's own son, too).

C. We are in the clear after all, heading for "heaven" instead (provided, of course, we believe it).

Many preachers and teachers put it much more subtly than this, but this is still the story people hear. This is the story they *expect* to hear. In some churches, if you don't tell this story more or less in this way, people will say that you aren't "preaching the gospel."

The natural reaction to this from many who have grown up hearing this message and feeling they *had* to believe it (if they didn't, they would go to hell) is that its picture of God is abhorrent. This God, such people instinctively feel, is a bloodthirsty tyrant. If there is a God, we must hope and pray that he (or she, or it) isn't like that at all. So they react in one of a number of predictable ways. Some people reject the whole thing as a horrible nonsense. Others, puzzled, go back to their Bibles and to the great teachers of the early church, and there they find all sorts of other things being said about the cross, for instance, that it was the means by which God's rescuing love won the ultimate victory over all the forces of darkness. Or they find early writers urging Christians to imitate the self-giving love of Jesus, and they seize upon that as the "answer": the cross, they say, wasn't about God punishing sin; it was about Jesus giving us the ultimate example of love. Thus many different interpretations have arisen, affecting the ways in which people have been taught the Bible and the Christian faith. This has been a recipe for confusion.

—*The Day the Revolution Began* 38–39

A Major Blunder

The danger with this kind of popular teaching—and examples of it are not hard to come by—is that ultimately we end up rewriting one of the most famous verses in the Bible. I already quoted the King James Version of John 3:16: "God so loved the world, that he gave his only begotten Son." Look at the two verbs: God so *loved* the world that he *gave* his son. The trouble with the popular version I have described is that it can easily be heard as saying, instead, that God so *hated* the world, that he *killed* his only son. And that doesn't sound like good news at all. If we arrive at that conclusion, we know that we have not just made a trivial mistake that could easily be corrected, but a major blunder. We have portrayed God not as the generous Creator, the loving Father, but as an angry despot. That idea belongs not in the biblical picture of God, but with pagan beliefs.

—*The Day the Revolution Began* 43

The Abuse of Love

Many people have pointed out that the idea of an angry, bullying deity who has to be appeased, to be bought off, to have his wrathful way with someone even if it isn't the right person fits uncomfortably well with the way many human authority figures actually behave: tyrants, rulers, bosses, sometimes tragically also fathers, within families older men in general. Sometimes, of course, clergy. People who have grown up in a family with a violent, perhaps drunken, father or who have been abused one way or another by people in authority hear someone in a pulpit telling the story of the angry God, and they think, "*I know that character, and I hate him.*" It doesn't do any good to tell people in that state of mind that this angry God is really a loving God in disguise. "*If that's love*," they think, "*then I don't want it.*" They have quite possibly been told by an abuser how much he "loves" them. You cannot rescue someone from the scars of an abusive upbringing by replaying the same narrative on a cosmic scale and mouthing the word "love" as you do so.

—*The Day the Revolution Began* 44

A Covenant of Vocation, Not Works

The "works contract" functions in the popular mind like this. God told his human creatures to keep a moral code; their continuing life in the Garden of Eden depended on their keeping that code perfectly. Failure would incur the punishment of death. This was then repeated in the case of Israel with a sharpened-up moral code, Mosaic law. The result was the same. Humans were therefore heading for hell rather than heaven. Finally, however, Jesus obeyed this moral law perfectly and in his death paid the penalty on behalf of the rest of the human race. The overarching arrangement (the "works contract") between God and humans remained the same, but Jesus had done what was required. Those who avail themselves of this achievement by believing in him and so benefiting from his accomplishment go to heaven, where they enjoy eternal fellowship with God; those who don't, don't. The "works contract" remains intact throughout.

This scheme is regularly explained by reference to the first three chapters of Paul's Letter to the Romans. There, one of the key technical terms is "righteousness," in Greek *dikaiosyne*. For many centuries in many traditions, "righteousness" has been understood as the moral status we would have if only we had kept the "works contract" perfectly, and then (by various explanations) as the status we can have by faith because, despite our moral failure, Jesus has taken the punishment and so provided the "righteousness" as a gift ("the righteousness of Christ").

The problem—to put it bluntly—is that this is not what Romans is all about. Such a view of the relationship between God and humans is a travesty. It is indeed unbiblical. It insists on taking us to a goal very different from the one held out in scripture. It ignores, in particular, the actual meaning of Israel's scriptures, both in themselves and as they were read by the earliest Christians. And it insists on a diagnosis of the human plight that is, ironically, trivial compared with the real thing.

What the Bible offers is not a "works contract," but a covenant of *vocation*. The vocation in question is that of being a genuine human being, with genuinely human tasks to perform as part of the Creator's purpose for his world. The main task of this vocation is "image-bearing," reflecting the Creator's wise stewardship into the world and reflecting the praises of all creation back to its maker. Those who do so are the "royal priesthood," the "kingdom of priests," the people who are called to stand at the dangerous but exhilarating point where heaven and earth meet. In saying this I am echoing what many theologians (including John Calvin, the founder of all "Reformed" theologies) have said before me. This is not surprising, because it is all there in the Bible. But this is not the story that normally comes through in popular preaching and teaching.

—The Day the Revolution Began 75–76

Bearing the Scars of Jesus

God's kingdom is indeed breaking in, but belonging to that new age, that new divine rule, will mean undergoing suffering. The "present age" and the "age to come" are grinding against one another, like upper and lower millstones, as God's new world is brought to birth. Those who find themselves seized by the message of Jesus will be caught in the middle *and will thereby provide in themselves further evidence of the message,* the news that the crucified Messiah is now the Lord of the whole world.

The paradoxes of Paul's apostleship are thus laid bare right from the start of his traveling career. There is a sense in which all the writing that would later flow from his pen becomes a complicated set of footnotes to the reality he was already discovering and modeling. When Paul writes to the churches in Galatia and refers to his first visit to them, he mentions that it was "through bodily weakness that I announced the gospel to you in the first place."

I think it likely that the poor physical condition to which Paul refers is the result of the violence to which he had been subjected. In the ancient world, just as today, the physical appearance of public figures carries considerable weight in how they are assessed. Someone turning up in a city shortly after being stoned or beaten up would hardly cut an imposing figure. The Galatians, however, had welcomed Paul as if he were an angel from heaven or even the Messiah himself. As Paul would later explain, the bodily marks of identification that mattered to him were not the signs of circumcision, but "the marks of Jesus"—in other words, the signs of the suffering he had undergone. When, later on, he faces suffering at other levels as well—including what looks like a nervous breakdown—he will, through gritted teeth, explain that this too is part of what it means to be an apostle.

—*Paul: A Biography* 123–24

The Promise

Truly, if we believe in Matthew's God, the Emmanuel, we must learn to see God in that way. Remember that when Jesus died, the earth shook and the rocks were torn in pieces, while the sky darkened at noon. God the creator will not always save us *from* these

dark forces, but he will save us *in* them, being with us in the darkness and promising us, always promising us, that the new creation
begun at Easter will one day be complete, and then there will be
full healing, full understanding, full reconciliation, full consola-
tion. The thorns and thistles will be replaced by cypress and myrtle.
There will be no more sea.

—Surprised by Scripture 127

Have You Belittled the Cross?

All this, I submit, generates a vision of the cross and its achievement so large and all-embracing that we really ought to stand back
and simply gaze at it. All the "theories" of "atonement" can be
found comfortably within it, but it goes far, far beyond them all,
into the wild, untamed reaches of history and theology, of politics
and imagination. We have, alas, belittled the cross, imagining it
merely as a mechanism for getting us off the hook of our own petty
naughtiness or as an example of some general benevolent truth. It
is much, much more.

It is the moment when the story of Israel reaches its climax;
the moment when, at last, the watchmen on Jerusalem's walls see
their God coming in his kingdom; the moment when the people
of God are renewed so as to be, at last, the royal priesthood who
will take over the world not with the love of power but with the
power of love; the moment when the kingdom of God overcomes
the kingdoms of the world. It is the moment when a great old
door, locked and barred since our first disobedience, swings open
suddenly to reveal not just the garden, opened once more to our
delight, but the coming city, the garden city that God had always

planned and is now inviting us to go through the door and build with him.

The dark power that stood in the way of this kingdom vision has been defeated, overthrown, rendered null and void. Its legions will still make a lot of noise and cause a lot of grief, but the ultimate victory is now assured. This is the vision the evangelists offer us as they bring together the kingdom and the cross.

—How God Became King 239–40

Make the Cross Your Story Too

We do not (of course!) have to give up the idea of Jesus "dying for our sins." Indeed, that remains at the very center. But that idea is refocused, recontextualized, placed within a narrative not of divine petulance, but of unbreakable divine covenant love, embodied in the actual person, life, actions, and teaching of Jesus himself. This means that in order to appropriate this for ourselves, to benefit from this story, it is not simply a matter of believing a particular abstract doctrine, this or that theory of how "atonement" might be thought to "work." No doubt that can help, though with the abstractions can come distortions, as we have seen.

No, the gospels invite us to *make this story our own,* to live within the narrative in all its twists and turns, to see ourselves among the crowds following Jesus and witnessing his kingdom-bringing work, to see ourselves also in the long-range continuation of that narrative that we call, in fear and trembling (because we know its deep am-biguities), the life of the church. In particular, as followers of Jesus from the very beginning have known, we are to make the story our own by the repeated meals in which the Last Supper is brought to life once more. If that was how Jesus wanted his followers not only to understand, but also to appropriate for themselves the meaning of the death he was to die, there is every reason to take it seriously as the sign and foretaste of the eventual kingdom, carrying within it the assurance that we too are those who share in the "forgiveness of sins." And, with that, the gospels give to those who read them the energy and the sense of direction to be Beatitude people for the world, knowing that the victory was indeed won on the cross, that Jesus is indeed already installed as the world's rightful ruler, and that his way of peace and reconciliation has been shown to be more powerful than all the powers of the world.

—*The Day the Revolution Began* 224–25

Dare to Believe

The gospels pose questions to us at every level, questions about what we have called the atonement as well as questions about what we have called the problem of evil. Dare we stand in front of the cross and admit that all this was done for us? Dare we take all the meanings of the word *God* and allow them to be recentered upon, redefined by, this man, this moment, this death? Dare we take the chaos of the dark forces within ourselves and allow Jesus to rebuke them as he rebuked the wind and waves on the Sea of Galilee? Dare we address the consequences of what Jesus said, that the rulers of the world behave in one way but we must not do it like that? Dare we put atonement theology and political theology together, with the deeply personal message on one side and the utterly practical and political message on the other, and turn away from the way of James and John, the way of calling down fire from heaven on our enemies, to embrace the way of Jesus? Dare we live out the message of God's restorative justice, claiming the victory of the cross not only over the obvious wickedness of the world but over the wickedness of those who fight fire with fire, bringing a solution by creating further problems? Dare we stand at the foot of the cross, feeling the storm clouds darken overhead and the earth tremble beneath our feet, and pray once more for God to finish his new creation, to make the wolf and the lamb lie down together, to bid the mighty waves of the sea be still and depart for good, to establish the new heavens and new earth in which justice and joy will dwell forever?

Evil is still a four-letter word; so, thank God, is love.

—Surprised by Scripture 127–28

LOVE

Who shall separate us from the Messiah's love? Suffering, or hardship, or persecution, or famine, or nakedness, or danger, or sword? As the Bible says,

Because of you we are being killed all day long;
We are regarded as sheep destined for slaughter.

No: in all these things we are completely victorious through the one who loved us. I am persuaded, you see, that neither death nor life, nor angels nor rulers, nor the present, nor the future, nor powers, nor height, nor depth, nor any other creature will be able to separate us from the love of God in King Jesus our Lord.

—Romans 8:35–39, *The Kingdom New Testament* 324–25

He Loves Us to the Utmost

John's gospel is a great love story, *the* great love story of all time. John plants love at the very center of his book. From there, it reaches out its arms to what went before and to what comes after:

It was before the Festival of Passover. Jesus knew that his time had come, the time for him to leave this world and go to the father. *He had always loved his own people in the world; now he loved them right through to the end.* (13:1)

I love that "right through to the end." The Greek is even crisper: *eis telos*, "to the goal," "to the utmost." This isn't just about timing ("he never stopped loving them"); it's about the quality of the action. There was nothing that love could do that love did not do, that Jesus did not do. "No one has a love greater than this," he says a bit later, "to lay down your life for your friends. *You are my friends*, if you do what I tell you" (15:13–14). So that sentence in 13:1 serves as a heading for all that is to come: the betrayal by Judas, the denial by Peter, the arrest, the mocking, the trial, the callous cruelty of Calvary. When Paul wrote, in perhaps the most moving moment of his most passionate letter, that "the son of God . . . *loved me and gave himself for me*" (Gal. 2:20), he was summing up exactly the same point. Read John's whole story, from the start of chapter 13 all the way through to the end of the book, as a single, simple act of love, costing not less than everything.

—*Broken Signposts* 39–40

Enfolded in the Arms of Love

John 3:16 ("This, you see, is how much God loved the world: enough to give his only, special son, so that everyone who believes in him should not be lost but should share in the life of God's new age"), then, applies to the whole book, and to the whole world. It invites us to see the entire drama of creation—the planets, the mountains,

the far reaches of cosmic space, the tiniest creature on earth, the refugee, the sick child, the grieving widow, the brittle and arrogant power broker, and the creator God who made them all, loves them all, and grieves over their folly, their wickedness, and their sorrow—from this point of view. John wants us to see this whole story as being narrowed down and focused like a bright, blinding laser beam on the single human story of this man Jesus, the Word who became flesh—the flesh that reached out and touched the sick, the flesh that was nailed to a Roman cross.

—*Broken Signposts* 41–42

Love Is Victorious

A new sort of power will be let loose upon the world, and it will be the power of self-giving love. This is the heart of the revolution that was launched on Good Friday. You cannot defeat the usual sort of power by the usual sort of means. If one force overcomes another, it is still "force" that wins. Rather, at the heart of the victory of God over all the powers of the world there lies self-giving love, which, in obedience to the ancient prophetic vocation, will give its life "as a ransom for many." Exactly as in Isaiah 53, to which that phrase alludes, the death of the one on behalf of the many will be the key by which the powers are overthrown, the kingdom of God ushered in (with the glorious divine Presence seen in plain sight by the watchmen on Jerusalem's walls), the covenant renewed, and creation itself restored to its original purpose.

—*The Day the Revolution Began* 222

Steps of Generous Love

Did we really imagine that, while Jesus would win his victory by suffering, self-giving love, we would implement that same victory by arrogant, self-aggrandizing force of arms? (Perhaps we did. After all, James and John, as close to Jesus as anyone, made exactly this mistake in Luke 9:54 and again in Mark 10:35–40) Once you understand the kind of revolution Jesus was accomplishing, you understand why it would then go on being necessary for it to be implemented step by step, not all at one single sweep, and why those steps have to be, every one of them, steps of the same generous love that took Jesus to the cross. Love will always suffer. If the church tries to win victories either all in a rush or by steps taken in some other spirit, it may appear to succeed for a while. Think of the pomp and "glory" of the late medieval church. But the "victory" will be hollow and will leave all kinds of problems in its wake.

—*The Day the Revolution Began* 374

The Motivating Power of New Creation

The thing about the new creation is that it simply overflows with the power of love. Read the Easter stories, especially the longer ones in Luke 24 and John 20–21. Jesus meets his followers. They are sorrowful, ashamed, and anxious. He calls them by name. He tells them not to be afraid. He explains what's going on. He deals with them individually. The meeting with the two on the road to Emmaus (Luke 24) is one of the most gently powerful stories ever written. The brief conversation between Jesus and Peter in John 21 is one of the most moving human encounters ever recorded. There is a love, a deep, moving warmth that goes out from Jesus. But this love is strong, powerful, life-changing, life-directing. New creation has begun; and its motivating power is love.

That is why, in Luke's gospel, the risen Jesus tells his followers to go and announce to the world that a new way of life has been opened, the way of "repentance" and "forgiveness" (24:47). To us Westerners, that sounds a bit gloomy, as though it's a perpetual act of contrition, dredging up our "sins" in order to hear someone declare them forgiven (until next time!). But it's far, far bigger than that. The old creation lives by pride and retribution: I stand up for myself, and if someone gets in my way I try to get even. We've been there, done that, and got the scars to prove it. Now there is a completely different way to live, a way of love and reconciliation and healing and hope. It's a way nobody's ever tried before, a way that is as unthinkable to most human beings and societies as—well, as resurrection itself. Precisely. That's the point. Welcome to Jesus's new world.

—*Simply Jesus* 194

The Resurrection Awakens Love

Then comes the third question to Peter in John 21. This time Jesus uses the word Peter had used. "Simon, son of John," he says, "are you my friend?" Peter was upset, says John, that this third time Jesus said it like that, and he replied eagerly. But I think the point is this—and it's a point that I suspect many of us need, in our varied discipleship and service. This is, for me, the heart of the Easter message as applied to those who would seek to be Jesus's friends, to follow him and serve him. "Very well," Jesus is saying, "if that's where you are, that's where we'll start." As with Mary and her tears, as with Thomas and his skepticism, Jesus comes halfway to meet Peter. He doesn't insist on Peter being able to say the big *L* word, the *agápē* word, right off. That will come. Peter is hanging in there: "Yes, Master; You know I'm your friend." "All right, Peter; that's where we'll begin. Feed my sheep. And, by the way, things are going to be tough; other people will have other tasks to do, but you must simply remember this: 'Follow me!'"

It is love that believes the resurrection. It is, conversely, the resurrection of Jesus that awakens love—love for him, love for one another, love for God's world. This is the message of Easter. This is the message of hope. This is the message for, and through, the whole church, through all of us together. This is the message of Jesus. May it be so for us, in us and not least through us.

—*Surprised by Scripture* 216–17

A New Reality

Love is the reality that belongs to God's future, glimpsed in the present like a puzzling reflection, but waiting there in full reality for the face-to-face future. And the point is that this future *has come forward into the present time* in the events involving Jesus and in the power of the spirit. That is why love matters for Paul—more even than "faith," which many have seen as his central theme.

Love is the present virtue in which believers anticipate, and practice, the life of the ultimate age to come.

That is why the final theological chapter in the letter, 1 Corinthians 15, dealing with the resurrection of the body, comes where it does. It is not a detached discussion tacked onto the end of the letter dealing with a distinct topic unrelated to what has gone before. It is the center of everything. "If the Messiah wasn't raised," he declares, "your faith is pointless, and you are still in your sins." Unless this is at the heart of who they are, he says (here is his own regular anxiety, now framed as a challenge to the Corinthians), their faith is in vain, "for nothing." But it isn't: the resurrection of Jesus means that a new world has opened up, so that, "in the Lord . . . the work you're doing will not be worthless." The resurrection is the ultimate answer to the nagging question of whether one's life and work have been "in vain."

—*Paul: A Biography* 256

The Generous Love of Creation

God creates "that which is not God" *out of generous love* in order that he may then, in the end, fill it, flood it, drench it, with his love and his glory.

Here is the paradox at the heart of the ancient biblical vision of creation, a paradox that reaches its height in the person of Jesus himself and then in the lives of all who are indwelt by his Spirit. God creates us to be precisely *other than God* because that is what love—the divine love—is like. God has taken great delight in the whale and the anteater, in the cedar tree and the rosebush, in the wild asses and the slimy, creeping things of the sea, in the lions roaring for their food and the little furry animals scurrying around the mountain rocks. All that is already there in Psalm 104 and else-where. This is the sheer matter of the world.

—*Case for the Psalms* 136

Why Did God Make the World?

Again and again, the early Christians came back not to theory but to gratitude and to answering love. "This is how we know love: he laid down his life for us" (1 John 3:16). "Love consists in this: not that we loved God, but that he loved us and sent his son to be the sacrifice that would atone for our sins" (1 John 4:10). "We love because he first loved us" (1 John 4:19). "The son of God . . . loved me and gave himself for me" (Gal. 2:20). "This is how God demon-strates his own love for us: the Messiah died for us while we were still sinners" (Rom. 5:8). "He had always loved his own people in the world; now he loved them right through to the end" (John 13:1). This is at the heart of the good news of God. What God *has* done in Jesus and what he *will do* at the end are united and held together in this: that he is the God of utter, generous love.

The thing about love is that it is *creative*. The great medieval Italian poet Dante ended his masterpiece by invoking "the love that moves the sun and the other stars." If today we hear that as a sentimental metaphor, it is because our vision of love is too small. Dante had grasped something deep within the thought of ancient Israel, deep within the good news of the first followers of Jesus, deep within the mind and heart and vocation of Jesus: the good news that there is indeed a God, a God who made the world, a God who made the world not because he was forced to but because his inmost nature is generous, exuberant love.

This is the basis of all other good news: that the power behind the cosmos is not blind chance, nor yet brute force, but love. It is a delighted love that celebrates the goodness and specialness of every part of creation and of the extraordinary, brilliant, pulsating entirety of it. A love that cares for and cares about the smallest creature and the farthest star. A love that made one creature in particular, humans, to share uniquely in the capacity to receive and to give love, and so to share uniquely in the vocation to work with the grain of the Creator's intention, to bring his work to its wonderful intended fulfillment. There are many things in the world as it now is that conspire to make us forget this great truth. The good news of Jesus is there not only to remind us of it but to transform us with it so that we in turn may become transformative people.

—*Simply Good News* 139–40

Love Allows the Other to Flourish

How then can we think wisely about God's present relation to the created order? If God is indeed the creator of the world, it matters that creation is other than God. This is not a moral problem, as has sometimes been thought (if a good God makes something that is not himself, it must be less than good, and therefore he is not a good God for making it). Nor is it a logical one (if in the beginning God is all that there is, how can there be ontological room for anything or anyone else?). As we said earlier, if creation was a work of love, it must have involved the creation of something other than God. That same love then allows creation to be itself, sustaining it in providence and wisdom but not overpowering it. Logic cannot comprehend love; so much the worse for logic.

That, though, is not the end of the story. God intends in the end to fill all creation with his own presence and love. God's creative love, precisely by being love, creates *new* space for there to be things that are genuinely other than God.

—*Surprised by Hope* 101–2

Unshakeable Love

The normal objection to theories of atonement and redemption that focus on divine *anger* is that this seems to run contrary to the deepest themes of the New Testament. Now, of course, divine anger at human rebellion and particularly at the rebellion of the chosen people features prominently throughout Israel's scriptures. Similar notes are struck in the New Testament, not least in the teaching of Jesus himself. And suggestion that "sin" does not make God angry (a frequent idea in modern thought as a reaction against the caricatures of an ill-tempered deity) needs to be treated with disdain. When God looks at sin, what he sees is what a violin maker would see if the player were to use his lovely creation as a tennis racquet. But here is the difference. In many expressions of pagan religion, the humans have to try to pacify the angry deity. But that's not how it happens in Israel's scriptures. The biblical promises of redemption have to do with God himself acting because of his unchanging, unshakeable love for his people.

—*The Day the Revolution Began* 132

Love Seeking Understanding— to Be More Love-Like

The aim, as in all theological and biblical exploration, is not to replace love with knowledge. Rather, it is to keep love focused upon its true object. We must not make the overwhelming experience of God's love revealed in the cross of Jesus an excuse for mere muddle. As in a marriage, love doesn't stand still. A passionately devoted young couple need to learn the long-term skills of mutual understanding, not to replace love, but to deepen it. It is, of course, better to hold on to love (whether that of God or of a spouse), even when we are confused, than to let go because we can't understand it. But it is far better to address the confusions. It isn't only faith that seeks understanding. Love ought to do the same; not, of course, in order to stop loving, but so that love may grow, mature, and bear fruit.

—*The Day the Revolution Began* 24

Love Is Indivisible and Jesus Is Indivisible

Where has this taken us? It has taken us to the point where we can see an integrated mode of knowing. All knowledge, suggests the biblical wisdom teaching, involves human beings in a much more complex series of relationships than simply that of the detached observer obtaining a supposed "view from nowhere."

There is an obvious biblical term for all this, and it is *love*. Our word *love* has tried to do so many jobs within the English-speaking world that it is hard to get this particular meaning into focus. But we must try. One of the primary things about love is that it strongly and radically affirms the person or thing that is loved. It doesn't try to manipulate him, her, or it, or to pull it out of shape; it desires the best for its object and works to bring that best about. But, at the same time, genuine love, whether for a person or an object, a tree, a star, a mountain, or a piece of literature, can never be objective in the sense of offering a detached, fly-on-the-wall perspective. Love draws together what the Enlightenment split apart at the level of knowing, just as—and for the same reasons—in my own field it tried to split apart the Jesus of history and the Christ of faith. It can't be done. Love is indivisible, and Jesus is indivisible, and the two rather obviously go together. And if you think that sounds like a pietistic short-circuiting of the whole thing, so that a leap of faith toward Jesus makes everything else irrelevant, that simply shows how deeply the split world has still got hold of us.

—*Surprised by Scripture* 147–48

The Far Better Way of Love

Love is sustained, as in Paul's famous passage, by faith on the one hand and hope on the other, all together looking at God the creator and recreator and at his promises, made sure and certain in Jesus Christ.

Western society has known something of this love. Forgiveness is held as a virtue by many in our world, in a way which is quite foreign to some other worldviews. We know we don't do it, by and large, but we think we *should*. The result of this, unfortunately, is that we have developed a corollary that is neither love nor forgiveness—namely, tolerance. The problem with this is clear: I can "tolerate" you without it costing me anything very much. I can shrug my shoulders, walk away, and leave you to do your own thing. That, admittedly, is preferable to my taking you by the throat and shaking you until you agree with me. But it is certainly not love. Love affirms the reality of the other person, the other culture, the other way of life; love takes the trouble to get to know the other person or culture, finding out how he, she, or it ticks, what makes it special; and finally, love wants the best for that person or culture. It was love, not just an arrogant imposition of alien standards, that drove much of the world to oppose the apartheid regime in South Africa. It was love, not a dewy-eyed, antibusiness prejudice (though that's what they said to him at the time), that drove abolitionist William Wilberforce to protest against the slave trade. It is love, not cultural imperialism, that says it is dehumanizing and society-destroying to burn a surviving widow on her husband's funeral pyre, or to kill the daughter who has eloped with a man of a different religion or race. Love must confront "tolerance" and insist, as it always has done, on a better way.

It is interesting how all the roads lead back to love. Love is often parodied, but its power shines through nonetheless. The greatest of the virtues, the first fruit of the Spirit—even the pagan moralists note it as the primary thing which sets Christianity apart.

—*After You Believe* 254–55

Love Is a Language to Be Learned

First Corinthians 13 is one of the best-known passages in all of Paul.

Fair enough to hold before yourselves that astonishing portrait. But don't imagine that you can just step into it on a cheerful sunny morning and stay there effortlessly forever. The last lines tell their own story: bearing, believing, hoping, enduring, never failing—all these speak of moments, hours, days, and perhaps years when there will be things to bear, things to believe against apparent evidence, things to hope for which are not seen at present, things to endure, things which threaten to make love fail. The phrase "tough love" now sounds hackneyed, a relic of social debates from the day before yesterday. But the love of which Paul speaks *is* tough. In fact, it's the toughest thing there is.

The love of which Paul speaks is clearly a *virtue*.

It is not a "rule" of the sort that is so out of fashion nowadays, imposed in an arbitrary fashion and to be obeyed out of a sense of duty. (We shall discuss the more serious question of proper rules and their relation to virtue later on.)

It is not a "principle," a generalized rule that a person either obeys or disobeys.

It is not a "prudential maxim based on calculated effects"; though it has to be said that if even a few more people lived in the way Paul describes, a lot more people would be a lot more happy.

Nor, especially, is it the result of people "doing what comes naturally." At every single point in Paul's catalogue of what love does, and what love doesn't do, we want to say, "Yes, I see what you mean. However, left to my own inclinations, I would be small-minded, unkind, jealous, fussy, puffed up, shameless, and so on. In particular, left to myself, there are some things I wouldn't bear, many things I wouldn't believe, several things I wouldn't be able to hope for, and a whole multitude that I wouldn't endure. Left to myself, doing what comes naturally, I would fail." But the point of love is that it *doesn't*.

That is why love is a virtue. It is a language to be learned, a musical instrument to be practiced, a mountain to be climbed via some steep and tricky cliff paths but with the most amazing view from the top. It is one of the things that will last; one of the traits of character which provides a genuine anticipation of that complete humanness we are promised at the end. And it is one of the things, therefore, that can be *anticipated* in the present on the basis of the future goal, the *telos,* which is already given in Jesus Christ. It is part of the future that can be drawn down into the present.

—*After You Believe* 181–83

Love Is at the Heart of the Surprise of Hope

The point of 1 Corinthians 13 is that love is not our duty; it is our *destiny*. It is the language Jesus spoke, and we are called to speak it so that we can converse with him. It is the food they eat in God's new world, and we must acquire the taste for it here and now. It is the music God has written for all his creatures to sing, and we are called to learn it and practice it now so as to be ready when the conductor brings down his baton. It is the resurrection life, and the resurrected Jesus calls us to begin living it with him and for him right now. Love is at the very heart of the surprise of hope: people who truly hope as the resurrection encourages us to hope will be people enabled to love in a new way. Conversely, people who are living by this rule of love will be people who are learning more deeply how to hope.

—*Surprised by Hope* 288

The Passionate Love of Paul

All this might seem to imply, however, that Paul was primarily, and perhaps only, a "thinker"—a detached brain box, a computer on legs. Not so. As we have seen repeatedly, he defined himself in terms of love: the love of God in the Messiah, the debt of that love that only love could repay, the love that bound him in a rich personal relationship with Jesus himself ("knowing him, knowing the power of his resurrection, and knowing the partnership of his sufferings," Phil. 3:10). The love that constantly overflowed into what we might call "pastoral" activity but that, for Paul, was simply love in action. We see that powerful but also vulnerable love in his very explicit anxieties over the Thessalonian church in the early days after its founding and in his deeply troubled reaction to the Corinthian church as he made his final journey from Ephesus to confront them once more. We see that love, powerfully and shrewdly in action, in the little letter to Philemon.

It is out of that love and pastoral concern that there flowed simultaneously the constant question of whether he was "running to no good effect" and the constant scriptural answer: *You are my servant.* Isaiah 49 played around and around in his head—along with many other passages, of course, but this one, and some phrases from it in particular, formed a lifelong mental habit. Isaiah's vision of the servant who would bring God's light to the Gentiles and of the troubles that this servant would have to undergo—including doubt about whether his work was actually doing any good at all—was Paul's constant companion.

—*Paul: A Biography* 410–11

We Are Made for Love

John's gospel says a clear, no-nonsense *yes* to the longing, the desire, the anguish of our broken and messed-up loves, our obsessions, and our self-absorption. Yes, that is (our distortion notwithstanding), to the reality that as God-reflecting human beings *we are made for love*, made to find ourselves in and through love, the love we give and the love we receive.

But John is totally clear that this love, embodied and dramatically lived out by Jesus himself in his utter seriousness and light-touch playfulness, comes to us through, and only through, the victory won on the cross over the dark distortions. It comes to us as part of new creation. The resurrection says God's *yes* to the whole created order and, with it, to the love that all humans know in their bones is central to what it means to *be* human. The love that Jesus's followers are then called to offer to one another and to the world—the love that is, as Paul says, the first element of the "fruit of the spirit"—this love is public truth. When the world sees it, it will recognize it as the genuine article.

—*Broken Signposts* 55

Love Lasts

The *agapē* ("love") we are called to practice in the present, to learn like a difficult but powerful language and to practice like a beautiful but complex musical instrument, will last into the future world—indeed, will be gloriously fulfilled in the future world—because it is the very essence of the God we know in Jesus Christ. The God whom Paul had come to recognize in the face of the crucified and risen Jesus is the God of utter self-giving love, and if we humans are called to reflect this God, to be "renewed in knowledge according to his image," then it is not surprising that love of this sort is the key element in that future life and in its anticipation here and now. It will "abide" (13:13); it will remain. It is the supreme example of the principle Paul articulates two chapters later (15:58): what we do in the present, in the Lord, is not wasted.

—After You Believe 188

Loving by Living Jesus

Precisely because the greatest Christian virtue is love, modeled on that of the creating and life-giving God, the individual Christian and the church as a whole must develop the settled habits of looking out for what's going on in the surrounding world, rejoicing with its joy, weeping with its grief, and above all eager for opportunities to bring love, comfort, healing, and hope wherever possible. And with all these it may bring faith, not necessarily by speaking of

Jesus all the time (though there will be such opportunities), but by *living* Jesus in public.

—*After You Believe* 237

The Source and Shape of All Christian Mission

The love, the "uttermost" love, that Jesus pours out is the sharply focused divine covenant love, which had made promises to Abraham, promises that his descendants would be freed from slavery and given their inheritance, promises that were fulfilled when this love came down to Egypt to rescue them. John is telling the story of the new Exodus, the new tabernacle, and, of course, the new Torah: "I am giving you a new commandment," says Jesus. "Love one another . . . just as I have loved you" (13:34). The people who are rescued by the cross and the love it reveals will then be shaped by the cross and the love it will reveal through them to the world: "This is how everybody will know that you are my disciples, if you have love for each other" (13:35). This is how we learn not only to *tell* the story of Jesus, but also to *live* the story of Jesus. There is a straight line from here to Jesus's commissioning of the disciples in John 20 and particularly to his recommissioning of Peter in John 21. This is the source, and the shape, of all Christian mission.

—*The Day the Revolution Began* 414–15

EASTER
The New Year

If it's only for this present life that we have put our hope in the Messiah, we are the most pitiable members of the human race.

But in fact the Messiah has been raised from the dead, as the first fruits of those who have fallen asleep. For since it was through a human that death arrived, it's through a human that the resurrection from the dead has arrived. All die in Adam, you see, and all will be made alive in the Messiah.

Each, however, in proper order. The Messiah rises as the first fruits; then those who belong to the Messiah will rise at the time of his royal arrival. Then comes the end, the goal, when he hands over the kingly rule to God the father, when he has destroyed all rule and all authority and power. He has to go on ruling, you see, until "he has put all his enemies under his feet." Death is the last enemy to be destroyed.

—1 Corinthians 15:19–26, *The Kingdom New Testament* 361

In the End—the Beginning

Jesus's resurrection is to be seen as the beginning of the new world, the first day of the new week, the unveiling of the prototype of what God is now going to accomplish in the rest of the world.

—Surprised by Hope 238

A Solid, Definite, and Practical New Life

Here, then, is the message of Easter, or at least the beginning of that message. The resurrection of Jesus doesn't mean, "it's all right. We're going to heaven now." No, the life of heaven has been born on this earth. It doesn't mean, "So there *is* a life after death." Well, there is, but Easter says much, much more than that. It speaks of a life that is neither ghostly nor unreal, but solid and definite and practical. The Easter stories come at the end of the four gospels, but they are not about an "end." They are about a beginning. The beginning of God's new world. The beginning of the kingdom. God is now in charge, on earth as in heaven. And God's "being-in-charge" is focused on Jesus himself being king and Lord. The title on the cross was true after all. The resurrection proves it.

—Simply Jesus 194–95

The Resurrection Declares That Jesus Is God's Son

The whole truth is that *Jesus himself, in his risen physical body, is the beginning of God's new creation.* He not only presides over that new creation; he *is* that new creation, in person. Everything about the larger Christian hope follows from this. "He is the start of it all," writes Paul, "firstborn from realms of the dead; so in all things he might be chief" (Col. 1:18). This is where the good news provides the launching pad, not for people to go to heaven but for people to discover that *God's new world has begun, and we can be part of it.* Welcome to the full meaning of the good news.

I hope it is now clear why the resurrection of Jesus is so central and vital—as Paul insists again and again, especially in 1 Corinthians 15:17. "If the Messiah wasn't raised," he writes, "your faith is pointless, and you are still in your sins." If the Messiah is not raised, the covenant is not renewed, creation is not renewed, and . . . he is not even the Messiah in the first place. The resurrection is the sign that the verdict of the courts has been reversed.

The Jewish court tried Jesus for blasphemy and found him guilty; the resurrection declared that he really was God's son. Pilate's court tried him for being a would-be rebel leader, and though Pilate didn't really find Jesus guilty, he handed him over on that charge. The resurrection declared that Jesus was not the ordinary sort of political king, a rebel leader, that some had supposed. He was the leader of a far larger, more radical revolution than anyone had ever supposed. He was inaugurating a whole new world, a new creation, a new way of being human. He was forging a way into a new cosmos, a new era, a form of existence hinted at all along but never before unveiled. Here it is, he was saying. This is the new creation you've been waiting for. It is open for business. Come and join in.

—*Simply Good News* 100–1

Fishermen and Shepherds

We find in John 21 (one of the most moving and profound chapters in the whole Bible) a multilayered statement of the new commission already announced in 20:19–23. The disciples go fishing but catch nothing. Jesus then helps them to an enormous catch but proceeds to commission Peter to be a shepherd rather than a fisherman. There are many things going on simultaneously here, but at the center is the challenge to a new way of life, a new forgiveness, a new fruitfulness, a new following of Jesus, which will be wider and more dangerous than what has gone before. This is a million miles from the hymns that speak of Jesus's resurrection in terms of our own assurance of a safe and happy rest in heaven. Quite the contrary. Jesus's resurrection summons us to dangerous and difficult tasks on earth.

In this story, fishing seems to stand for what the disciples, like the rest of the world, were doing anyway whereas shepherding seems to stand for the new tasks within the new creation. To develop that as a metaphor, it seems to me that a good deal of the church's work at the moment is concentrating on fishing, and helping others to fish, rather than on shepherding. Yes, there are tasks to be done in helping the present world to do better what it should be doing. Jesus will help us to do that. We are to be at work in partnership with the wider world. But if we only try to do alongside others what they are doing already, we will miss the really significant task. As with Isaiah's vision in the Temple, and many other scenes both biblical and modern, Peter's change from fisherman to shepherd comes through his facing of his own sin and his receiving of forgiveness, as Jesus with his three-times-repeated question goes back to Peter's triple denial and then offers him forgiveness precisely in the form of a transformed and newly commissioned life. Those who don't want to face that searching question and answer may remain content to help the world with its fishing. Those who find the risen Jesus going to the roots of their rebellion, denial, and sin and offering them love and forgiveness may well also find themselves sent off to be shepherds instead. Let those with ears listen.

—*Surprised by Hope* 240–41

One Small Gesture of Love

One great project in which I worked with others happened a few years ago in the northeast of England. I worked there as bishop, and for a week thousands of young people came together to be taught the scriptures in the morning, work on social projects in the afternoon, and hold celebratory and evangelistic rallies in the evening.

Among my favorite memories of the week was going with one of the dozens of afternoon groups to paint the back walls of a lane of dark and dismal houses in the wrong part of one of our old towns, and hang flower baskets all the way down the road. People were coming out of their houses—and that's something they didn't normally do, because they were afraid of those dark back alleys because of what used to go on there—and asking nervously whether we were from the Council or whether they were going to have to pay. No, replied the cheerful teenagers, we're from the church; this is just a present to you. They were astonished.

And the story doesn't stop there, because when I went back a year later, the residents had begun to do more things in that back alley, planting little gardens and holding barbecues and getting to know one another. One small gesture of love and generosity from the church cascaded into new life and new possibilities for a whole street. And when the lay church worker who had gone to live on that street spoke about Jesus, they knew it was true. They had seen the marks.

—Surprised by Scripture 214–15

Improvising in the Key of Resurrection Hope

We who call ourselves Christians must be totally committed to telling the story of Jesus both as the climax of Israel's story and as the foundation of our own. We recognize ourselves as the direct successors of the churches of Corinth, Ephesus, and the rest, and we need to pay attention to what was said to them as though it was said to us. We cannot relativize the epistles by pointing out the length of time that has passed between them and us, or by suggesting any intervening seismic cultural shifts that would render them irrelevant or even misleading. It is an essential part of authentic Christian discipleship both to see the New Testament as the foundation for the ongoing (and still open-ended) fifth act of God's great story and to recognize that it cannot be supplanted or supplemented. The fifth act goes on, but its first scene is non-negotiable, and remains the standard by which the various improvisations of subsequent scenes are to be judged. That is what it means for the church to live under the authority of scripture—or rather, as I have stressed all along, under God's authority mediated through scripture.

The New Testament offers us glimpses of where the story is to end: not with us "going to heaven," as in many hymns and prayers, but with new creation. Our task is to discover, through the Spirit and prayer, the appropriate ways of improvising the script between the foundation events and charter, on the one hand, and the complete coming of the Kingdom on the other. Once we grasp this framework, other things begin to fall into place.

The notion of "improvising" is important, but sometimes misunderstood. As all musicians know, improvisation does not at all mean a free-for-all where "anything goes," but precisely a disciplined and careful listening to all the other voices around us, and a constant attention to the themes, rhythms and harmonies of the complete performance so far, the performance which we are now called to continue. At the same time, of course, it invites us, while being fully obedient to the music so far, and fully attentive to the voices around us, to explore fresh expressions, provided they will eventually lead to that ultimate resolution which appears in the New Testament as the goal, the full and complete new creation which was gloriously anticipated in Jesus's resurrection. The music so far, the voices around us, and the ultimate multipart harmony of God's new world: these, taken together, form the parameters for appropriate improvisation in the reading of scripture and the announcement and living out of the gospel it contains. All Christians, all churches, are free to improvise their own variations designed to take the music forward. No Christian, no church, is free to play out of tune.

—*Scripture and the Authority of God* 125–27

Embracing the Vision of
New Heavens and New Earth

As we tell the story again, as we listen to the musical settings, as we contemplate some of the great works of art that help us to glimpse the way in which the horror and pain of the world and the powerful love of the creator God came rushing together on to one place; as we find ourselves battling an intransigent magistrate on behalf of someone suffering injustice or praying at a deathbed and feeling a soft hand squeeze at the name of Jesus; as we find ourselves singing "When I Survey the Wondrous Cross"; as we find ourselves stopped in our tracks once more by the forgiving love that won't let us go sneaking back to the place of slavery—on these occasions and on thousands more we know that we are in the presence of the Lover himself.

Christian devotion today has everything to gain and nothing to lose by exploring what the early Christians meant when they said that the Messiah died for their sins "in accordance with the Bible," by understanding better how the great story fits together and how it all makes sense. Christian theology, undergirding that devotion, has everything to gain and nothing to lose by abandoning its Platonized eschatology, its moralized anthropology, and its paganized soteriology and embracing instead the vision of new heavens and new earth with renewed humans rescued from the power of sin and death to take their proper and responsible place, here and now and in the age to come, within that new world.

—*The Day the Revolution Began* 409

Easter Should Be Raucous with Celebration

Consider Easter Day itself. It's a great step forward that many churches now hold Easter vigils, as the Orthodox church has always done, but in many cases they are still too tame by half. Easter is about the wild delight of God's creative power—not very Anglican, perhaps, but at least we ought to shout Alleluias instead of murmuring them; we should light every candle in the building instead of only some; we should give every man, woman, child, cat, dog, and mouse in the place a candle to hold; we should have a real bonfire; and we should splash water about as we renew our baptismal vows. Every step back from that is a step toward an ethereal or esoteric Easter experience, and the thing about Easter is that it is neither ethereal nor esoteric. It's about the real Jesus coming out of the real tomb and getting God's real new creation under way.

—Surprised by Hope 255–56

Our Greatest Day

All right, the Sundays after Easter still lie within the Easter season. We still have Easter readings and hymns during them. But Easter week itself ought not to be the time when all the clergy sigh with relief and go on holiday. It ought to be an eight-day festival, with champagne served after morning prayer or even before, with lots of alleluias and extra hymns and spectacular anthems. Is it any wonder people find it hard to believe in the resurrection of Jesus if we don't throw our hats in the air? Is it any wonder we find it hard to *live* the resurrection if we don't do it exuberantly in our liturgies? Is it any wonder the world doesn't take much notice if Easter is celebrated as simply the one-day happy ending tacked on to forty days of fasting and gloom? It's long overdue that we took a hard look at how we keep Easter in church, at home, in our personal lives, right through the system. And if it means rethinking some cherished habits, well, maybe it's time to wake up. That always comes as a surprise.

And while we're about it, we might write some more good Easter hymns and take care to choose the many good ones already written that celebrate what Easter really is rather than treating it as simply our ticket to a blissful life hereafter. Interestingly, most of the good Easter hymns turn out to be from the early church and most of the bad ones from the nineteenth century. But we should be taking steps to celebrate Easter in creative new ways: in art, literature, children's games, poetry, music, dance, festivals, bells, special concerts, anything that comes to mind. This is our greatest festival. Take Christmas away, and in biblical terms you lose two chapters at the front of Matthew and Luke, nothing else. Take Easter away, and you don't have a New Testament; you don't have a Christianity; as Paul says, you are still in your sins. We shouldn't allow the secular world, with its schedules and habits and parareligious events, its cute Easter bunnies, to blow us off course. This is our greatest day. We should put the flags out.

—Surprised by Hope 256–57

There Will Be No End
to the New Creation

It is true that faith and hope do at present seem to us to be looking forward to the new age, so that we might assume that when that new age comes, they will be redundant. But Paul sees much deeper than that. Faith is the settled, unwavering trust in the one true God whom we have come to know in Jesus Christ. When we see him face-to-face we shall not abandon that trust, but deepen it. Hope is the settled, unwavering confidence that this God will not leave us or forsake us, but will always have more in store for us than we could ask or think.

I do not imagine for a minute that in the coming age we shall arrive at a point where we shall have experienced everything the new world has to offer, and will become bored (as is imagined by some scornful contemporary visions of "heaven"). That is a gross caricature, born of the bland talk about "heaven" that has characterized "afterlife" speculation in the Western world over the last century or two. In contrast, because I believe that the God we know in Jesus is the God of utterly generous, outflowing love, I believe that there will be no end to the new creation of this God, and that within the new age itself there will always be more to hope for, more to work for, more to celebrate. Learning to hope in the present time is learning not just to hope for a better place than we currently find ourselves in, but learning to trust the God who is and will remain the God of the future.

—After You Believe 204–5

BIBLIOGRAPHY

All daily readings are taken from the publications below
and are used by permission of the publisher.

Wright, N. T. *After You Believe: Why Christian Character Matters*. San Francisco: HarperOne, 2012.

———. *Broken Signposts: How Christianity Makes Sense of the World*. San Francisco: HarperOne, 2020.

———. *How God Became King: The Forgotten Story of the Gospels*. San Francisco: HarperOne, 2016.

———. *Paul: A Biography*. San Francisco: HarperOne, 2018.

———. *Scripture and the Authority of God: How to Read the Bible Today*. San Francisco: HarperOne, 2013. First Published as *The Last Word*, 2005.

———. *Simply Christian: Why Christianity Makes Sense*. San Francisco: HarperOne, 2010.

———. *Simply Good News: Why the Gospel Is News and What Makes It Good*. San Francisco: HarperOne, 2015.

———. *Simply Jesus: Who He Was, What He Did, Why It Matters*. San Francisco: HarperOne, 2011.

———. *Surprised by Hope: Rethinking Heaven, the Resurrection, and the Mission of the Church*. San Francisco: HarperOne, 2014.

———. *Surprised by Scripture: Engaging Contemporary Issues*. San Francisco: HarperOne, 2014.

———. *The Case for the Psalms: Why They Are Essential*. San Francisco: HarperOne, 2013.

———. *The Day the Revolution Began: Reconsidering the Meaning of Jesus's Crucifixion*. San Francisco: HarperOne, 2016.

———. *The Kingdom New Testament: A Contemporary Translation*. Grand Rapids: Zondervan, 2011.